Within *the* Child's Core

Janiece Corevine

FULL CIRCLE PUBLISHING

Full Circle Publishing

ISBN: 978-0-578-18537-8

PRINTED IN THE UNITED STATES OF AMERICA

If you want to live in the light of day let go of the darkness from yesterday. From there is where you star to live! Live your life in the way of being loving, and nurturing. That is how it should have been from the start. The road to abuse truly began when the family's loyalty was tempered from my father's with violence, physical, mental, corporal abuse, drinking, drugs, secrets, submission, dominance and control. There is no reason, or responsibility, for these actions. Nor sense of love, or security, only pain to each individual. Your loyalty to yourself comes first. Trust me when I say this you are not alone.

Do not ever be ashamed of your past, nor of what the future will bring.

Dedications

I would like, to dedicate this book, to all, who are survivors, of incest, sexual molestation, emotional, physical, and psychological abuse. Also to all the tough women in my life who have passed on, I keep them close. Susan T thank you my friend. Susan you know you were a big part of this book. My book flows because of your help in therapy. Stay strong in who you are.

To my father Roman J. Steward for, acknowledging, and admitting on how he raised us was wrong. Accepting my father's apology, for placing our entire family in the depth of dysfunctional living was very important to me. His apology was a blessing worth waiting for. Thank you Dad

To Leslie my child, my daughter. I humble myself before you. I am truly sorry. For everything that has happen since we met in 2015. I know that any apology won't change the past. However, it can lead to a more positive future.

I love you. Your mother Janiece

I am Janiece Corevine. My precious core went into a deep sleep in 1963, and my protector awakened. She never slept; she always protected me. Finally, after 50 years, the protector finally went to sleep, and she is never going to wake up again, I finally let her go. April 21 of 2014, my precious core has finally awakened. I started writing this book in 1994, and I finally finished in August 18, 2015. I am for the first time living my life the way I want to live it. Healthy, strong and alive! I wrote this book to help myself grow and live.

The title Within the Child's Core is a true untold story of my life. The word Core is my center, my soul, my survivor of innocence. My core was full of, sadness, pain, and abuse. My survivor suffered the abuse. I fought for validation to know that what happened to me was not my fault. I am living my life in the present. I see things, differently, and everything is clearer. I know what I need to do for me alone, and it feels so good. This is my first book. I started with one word and it has turned into many words, and memories. This book is my only legacy and I am damn proud.

Prologue

My nickname is Jaynie. I will use name throughout this book. I was born in Lexington Iowa, on Feb 14, 1961. I have three brothers and one sister. Their names from the oldest to youngest. Maye was the first-born. She is six years older than I am. Towan is the first-born male, and the tallest of us all. He is five years older than I am. Then there is Antwon, he is six months older than I am. Last, but not least my twin brother Jeffery James Steward.

I am sad to say, my twin brother Jeffery died at the age, of two years old on May 20, 1963. He died of a heart ailment. Maye told he was a fighter. My mother's name is Othea and my father's name is Sylvet. I guess you can say Sylvet was the breadwinner in the family among other things. You can call us the crumb snatchers. We were just an ordinary, average middle class American family living in a traditional metropolitan city.

I want to share my story with everyone.

Contents

My Core Part One

AS A YOUNG child my memory was not strong, but I re-member enough of the past to put on paper and make sense out of everything. As far as I can go back into my life, we lived at 617 10th avenue in Cedar Rapids, Ia. The house was white with gray trim on the bottom, had a chain- linked fence around the whole yard, and the garage was next, to the house and in between was a gate my father dad built. You can open the gate by raising the handle with your hand; I could not because the gate much bigger than me, so I could not reach the handle. I do not think they had invented electric garage door openers yet, because if they did we would have had one by now. We had a clothesline so my mother could hang out the laundry in the summer time, and a nice big backyard to play in. We had a nice sized porch, with chairs so you could sit outside to watch who ever walked by. I loved our house; it was so big. As you walk into the house, there is a little breeze-way. There you can take off your shoes and there are coat hooks to hang coats. You walk through one more door. Then you are in our house. Once you are in then you are standing in the kitchen. Then you go through one more door, and then you are our house. Through the door, you would be standing in the kitchen.

Our kitchen was painted yellow, and the floor had this ugly gray tile with specks of black in it. I really hated tile because I had to wash the floor with a sponge on my hands and knees when I was old enough. Right in front of you is the kitchen table. Directly to the left is the refrigerator. Passing the refrigerator is our bathroom. From the bathroom is our kitchen again.

Starting from the wall of the bathroom is the kitchen cupboards. Which are on both sides of the sink. The kitchen window faced our garage and part of Annie and Jacob's yard. On the right of the sink was the stove, and the way upstairs to where Jeffery, Antwon and Towan bedrooms, and where we would play.

As you walked up the stairs there was paneling along the whole staircase. A ledge went around the staircase at the top of the stairs. As you walked up the stairs, the walls on both side of the stairwell were wood paneling. As you came to the top of the stairs and looking to your left, you could see the two beds, to the left along with Jeffery's crib in between them. The beds upstairs faced the front, of the house. Their bedroom was big as far as I could tell. To the right was little nook I would play in. It was kind, of like a den, but there was no door. It was the corner, of the house, and we used the nook if we needed an extra bed space when we had company.

You could look out the window, and see the tops, of people's houses, even Annie. (Annie and Jacob are married. They are an older couple. They are about 60 to 70 years old.). You could also see Annie and Stan's house from our back yard. Along with Stan's house who lived right next door to Annie and Jacob's. Then there was the dining room, which we never used except, for special occasions. Maye and I had the bedroom, which faced the dining room. I actually liked our bedroom. You could see the alley outside of our bedroom window. Across the alley was an old dirty decrepit apartment building where homeless people lived, and houses farther down the block. At night when the street lamps come on at night, I liked to watch the cars with their taillight go by. Listen to the sirens and the noise the trucks made and drift off to sleep. You moved forward from the dining room you walked into the living room, and a little further ahead was my parent's bedroom. I remember playing house with my dolls one day, I also remember on time when my brother Antwon and I were playing with matches. He lit some paper on fire; the ashes started flying all over the place.

As quickly as the fire was started Antwon just a quickly put the fire out. Thank God. If we would have been caught playing with matches we would have had both, of our asses beaten, to a bloody pulp. We were both so scared day and we said we would never play with matches again. We also promised we would never mention what we did for the rest of our lives. I kept the promise of never playing with matches again until later. At the top of the stairs, all of us kids would sit up there scared, crying and listening to my parents fighting, and yelling at each other. It would be very quiet for a minute and then we would hear my mother crying, from my father hitting her. You can actually hear him hitting her, and my mother begging my father to stop hitting her. It seems almost every day my parents were arguing about bills, utilities, food; clothing anything, my dad was mad about he would take it out on her. When he stopped hitting her, he then would turn his anger on us. He would be so angry he would look for something for us to do.

Clean the house from top to bottom. Wash the floors, not with a mop, but on our hands and knees. Wash, wax, and clean out both cars, mow the lawn, trim around the yard with a hand trimmer on our hands and knees. Pick up garbage, around the yard and in the street. Cleaning out the entire refrigerator, or cleaning out all the closets. Washing and cleaning out the garbage cans. Picking up any lent off the floor on our hands and knees. We all were doing the entire jobs my father told us to do. My father would follow behind us making sure we did it to his liking.

As soon as we would complete one task were off, to another one. This abuse would continue for hours. Until my father tired himself out so much, he would fall asleep on the couch watching TV. As a child what I thought was strange was he would beat my mother for spending money or using charge cards, to buy us clothes anything, but it was ok for my father to play poker and lose $500.00 or more. It just did not make sense to me. I remember so many nights' when my father would go out, and play poker with his friends, and he would not come home for hours. Which was nice because, we did not have, to hear his mouth. When the phone would ring at 3:00 or 4:00 in the morning.

It would be my father calling my mother to bring him more money or food because he was losing in poker, or sometimes winning. My mother would have, to get out of bed make him a plate, to take him some food and money. My father was a tyrant. He exerted so much dominance over my mother as well as us kids. When he finally did come home, which would be maybe 5:00 or 6:00 a.m. he would be drunk. If he lost money, he would take it out on my mother and us kids. Sometimes he was so drunk, and angry he would start, to fight with my mother. She would make us get up, and out of bed, while crying, and trying to hurry, and get us together, and we would be crying too. Because we did not know what was going on. My mother is telling us to hurry because she was scared of what my father might do, to her or us We are crying, and getting dressed at the same time. Maye had, to take care of the two of us.

My mother would put us in the car, and we would show up on the front door at our cousins Jessie, and Tonda's house who lived about eight blocks away from us. Now remember this is happening 4:00 o'clock in the morning all because of my father being drunk, and having a violent temper. We would stay sometimes two to three days until he would calm down enough for use to come back home. It is not as if my father didn't know where we were. Because there were also times he would come over to get us, at uncle Malik (my father's brother), and my aunt Malik wife Tracine and kids Tonda and Jessie.

Uncle Malik would try, and talk my father into going back home,

"Sylvet you are drunk! Go home, and sleep it off, and come by tomorrow, to Othea, and the kids in the morning."

I'm coming to get them now bring them out here Malik. Then my father and Malik would yell back and forth for a while, but eventually my father would tur around and go back home. In addition, we would eventually be able to sleep. I wish my father would not behave have the way he did when he would be drink. We were all little kids, what did we know? When this was going on, I was about two years old, not old enough to understand. Early on, I remember one time when my father came home he was so drunk he made it into the house, but not to the bathroom. I don't think my father meant, to puke all over the dining room floor right smack in front, of Maye's, and my bedroom. Maye and my brothers, had to clean it up. By the time we were finished it would be around five a.m. in the morning. When we were done, we went back to bed, and my father would be sleeping really had in his bedroom snoring away.

Now if he won in poker, which was a different story. He would come home in a good mood, and was when we would hit him up for our allowance, which was five dollars. In the year, 1963 candy was cheap so you could buy a lot of candy for five dollars. Throughout my childhood, I could remember there were times when my father would be in one of his bad moods. He would be yelling and hitting my mother and he would not even be drinking at all. Sometimes my father would have bad days at work, and when he would come home, and not say anything at all. We knew something was going, to happen. Therefore, when all, of us kids would hear my father say, "Kids get yo' asses upstairs, and don't come down until I call ya." We all knew then that my father was in one of his moods. Up the stairs we and upstairs was where we stayed, sometimes two to three hours. Or when my father told us we could come down. However, we did not hear anything. We had no garbage in our yard at all. There is absolutely no litter around, or along the fence. Not even alongside the house in the alley, not with My father around, to tell three older kids, to pick up the trash. Maye told me that Jeffery cried a lot, and he could not walk at all because of his heart. Maye told me later his heart did not develop properly.

So most, of the time he spent his days in the crib crying all the time. Maye told me when Jeffery would cry so would I. I guess I cried along with him so he did not think he was alone. When we were out of our crib, he would be trying to scooch around on the floor. All I knew was I had a constant playmate; someone I could tug, pull, hit, and push around. Maye told me we were inseparable. Maye told me later on, as I grew older to understand more about Jeffery. She told me when Jeffery would cry so would I. I guess I cried along with him because I did not want him to think he was alone. My sister said he was in such terrible pain. She said I would always try, to get Jeffery, to play with me. So when we were not sleeping, we were playing all over the house. It would irritate my mother so much she would all yell at us, but we did not know what she was saying, so we just kept playing. I hope we did not get carpet burn on our knees from crawling all over the floor. Jeffery and I were growing up in this large house full of curiosities and mischief. My father of course, at work.

Maye, Towan, and Antwon were at Tyler Elementary School, which was three blocks from our house. We lived just around the corner from Stan's house. My mother was in the kitchen doing I don't know what. I think we like the kitchen and dining room table the most. We always hide under the tables, and hide all of our toys in the corners behind the chairs. We would take our bottles under the table and drink our milk. Its early morning and I heard my mother yelling from the kitchen for Maye my older sister. Maye was usually at school I. However, today she stayed home because she was not feeling well.

Maye had stayed home from school today because she did not feel well

"Maye."

What momma?

"Don't say what to me again."

Yes, mam.

"Go wake up Jeffery and Jaynie, and get them ready for breakfast."

Jeffery wake up.

I see her shaking Jeffery!

I ain't playing now wake up.

Momma momma...Jeffery ain't moving, at all. I tried to shake him, and he ain't moving. Maye picks up Jeffery from our crib, and takes him down stairs to momma.

She left me upstairs in our crib.

My mother comes back to get me. I thought they forgot about or me.

My mother and Maye looked at Jeffery, and they both started to cry. I am sitting in my high chair. Just watching everything, and not knowing a damn thing is going on (Hello I am starving over here.). I start to cry to because my mother and Maye are crying.

"Maye you watch Jaynie and I'll go call ya' daddy."

The next person I seen was two men in white coats with a rolling table. My father could not come home. My mother, Maye, and I are crying at the same time. One of the two men picked up Jeffery and placed him in a bag on top of the rolling bed table, and took him out the back door.

I am still wondering when I get to eat. We are all sitting in the living room. Maye is holding me. After, they never spoke his name again not I can recall. Jeffery and I was two years old. Jeffery died in the month of May in 1963. I never saw him again until years later in a picture lying in a casket. It must have been hard emotionally on a eight year-old child. To find her little brother dead in a crib. Let alone to handle his death on her birthday. The image of seeing a dead body let alone her baby brother lying in bed will be with Maye for the rest of her life. As I grew older, I used to beg my mother to take me to his visit his gravesite, but she kept telling me not to ask again. Why was my mother so stubborn in not wanting to take me to see my own twin brother is grave? Finally, Maye took me to his gravesite when I was older; I think I was about twelve years old. Maye told me that after Jeffery died, I changed. I was no longer that independent little girl who always played by herself. Before we were off doing our own thing and we did not have a care in the world. After Jeffery is passing, everybody changed in my family. I started to cling to my mother more. The more I tried to cling to her the further she pushed me away. She pushed me so far away I loved her less. I resented my mother more than I resented my father. My mother was never there for me.

My mother hurt me emotionally by abandoning me be- cause she lost her child. I always felt I was being punished for his death. I did not take Jeffery away from you, God, did. Why punish and push me away because you are hurting, I just want to know why? When I saw his head stone, I just started to cry. You could hardly see his name or even the year he was born. It was like since Jeffery is no longer alive, so why worry about his grave. This is their son for God's sake! With the information, Maye told me and what I remembered was Jeffery J Steward, Born Feb 14, 1961 died May 20, 1963. I remember Maye told me he died on her birthday. She also told me the doctors had said he would not reach 5 years of age. Jeffery had just turned two years old. He died four months after his birthday. I thought is fitting since she was mainly our care provider not my mother. Maye, would always got us up, bathed us, and helped fix our breakfast. I wonder what life would have been like if Jeffery was still alive. I just wanted my mother to hold me have her tell me what happened to Jeffery." Why isn't Jeffery coming back home to me? Why couldn't I go with him? Before Jeffery died I never felt love from my mother. All I felt was hostility from her. If my mother had it, her way she would never picked me up.

As Jeffery passed away in his sleep, my mother passed away in my life. Why momma?

What did a two-year-old child do to you for you to treat me the way you did all these years? I thought you would be there for me if, and when I needed you! I thought you loved me! I do not understand why you are pushing me away. I did not do anything wrong; why am I being punished? Why didn't my parents show love to me, but shows love toward my other siblings? I am only two years old! What do I know about grief or death? How do I face this by myself? Do I have to face the hurt and pain on my own? I always felt my mother was treating me, as I was a problem for her. She went through the responsibilities of raising children, but there was no love there at all when came to my wants or my needs. I felt like I was a job to her. All I knew was I needed my mother at time in my life, but she just kept moving further away from me. By the time, I knew what was happening she was so far ahead of me my little heart couldn't catch up to her. I know I had not done anything to her except be born. I know losing a child is very difficult to manage.

Seeing your child lying in bed dead can be a severe blow to anyone. However, my question is, why abuse the child is living? It is not a child's fault when a child dies. I wanted my mother to try a little tenderness. Just love me and hold me. Alternatively, I would love to hear you say the words "I love you Jaynie" I have waited for a longing to hear you say those words. However, I know it would take many years. I have to be honest in 43 years of me being alive you have said I love you a matter of three times. That is sad. Attention, all parents, if you experience a death of a child in the family please does not treat the other surviving children wrong or indifferent. The surviving children have done nothing wrong, and they did not cause sibling to die.

They have done nothing wrong and they did not cause the child to die. Children are so naïve, innocent and trusting. All we try to do is love anyone meets us. We know of nothing else, they only know to trust anyone holds them. As I grew, I would see and hear so many things in our house. I would hear so much sadness. Many times when we were growing up my father would be beating on my mother, and it caused much pain in my heart. If I could stop him, I would have. He would beat her so hard she would have black eyes, swollen lips, her aches, and pains we could not see. However, the bruises were visible. We could see the pain was there by the way she walked. My mother is working now. There was no one to watch me so my mother asked our neighbors Annie and Jacob to watch me until she got off work.

One day my mother took me over to Annie's house. They lived right around the corner from us. I cried so hard when she dropped me off! (Remember our back yards are connecting to each other. Sometimes we kids would be playing ball in our yard, one of my brothers would kick the ball hard, and it would go over to Annie's yard. Annie would call out, "Towan, you keep your ball in your own got damn yard, ya' hear me!"

I always liked Annie. When I arrived at her house there was a little boy name Wanya Plumett. Annie was to watch both of us until our parents picked us up. Wanya, and I got to play together every day. So in a small way, I have another little brother again to play with. Wanya is just a little younger and just a little shorter.

However, I don't care I had someone to play with. Annie would yell from the back door in her little squeaky voice, "Jaynie, Wanya it's time for lunch come in and wash your hands and faces."

We said at the same time, "Okay."

We ran into the house and we both go went over to the sink and Annie wiped us down. I could not wait to eat. She made good lunches. I see Stan, my dad's friend going in and out of his house. I can see he was watching us. Wanya, Annie, Jacob, and I all hold hands and we had to say this little prayer every day before we started to eat: We all hold hands and we had to say this little prayer every day before we started to eat:

"Bless us oh Lord for these thy gifts, which we are about to receive
From thy bounty through Christ our lord amen"

Finally, we get to eat and after lunch, Wanya and I would run outside, and play around in Annie's fruit trees. Annie had a cherry, apple, and pear tree. The tree I liked most of all was the cherry tree

Stan was a black man who lives next door to Annie, and Jacob. He is the man I have been talking about in the last several pages. One day we are, outside, playing ball, and Stan came over to the fence.

"Hi there! Can I play too."

No! Your too old!

"Come over to my fence and talk with me for a while."

I went over to the fence. In the meantime, Wanya yells for me to hurry up, come back, and play. I waved at him to let him know I heard what he said.

Wanya wait a minute!

Mister what do you want? ….. "What's your name?

"Well you can call me Stan Moleslime."

"I know your father…What's your name? ….. How old are you?"

I'm Jaynie.

Stan is looking at me with a big smile.

Annie and Jacob take care of me.

Stan, do you have any kids I can play with?

"Yes, but they don't live with me.

"Jaynie would you like to come over to my house and play some fun games fun with me?"

You are so pretty for just being three years old!

"I have all kinds of games like; toss the ball, chase the worm, or hide the snake!"

You know the game I liked the most.

"No, what game is?"

I like duck duck goose, jump rope, and hopscotched.

"Jaynie," Stan said, "I want to show you some of the other games I have at my house if you want to see them and play with them!"

Okay.

As Stan starts to lift me, up over his fence to walk toward his house. I looked back at Annie's house.

Stan I better go back and ask Annie if I can come over to your house to play! ... I don't want Annie to be mad at me ... She spanks really hard.

"Annie won't be mad at you because she told me it was all right if you came over to his house, and also Annie and I are friends."

Are you sure Stan?

"You won't, I promise."

I am afraid Annie will tell my parents that I left the yard.

"It's okay."

I guess so. Okay.

Stan was right because later on day when she saw me again.

Annie did not yell or tell me to stay in the yard, so I guess Stan and Annie were friends.

I never saw or played with any children at Stan's house. I do not even know if I was the only child he was molesting. She allowed this man to take me out of her yard and she had to have noticed how long I was gone. I could never understand how Stan knew when I would be playing out in the front yard of Annie's house. Through the side window of his house, he could also see Annie's front side porch and the front yard. When he saw, it was just me in the front yard he would call me over to play with him in his house. Then once I was inside his house was when he would start to touch me. In addition, I finally find out how he knew when I was outside. As you walked into, his house and to your left, you noticed his living room. On the wall he had wallpaper, colors were gray with red, pink, and blue flowers, and you also noticed on your left was his bed, which was full size bed. As you circled the room with your eyes, you could see a lamp on the table, and then you would see the hallway to the kitchen. I assumed he had a bathroom, but I never used it.

Directly to the on the right you would be in his living room and out the side window was Annie's back yard Therefore, is where this pedophile would watch me and eventually coerce me to his house. Stan first got the idea to take me to his house by watching Wanya and me, as we would be playing outside. We would be in either the front or back yard. It was as if he was a stalker, but behind closed doors. Stan knew when I was outside. He could see Annie's side porch through his side window. I could see his side window facing Annie's yard, His back window in the kitchen facing our back yard. Stan was able to watch me all the time. In the front of his house was a sitting room with a chair and to the right of his house was his bed.

The room was dark because his shades were always down. The front part of the house was the only part of his house I would ever see for the next eleven years. Stan started me out by sitting on his lap in the same chair he uses to watch me play in Annie's yard. With my legs spread of over his. He lifts up my shirt. Stan had a long brown thing looked like a worm with a hole in it between his legs. thing was shiny, and it was sticking up between his legs. thing can touch his belly button.

What's long shiny thing?

"It's a penis, touch it? As Stan pulls my hand toward it.

No, I'm scared. I pulled my hand back!

"It is okay Jaynie, it won't hurt you See I am touching it. It's not hurting at all."

I can see Stan touch himself, but he does not take my hand again for a while.

Well what do you call it?

"It is called a penis."

I just kept looking at it.

Okay.

I let him take my hand, and then he places my hand on his penis.

He starts moving my hand up and down on his penis.

I pulled my hand away.

"It is okay Jaynie, just keep touching it."

I did. He just sat there with his hand over mine; touching his penis.

It felt yucky because it was slippery. He wanted me to play with it as a toy.

I never played with any toy like before. His penis was getting bigger.

I looked up at Stan and said, does it hurt?

"No!"

It is getting real big and I don't want it to break!

Stan just laughed and said, "It's not going break."

He kept rubbing his penis against my hand, and he said it feels good. He goes faster and faster, as I watch my hand in his going up and down. Stan grabs some tissue with his other hand from the table next to the chair where were sitting.

Stan replied in a quick voice, "Jaynie watch this!"

I am watching him, and all of a sudden, this milk comes out of the top of it. It just oozes all over our hands.

He took his finger, and put some of it in on my lips and he sticks his finger inside my mouth.

"Do you like how it tastes Jaynie?"

No!

What is that stuff?

"It's milk."

I knew what milk tastes like, and was not milk. However, it was warm on my stomach. Stan proceeds to wipe off my stomach and my hand.

"Wasn't that fun Jaynie?"

No.

"Well I liked it a lot. I will show you more games we can play once you understand them."

Okay Stan, I hope they will be a lot more fun then what we played today.

"Here Jaynie this is for you."

Stan gave me 1.00 and said for me to spend it any way I want to.

Wow thank you Stan.

A whole dollar and was all mine. I could not wait until I get back to Annie's yard so Annie could take us to the store. I am going to buy some candy for Wanya.

Stan took me back to Annie's yard.

Good-bye.

"I will see you tomorrow."

Okay.

"You were a very good girl, Jaynie."

He then gives me a big hug and he even kissed my cheek.

I gave him a hug and kiss too. The next several years, I go over to Stan's house almost every day until school starts. Then it would just be twice a day. My age was three years when the molestation started and through eleven years of age when it ended.

I will be going between Annie's, Stan's, house, and school until we move to our new home and will not be until 1974. During all those years, Stan conditioned me to perform oral and sex gratification. When he put his penis in in my mouth, it felt funny. In addition, he taught me things to do to him to make him feel good. Stan would treat me, as if I was his lover when I would come to his house to have to play and have sex. When I was first learning my ABC's and my sister was trying to teach me. But my father was trying to beat learning into me.

My father holds a paddle in his hand so when I would

miss a letter my father would hit my hand repeatedly until I didn't miss any.

My hands hurt from the beating and after a while, he stopped beating my hands because I kept crying so much and could not remember anything.

Maye told my father that she would practice with me.

Stan. I said, when I was over at his house, I'm learning my ABC's.

"Can you say them to me?"

Yes.

After I was done, I knew I missed some, but Stan didn't get mad at me.

"You missed some letters Jaynie, just keep practicing."

He gives me a big hug and he even kissed my cheek.

I gave him a hug and a kiss too. He then tried to stick his tongue in my mouth, and I did not like that at all.

I love you Stan. I wished you were my father!

"I love you too Jaynie. … Jaynie I want to play with you every day okay?"

We can play with Wanya too right?

"No Jaynie, only you and I can play these games."

Okay. I still did not understand why we all can't play together.

I never told anyone about Stan because he never mentioned it and he never told me not to.

It was as if what we were doing was a normal thing to Stan. In addition, it was normal to me too.

He never said this is our secret, or do not tell anyone, or this is just between you and me.

Stan never said if you tell I will hurt your family. I was afraid that someone would take Stan away from me just like they did Jeffery. In my mind Stan was the adult who love me, and my only friend besides Wanya. He was always good to me; he gave me money every day.

Why was Stan so nice to me, and my father was so mean to me? Stan would let me play with him, and I was able to watch Stan play with his penis and not be scared. Sometimes Stan would buy me candy and he would play hide and seek with candy. I would have to check in his pockets for candy or money. When I would find it and I would say thank you. Following those weeks of going over to Stan's house, every day he was teaching me some new games. Stan was fun to play with. I liked the game called hide n seek. If I found Stan than I had to kiss Stan, and if he finds me, he gets to kiss me. After a few months, I am touching his penis and I was not afraid at all, and it still felt slippery and still was shiny. I still didn't like it because it was so long, and big. He still tried to put thing in my mouth, which tasted funny because of the Vaseline. Sometimes, I liked it and sometimes I didn't.

My mouth was not big, and he tried to make my mouth bigger by moving his penis in and out of my mouth, faster and he started moving his hips back and forth.

His pushes too far and I would stop. Then the milk would come out, and run down the side of my mouth, and still tasted yucky. Most of the time I wanted to spit the milk out. It was so yucky.

Stan, does it feel good to you when you put your fingers inside me?

"Yes it does Jaynie it feels really good."

Does it feel good when you put your penis inside me and lift me to go up and down?

"Yes."

"Jaynie, do you like it when I touch you?"

Yes, I do. It makes my tummy tingly inside.

Stan what do you call the thing inside me?

"It's a vagina."

What?

"A vagina."

I think I know what that is.

"You do huh? Okay tell me what it is."

Yes. It gets wet and it tingles and it feels good when you touch me.

"Yes."

He also told me I was a very special girl because I make him feel good.

Stan did something different to me he has not done to me before. One time he put his tongue in my vagina, and it felt funny and very wet. He did not do it often, but when he did, I started to like it after a while. Every day from the start, he gave me a 1.00 to $1.50 sometimes $2.00 and I always said thank you. I left, and as I walked back to Anne's house just smiling because I have my own money, and cannot wait to show Wanya the money Stan gave me. I missed not seeing Stan. The holidays took forever. I felt he did not care about me when the holiday arrives. I wanted to be with Stan all the time, not just during the week. I really liked it when he puts his fingers inside me. I just like everything. Every time he would put his fingers in me, it hurt less. Sometimes he would try to use three fingers it would hurt. I felt those same kinds of feelings when I saw the naked girls in the shower when I started kindergarten a few years down the road. I liked it when he would lift me up on him, and his penis would be sticking up in the air and he would slowly lower me down on his penis. I thought was very nice. I wondered how Stan doing? Does Stan miss me at all? Does Stan think about me? I wish I were his daughter. I cannot wait to see him. I like going to kindergarten. **I am five years-old** I also get to see Stan as just much as I did before I started school. Every day I would have to walk by Stan's house to go to school.

Stan would always be watching for me. When he seen me coming, he holds his arms out and I run into them to give him a big hug. In addition, I get to sit on his lap again, in the same chair facing the side window overlooking both yards. However, this time he wants me to lay on his bed with him and I did. We are both naked, he lies on top of me, he puts his weight on me, and I can smell his body. He smells like cigars. He always chewed a cigar wherever he went. I would be out with my mother and I would see Stan and he would have cigar in his mouth. I would see Stan somewhere, and he would be chewing on cigar. However, Stan's cigar is just sitting in his mouth and he is chewing the end of it. How do you chew on a cigar with no teeth? Anyway, I told him he was too heavy, and I could not breathe. Therefore, he would hold himself up. He wiped the milk off my stomach and helped me to get dressed gave me more money and sent me off to school. In kindergarten, we had a swimming pool right across from the playground called Tyler Pool. We had to learn how to swim, but my mother did not want me to get my hair wet. My class had swimming lessons three times a week. My mother would write a note to my teacher saying I cannot go swimming because I was sick. Which wasn't true. I would be standing by the pool and I would pretend to slipped so I could get wet. I thought hey why not go ahead and swim.

I knew I would get in trouble from my mother coming home with wet hair, but I couldn't help it if I slipped. There was this girl in my class named Jonessa Willings. She is my height my age and I really wanted to get to know her. She was nice and she swam pretty well too. Anyway, back to my mother, she just did not want to take the time to be fussing with my hair every time because it was so long. I would come home from swimming, my hair would be messy, and she would be yanking and pulling my hair. I would be crying and saying ouch and telling her it hurts, but she did not care because she was mad and would tell me to shut up. I remember before and after swimming class, we would have to change in front of everyone, and felt so embarrassed when I was naked because I was a big girl and my mother would always call me a big ass cow and I did not want the girls laughing at me. I always change behind the shower curtains. Thanks to the confidence building from my parents. I found out when I was in the locker room I would see the girls and it really excited me to see these girls naked. I would get a tingly feeling in my stomach. I wanted to touch them and to see if I got the same feeling when Stan would touch me. One time we had to go to the nurse's office and take an eye test to see if we needed glasses.

I could not read some of the letters on the wall so the nurse said

"Jaynie, we need to tell your mommy know you needed glasses."

Okay.

The nurse calls my mother and tells her the problem I have having with my vision. My mother listens to the nurse on the phone.

Jaynie's eyes are fine, and she don't need glasses.

However, when Maye had eyes checked and the nurse noticed Maye needed glasses too. When Maye came home from school, she had glasses.

With his arms, holding me on top of him, he starts going faster, and faster, and he making sounds like he is running out of breath. Then I hear him moaning sounds. Then he pulls his penis out of me and he puts yucky milky stuff, all over my stomach. He, he finally stops whatever he is doing to me and he just looks at me he and smiles. Then he would lay me on his bed and started licking my vagina for a while, and I just laid there it felt nice and tingly.

Stan are you okay?

"I am feeling just fine sweetie." (He sounds like he is out of breath).

He always called me sweetie; as he wipes my stomach off. I do not like touching it milky stuff.

He said I should get off to school. He gave me another dollar. I headed off to school. I had to pass Wilber Store on the way to school; so I went in and purchased lots of candy for my friends. I could not wait to go to school and play with Jonessa.

Candy was five cents, a bag of chips were ten cents 10 cents and a can pop was 25 cents. I remember this gum called Bubbs Daddy and it was long and shaped like licorice; only thicker Bubbs Daddy came in different flavors. My favorite was cherry and watermelon. I would buy ten of those with the money Stan gave me every day. Bubbs Daddy would cost 50 cents apiece. I would pass it around to my friends. Candy was cheaper to buy than it is today. I started getting alot of cavities. **I'm six years-old**. Our teacher said we were going to make a kitchen towels for mom's. I worked hard on mine. We had to put all kinds of sparkles and stars on them. I am thinking my mother would like this towel for the kitchen. We work on the towels for a long time and we finally get to take them home. After school, I was running home and Stan saw me coming. He asked if he could come in and talk for a minute and I said okay. He made sure I was never late coming home from school. He acted as if he had never seen me before. He would be so excited. He was so excited he hurried me into his house. I thought it was okay because I knew I could not wait to see him either. Stan would always be in my thoughts.

When I would be on my way to school, and when I saw him standing at the door I knew I would be getting 1.00 or more for school the next day. We walk into his house and he has his pants down before he even sits down, in addition, his penis is sticking up again; he pulls my skirt up, and pulls down my panties. My mother let me wear a skirt to school day.

Stan puts me on his lap; I am sitting right in front of his face.

"Jaynie you want to try something different?"

Will it hurt?

"No it would it hurt."

Stan lifts me up, and turns me around so my back is facing him. He spreads my legs across his lap. He starts to move his penis around my vagina, and then he puts it in side me. I do not like shiny stuff on his penis. He starts to pick me up, and down on him, and then he goes faster; I think it is fun because I feel like I am riding a horse. So then, he finally stops he pulls his penis out of the milky stuff and me is all over my back. He just sits there and he holds me.

Why do you use Vaseline all the time?

"So when I put it inside you it won't hurt, and it will go in nice and easy."

It's the same stuff my mom puts on our faces before we go to church. Then he puts me down and pulls up my panties, and I pull my skirt up. I want to go home so I can show my mom the towel I made for her in class… Do you like it Stan?

I held my mom's towel up in front of Stan.

"Yes Jaynie, it's beautiful. I think my mother will like this towel very much."

Thanks. I hope she does because I worked on this towel for a long time.

As I walked toward the door, Stan gave me another 1.75 cents he must have quarters lying all over his house. I forgot to use the bathroom and I never used it at Stan's house. I do not think Stan even has a bathroom. I never used it and I never saw him use it. I do not even think Stan has a bathroom. All know is I had, to use the bathroom bad. I got home from Stan's, I knocked on the door; no one answered for about five minutes. However, I knew my mother was home because I could hear the TV playing. By now, I am yelling I have to pee! I have to pee! My mother please let me in! I could not hold it, any longer, and I peed all down my white stockings. My mother is going to be so mad at me, but it was not my fault; I tried to knock.

Finally, my mother opened the door and saw what I did. Therefore, she pulled me inside the house, and called me names as she cleaned me up. I never asked her why she took so long to answer the door. Look, mom I made this for you; we made it in art class... Do you like it? My mother did not even look at it, and she never even answered my question.

I just laid it on the table, and I went off to play in my room. I was so proud of the towel. Later on, afternoon I had to throw some papers away I looked down and I say my towel in the garbage can. I took it out and it walked up to my mother.

Mom, why did you throw my towel in the garbage? .... Didn't you like it?

"Shut up Jaynie and put it back in the garbage."

I did, and later evening, I took it out of the trash, and cut it all to pieces. I am thinking, if she decides she wants it, well it is too late now. I went to my room and I cried so hard in my pillow, I cried myself to sleep.

I will never make her anything else again! Why does my mother hate me so much? Why is my mother so mean to me? I did not do anything to her. Does she even love me? I never mentioned towel again. Everything I tried to make for her she did not want. I am in the I remember one time I had to summer school; we were to make anything out of clay so I put together an ugly ashtray.

At the time I made it, I thought it was so ugly. Of course, I took it home to my mother and she said she didn't want it so this time I showed my father.

"Jaynie is nice. Go put it over there where the other trophies?" I did. It felt good my father would let me put my little ugly ashtray next to Towan's and Antwan's trophies. I didn't want my mother to throw my ashtray away as she did with my towel.

That is why I went to my father.

There were times throughout my childhood my father did show real love to my mother and to us. However, it was far, and in between.

I remember my father always watched the evening news. It would always get dark fast. My mother always told us if we fall asleep before dinner then we would not eat. My father said without even looking at her. Othea go make me some popcorn.

She would go and pop him some. Sometimes he would give us some, and sometimes he wouldn't. My father was never a big person when it came sharing period. One night we had to stay in the house because it was snowing.

CHAPTER **2**

WE WERE ALL in the living room with my father again watching the news. I knew supper would not be ready for a while. I tried my best to keep my eyes open. I fell asleep. My mother made me go upstairs with no dinner. I was so hungry. Hours later, my siblings felt sorry for me. Towan brought me up some cornflakes, and Maye brought me up a slice of cornbread. Anthony brought me Kool aide. I really thought was nice of them to have brought me food. Having to go to bed with no food would happen many times to me. It is very hard, for a child to be interested in the news and let alone understand it. I really wanted to tell Stan about my best friend Jonessa, but I was afraid Stan, would like her better than me and I didn't want to lose Stan. He has been my best boyfriend since I was three. Stan is like the father I wish I had. I do not want to share him with anyone so I just kept Stan to myself. Jonessa was my real friend in school and we did almost everything together. All the kids in the neighborhood wanted to play with her all the time.

Her mom's name is Dianna and her father's name is Kendall. I liked her parents. I wish my father were as nice as Stan or Kendall. I always thought Kendall was very good looking. Jonessa had one brother, and his name is Jadeson. He's about one inch taller than Jonessa, and one year older. I really didn't like him too much. I thought he was a stupid boy who talks too much. As I gotten to know him, I found him to be nice and I developed a crush on him. I also I had a crush on Jonessa's dad. However, I had a giant one on Stan. I really loved Stan.

I am 7 years-old Grandma Odemesse would say, "I am just growing like a weed." This was a bad year for me because I got in trouble a lot. I was always in trouble for something. There was this boy named Brian Kipp he was in the same grade I was. Brian always wanted to play around with me in class, always wanting to touch me. I let Brian touch me for a while under the desks.

At some point, I told Brian we would have to stop because of the desk. He could not get his hand down my pants and we could not move the desks because the desk and chairs where nailed to the floor. We did not want Mrs. Dennisstone our 2nd grade teacher to yell at us. So sometimes, I would let him put his penis in me as I did with Stan. Behind buildings, in old garages and wherever we could. One day in the classroom, I was daydreaming, and I was looking out at the rain pouring down on the windowpane. I just happened to look over at Brian Kipp, and noticed he has been trying to get my attention I finally noticed him looking at me, and he is holding his penis in his hands. He points his head toward the bathroom as if he wants me to follow him. Therefore, I did.

I asked, "Brian why are we here?"

Brain replied, "Because I want to stick my thing in you!"

I replied, "Why don't we wait till after class; I don't want to get in trouble?"

So, we waited; we did hook up, but not in class. Some weeks go by we are in class Brain wanted me to go into the bathroom with him so I did. When we were in there he tells me to pull down my panties and lean against the wall, so I did.

I was watching him he pulled down his pants, and his penis looks just like Stan's, but only smaller, and not as shiny as Stan's. Brian walked up to me and I spread my legs open the way Stan taught me. I am leaning against the wall, he puts his penis inside me, and all of a sudden, the teacher came in. She saw us and sent us down to the principal's office. He spanked Brian with a paddle and he called my mother. She had to leave work to come, and get me, and I am wondering what the big deal is. I thought every child did this. I never got in trouble with Stan and he has been putting me on top of him since I was three years old, and nobody said anything. I never told anyone is why but nobody ever caught us.

So anyway, I must have done something terribly wrong because my stomach feels like there are knots tied up inside. However, I still did not know what I did wrong. I did not lie or fight in school. The school had called my father. When we got home I saw his face I knew I was going to get an ass beating. My father was extremely mad and he had the paddle in his hand. My father used a 24-inch-long and 1 to 1/2 thick wooden 2 by 4. That he had made into a paddle. He took nails, and hammered them into the paddle, and then took a screwdriver to make sure the nails went even deeper than the wood's surface. Therefore, when he uses the paddle on our skin you would see circles left from the nail holes. I had knelt in front of him on my knees facing him because he told me to.

My father said, "Hold out your hand Jaynie, and I am not going to tell you again."

I did and he went to hit my hand and I jerked it away, and he missed it.

He looked at me with such anger in his eyes I thought he was going to hit me in the head. But he didn't.

My father repeated his demand, "Jaynie give me your hand."

He took my little hand in his, and held my hand real tight and he hit me so hard and just kept hitting me and hitting me! When my right hand was as red as red could be, he did the same to my left hand. All this time he had not said one word. Neither parent told me what I did wrong. So why was he beating me? I thought it was because we did it in the school bathroom! I do not know. I just cried, and cried; I just kept thinking about how much hated my father for beating my hands, and Brain for getting me in trouble. After my father was done, beating my hands my mother took me to the bathroom to soak my hands in warm water. My Gosh did water sting. I do not remember how long I was in the bathroom.

My mother dried my hands; I went to bed. I just cried myself to sleep. The next day no one said anything to me, about the other night. I still do not know what I did wrong. They were red and swollen. My hands were sore. At school, I could not even hold my pencil to write. Look what happened! I get into big trouble because of Brian. So why didn't I get in trouble having sex with Stan? Maybe because I did not think to tell anyone because he never told not to; Stan did more to me than what Brian ever could do to me, so why was it okay. to do this with Stan, and not Brian? Alternatively, was it because I did not know I should not be doing this in school, or I should not be having sex in second grade or having sex with Brian? All I remember is my mother said I should not say hi, to everyone I meet. I never spoke to Brian again. I wished he were dead. I know everybody heard what Brian and I did in the bathroom.

At least it never came back to me. No one ever spoke about it again thank God. It also never happened again. I told Jonessa about it and we just laughed about it, after my hands stopped hurting, of course. Even though I told Jonessa about Brian, I never told her or anyone about Stan. You would think parents would be wondering what is happening to their child if they know what goes where and what to do in second grade. If your child is acting differently than they normally do, and cannot wait to see a particular adult. There might be a problem. If she/he always has candy, but they are e not doing anything to earn the money through an allowance or from relatives to buy the candy. You need to ask the child is what is going on? Build a strong foundation together first. Because if you don't you lost child even before you knew it. If your child start having alot of cavities at an early age. Then you should look into what is going on. Do you remember back when the dentist would come to your school, and they would give you these little red tablets to see if you brushed your teeth and your tongue good?

If you didn't brush your teeth, you could see all the plaque in your teeth from red tablet. Then the dentist would give all the kids, a small tube of Crest and a new toothbrush? When I first went to the dentist, I had five cavities, and this was the first time I ever went, I remember the dentist.

The dentist said, "Jaynie where did you get so many cavities from? ... Did you eat all the candy in the candy store or what?"

I replied, "I don't know! I guess I must really like candy."

The first visit to the dentist and all the drilling they had to do on my teeth, made me scared to go back to the dentist. However, I never stop going. I go every six months for a cleaning. I love my dentist. I was not really doing well in school. My grades were bad. So now I had to repeat second grade again and eight years old. I kept getting beat for my bad grades.

Parents please have a clue there must be something wrong with your child for having to repeat the second grade. With me repeating the second grade over again was just like first grade just with more things to do. There must be something wrong with me. I was sad I had to repeat second grade over again. Jonessa knew I failed second grade she did not laugh at me. She still liked me, and I was happy. I was somewhat mad because at first, we were in the same grade and now she, and everybody in my class was a grade ahead of me. Grandma Odemesse is my mother's mother. We all love my Grandma O. She will be staying with us for the summer and I cannot wait to see her! I still see Stan and I worked harder this time in second grade so I could pass. There was not going to be a repeat with Brian, no matter what.

I said, "What did the principle Richards do to you after we got caught in the bathroom?"

Brian said, "Mr. Rickard asked what we were doing in the bathroom."

Brian had replied, "Hunching!"

Mr. Richard had replied, what is Brian?"

Brian proceeded to show me what he showed Mr. Richards, what we were doing in the bathroom. After Brian showed him, he sent Brian home with his parents.

I asked Brian if he got a spanking, and he told me no. However, he did say his friends laughed at him the next day.

After conversation with Brian, I told myself I would never speak to him again. I never did. It would be 46 years before Brian, and I would speak again. Stan is still giving me money every day. When I went over to his house, he would look at me.

Stan asks, "What do I want to be today the mommy, child, or girlfriend?"

I replied, "I want to be your girlfriend today."

I liked being Stan's girlfriend because he gives me hugs and kisses.

Nevertheless, his breath always smelled like a cigar. Cigars is all he smoked, and chewed on. He touches me very softly, and I get excited when he touches me. I feel so good and tingly inside. Sometimes he asked me what I want him to do to me and I told him I like it when he spanks me not hard at all.

He takes my panties down, he lays me over his lap, he spanks me, he touches me inside with his fingers, and I pretend I am crying. Then when he is done spanking me, he rubs my bottom very softly. He sits me back up. By now, he is excited, and his penis was sticking out again. Therefore, he lifts me up on top of him and starts to lift me up, and set down motion again. **Now I am in third grade and 9 years old**. I enjoyed going to school every day because I was able to see Stan everyday twice a day.

At school, I would play with my friends and buy candy so I could make more friends. I made sure I always bought candy for Jonessa. She was my only real friend I ever had, but sometimes she just did not want any. Jonessa and I were always trying to make time to play together and I felt we were good friends because we always hung out together. I would go over to her house or vice versa, but mostly I would hang out at her house. We would play at in their back yard, which was cool. Behind their fence was an alley. The fence went around their back yard which was almost gone from us kids crawling over it. There was little fort Jade built with his friends. When the boys were not there Jonessa, I would play in it until the stupid boys heard us laughing inside, then Jade, and his friends would throw stuff at us. So we threw stuff back. They did not like too much. After a while, Jonessa and I would go in the house and up to her room.

I really like Jonessa's and Jades room. She had her side and Jade had his side. Jonessa room was so cool because her ceilings were slanted. You could look out the window, see the next-door neighbor's house, and a little bit of the street. Jonessa's room was messy, but a nice messy. Jade kept hanging around Jonessa and I, and wouldn't leave us alone. When Jonessa went into the house to tell Dianna Jade was bothering us. He whispered in my ear he wanted me to have sex with me sometime I said sure. However, I was scared because I did not want to get caught like the last time with Brian in the bathroom. He said we wouldn't, and he was right. When Dianna would go to choir rehearsal was when we would do it. We hooked up for a short time. All I knew was I had a gigantic crush on Jade, but around his friends he makes fun of me, but when we are by ourselves he was pleasant to me, and I could not figure it out yet.

Getting together eventually slowed down to where we never did it again. However, stuff with Jade did not bother my friendship with Jonessa and I do not think she even knew. I am happy about; maybe she did know, and if she did, she never brought it up to me. All I knew is we liked spending time together and had fun playing with each other. When we were at school, I would want. Jonessa to play with me, but she had other friends also so I had to share our friendship. I could only go over to her house if one of my brothers would take me because I was not old enough to go over there on my own yet! Only if my mother was in a good mood. I would always glace at Stan's house, as we would cross the street. Many times, I wished he was my father. After I would tell to Stan, he would hug and kiss me. When he would touch me it would really be nice and it does not hurt and you always tell me I am such a good girl.

He never treated me the way my parents did. Growing up in our house was had always bad memories then good ones. I remember my father would call us names as we were growing up. One names stand out to me. He would call me "an ignorant big-footed galunt." (Still to this day, I still do not know what a galunt is!) I guess it is bad or insulting because of the tone in his voice when he was mad at me. When my father was mad about something or someone, he would take his anger out on us. On the other hand, if we didn't do something right that he wanted us to do. That would be when he would call you names. As a child, I had big feet and my father would always insult me about my feet. I hated my feet and always wished they were smaller. I did try like hell to be an obedient child for my mother and father. But the more I tried the worse I became. I remember so many times my mother would cook dinner and would call us all to come and eat, except for my father. He would stay in the living room watching TV. Therefore, we would be eating and my father would make one of the kids bring him a plate of food. Once he had the food we would be all eating then you would hear my father say bring me this, bring me, I need something else to drink.

How I hated my father for making us bring him food, waiting on him as if he was a king. Why couldn't my father eat at the table like the father's we see on T.V? The only time we did not have to take food to him was during the holidays. Taking food down stairs to my father did not stop until he was full. I do not think my father ever took the time to think maybe just maybe we would like to eat our food while it was hot. In his mind, and what you see in his behavior, he is the king of his castle and we are his servants.

My father always stayed on us to keep house clean and our rooms straightened up. We never had any privacy. When we would use the bathroom my father would just come in without even knocking. He just would walk in. It did not matter if we were peeing, or number two, or taking a bath. Many years I hated my father so much, I wished he were dead. I felt sorry for my siblings. Little did I know that in the future it would be me taking my father his food? Why do the parents treat their kids like puppets? Why is it when I go to someone else's house I and feel the comfort the happiness and love? I see the work the kids did for their parents hanging on the wall, on the refrigerator; and at our house. I felt sad and I felt unwanted. Nothing I did in school was ever out for show. I was non-important I was a chore. One-time my father asked me to go to the store. I had gone into my brother Towan's wallet and I had taken $10.00. All I know is I wanted to have my own money. I was jealous of the fact Towan and Antwon never had to beg for their allowance. I had to beg for mine. With the money in my pocket, I was on my way to the store thinking about what I wanted to buy. I Think I bought too much candy. How would I get it into the house? When I got home, I gave my father the stuff he sent me to the store for originally.

My father said, "What was in the sack?"

I replied, "As I walking home I found this sack with candy and money in it?"

Can you believe my father didn't believe me? I was lying to avoid an ass beating, but I got one any way. He took the money and candy away from me. I would not do something like until I get older. It really does not pay to lie.

Grandma O is here and I am so happy. (I will call her Grandma O) for short. Grandma O gets to sleep in our room, I have to sleep upstairs with my two stupid brothers, and Maye gets to sleep with grandma. I hate her. I wanted to sleep with Grandma O because I honestly loved my grandmother more then I loved my own mother. When Grandma O would be cooking and I would just walk up and would kiss her and I would put my small arms around her big body, and just squeeze her so tight. Grandma O would never tell me to get away from her or do not touch her, or stop feeling on her. She would tell me she loved me.

Maybe that is why my mother could not stand me because

I never told her I loved her even though I did. My mother would push me away or she would tell me to stop touching her, my mother would always say to me I was always kissing up on somebody. Now Grandma O is finally settled in and everything is put away. Now everything is back to normal. There are times during the year we would drive to in Metwood Tennessee. We would go and visit all of our cousins. It was nice down there and very hot. I would love to live there with grandma and Aunt Joslyn. It was a very long drive, but worth because when we turned down gravel rode I would be able to see Aunt Joslyn's house over the hill and across the railroad track. Sometimes we would have to wait for the train. The train would be traveling at very fast speed. I could not wait to get out of the car, fall into her arms, and get many kisses. Gabriel was a part of our family. I have to say it because I think this affected my father and is why he acts the way he does.

In 1971, my father says his other son is going to stay with us. Gabriel is from my father and other woman he used to be with before he met my mother. I truly don't think my mother was happy about it. His name was Gabriel David Corevine. He was only seventeen years-old. He was the same age as Maye. All I know is he was at the same high school Maye and Towan went to. Gabriel tried out for wrestling along with my brothers Towan and Antwon. He made the team. He was not even with us one year. Gabriel and some of his friends were on the way to a wrestling meet and there was a tragic car accident. What my sister told me was they found Gabriel head pinned between the seat and they said his neck was broken. This time my parents took me to the funeral and I really did not know what was going on, but I see Gabriel lying down in a casket and he would not be waking up again. He looked just like he was sleeping. My mother and Maye were taking pictures of Gabriel. I will miss him. I wonder if he is with or sees Jeffery. This is why I think why my father changed and became angrier with my mother and us kids. He not only lost his baby twin, but he also lost his first-born son. The beating became more frequent and more sever. It was an early Sunday morning and the sun was already rising for the day. My father and I were up early. The sun is starting rise. The living room front door was open at to cool the house down.

My father and I were sitting in the living room Grandma O was in the kitchen making breakfast.

My father said, "Jaynie go get the newspaper of the porch."

I replied with, "Yes sir."

I see man touched me several months ago.

The man was one of many pedophiles who lurked in our neighborhood.

Months ago, I met this old man. I am in the fourth grade. He asks me if he could play with me and I said yes. He takes me into our alley where the apartments are across from our house. He placed his fingers inside me for a few minutes, and then he stopped. I pulled up my panties, he walked away, and I didn't see him for a long time. I was scared of him because of the way he had touched me before.

I didn't like it because his nails were very long and they hurt me inside). I noticed him walking by our front porch. As he passing our house and I was picking up the paper and he stopped right in front of my house. He was wearing a long black trench coat.

The old man asked, "Do you want to meet me over there in those apartments?"

I replied, "No I can't I have to go back inside. … I am shaking my head back and forth. As he walks by, I went back inside the house hoping nobody was watching. My luck just ran out today because as soon as I stepped back into the house.

My father said, "Jaynie, what did old man say to you?"

I replied, "He asked me if I would like to meet me over there in those apartments?"

I did not think to lie and I do not think I could come up with a lie good and fast so I just told the truth. As soon as the words came out of my mouth, my father was out of the house. I had never seen my father move as fast as he moved that day. I knew the way he left the house either that old man was going to get his ass beat or it was going to be mine. Nevertheless, I knew my father would believe me, not dirty old man. I think there was a reason why my grandmother stayed as long as she did. Thank God for small miracles. I honestly felt she knew something was going on with me, but I do not think she knew how to mention it to my parents. Even if she did mention it to them, would they even believe her? Would they have understood? Would they have claimed that it was my fault? A child in fourth grade and it's her fault the next-door neighbor is a pedophile. My father came back fifteen minutes later (My luck just ran out for me.) Because he had that, I'm gonna beat your ass look. He told me to get the paddle.

I'm really shaking badly inside, because I know my father is going to beat my ass. I want to run away, but I do not know where I would go So I did. When I came back into the room, he was gone. I notice he is on the back porch and I notice Grandma O was out there with him. I am waiting for him to call me to him so he can beat me. But in the meantime, I remembered I had been playing a few weeks ago and I scratched my leg really bad I was so nervous and scared, and still shaking I started picking at my scab. Grandma O talked to my father for over an hour. Grandma is devoted Baptist Christian woman. She never said words like my mother and father says. She had a way with words and she always read the Bible. Grandma lost her husband before I was born. So

I never had the chance of seeing my grandfather. Although I see him in pictures. She had to raise three kids on her own and her kids never wanted for anything. My grandma O only used a switch, and even then she would not beat us the way my parents did. I felt inside my father still wanted to beat me. I swear my father loved beating us. It is as if he was taking his anger out on us. It seems the more we would yell and beg my father to stop the harder he would hit us. He had that look in his eye.

I wonder what that man said to my father to make my father believe him and not me and this time I was telling the truth. Why would a parent believe a complete stranger over his or her own child? Grandma O never wore pants except when she went fishing every Sunday. So finally, my father calls me outside and Grandma is nowhere. I guess she went back into the house. Now I am really shaking and I am thinking he is going to beat my hands again so I go out and he sits me down and looks at me and says.

"Jaynie, why are you so fucking stupid...Don't you know better not to talk to strangers?"

(By this time, you would have thought my father would have started asking me a whole bunch of questions, but none came).

I replied, "Yes Sir."

My father replied, "Shut the fuck up, you're lucky your grandmas here or I would've tore your ass up."

In my head, I am thinking there is a God, thank you for having grandma here with us. I know Grandma knew something bad was happening to me. Why could Grandma O see it, but not my parents? Grandma O had ability absolutely no one else had. Which was she was able to talk to my father when he was angry. Not even my mother. By the time she was done he had calmed way down. When my father is angry, his anger is so strong the look alone can make you start to cry. Was all he said to me and I just sat there not knowing what I was supposed to do. Because normally he would beat us until he felt we had enough, then we would go to our rooms. So understand this has never happened to me before so behavior coming from my father was new to me. I honestly felt my father and my mother just did not want me!

My mother in particular, I felt so much resentment from her. You could cut her resentment toward me with a knife. I remembered telling my mother since she wished I had never been born why I couldn't take Jeffery's place and die. I told her I was running away and I'm never ever coming back. She didn't say anything, or look at me. So I walked out of the house crying hard. I believed she really did not care if I was gone. When I was growing up, I felt I was just her job instead of her child. I noticed my mother just didn't want to talk to me when I was growing up.

I noticed when she had to buy me clothes or shoes she really didn't want to. When we would eat dinner, I would like second helpings, and she would call me a big ass cow.

My mother was a very cruel, non-feeling, woman towards me growing up. One day I overheard Grandma O talking to my mother.

"Othea you should not treat Jaynie the way that you do. You act as if you hate your child. Jaynie needs your love and you are just ignoring her!"

When Jaynie grows up, she is going to resent and hate you. My mother just sat there and listed to Grandma O.

My mother said "I don't hate Jaynie."

Boy was Grandma O right on the money.

We are back in school and I am in the fifth grade. I am mad as hell at teachers and the other kids. My teachers are always sending me to the principal's office at least five times a day. In addition, she would call me into her office and ask me the same question,

"Jaynie what is it with you beating up on boys?"

I said, "I like some of them, but not all of them."

Mrs. Nathaniel asked again, "But why do you think you need to fight or beat them up Jaynie… this is what I want to know?"

"I don't know why, maybe because they're mean, and I see my father in them. The mean boys beat on kids who are afraid to fight…. Can I go please? "

"Yes Jaynie you may be excused."

I never heard any more from the teacher about why I beat up on boys.

Where does it come from? I truly don't know. There was this girl named was Celeste Stankbooty. She was this black ugly girl and a bully at our school. She had teeth that stuck out of her mouth because she sucked her thumb. To this day, I still do not know what her problem was. I guess she just wanted kids to be scared of her, and it worked because I was. She was the school bully. Celeste wanted to beat me up. Why I don't know. It was almost an everyday occurrence. I didn't say anything to her. I didn't bother her. I didn't even look at her. I went out of my way to ignore her. In addition, every day I would run from her instead of fighting her. I saw how Celeste acted towards my brothers and sister.

She liked them. She never wanted to fight them, just me. My parents said never run away from a fight or you will get your ass beat. I just don't think she liked me. When she pushed me, I would just start crying, and all she did was laugh at me. The more I cried the more she knew I was scared. Sometimes my cousins Vanessa and Dedria Hillton would walk home with me and see her pushing me. They would tell her to leave me alone, and for me to go home. Celeste would leave, but the same thing happened again the next day and the day after. I got beating almost every day for running home. There would be days when I would run all the way home from school to get away from her. My mother would arrive home early from work and she would ask me why I was home so fast. I told her and she made me go back outside so Celeste could see me. I was so embarrassed. Celeste kept pushing me to fight her throughout the school year, but still I would not fight her. Many times when I would get home my mother would whip me with extension cords.

From running away from a fight. She would whip me all over my body. Maye and I both were tired of me getting my ass beat because she told me I was going to fight Celeste, and I was going to beat her ass.

"Maye I didn't want to fight her and I don't know how to fight."

Maye said, "You don't have a choice."

The next day my brothers and my sister and I went to find Celeste and her friends. My sibling promised they would stay incase her friends would try to jump me.

I said, "Celeste do you want to fight me." (You don't walk up to your enemy and ask if they want to fight. I have to admit I was a big fat coward.)

Celeste said, "Yes let's get to it."

Thank God, they were all there. She started to tease me about my brothers and sister being there and I again wanted to run. However, I looked at my siblings and they shuck their heads no. Celeste called me some names and a big booty bitch and I called her one back, and boy I tore into pile of shit. I beat the holy shit out of girl so badly she ran home crying and she never bothered me again.

My mother told me we were moving and I have not even completed all of fifth grade. I told Stan we were moving. I started to cry, he picked me up, held me, and said not to cry. It's going to be alright. Then Stan said the last day before I leave, he will give me something special.

I don't know when we are moving and I don't know where. All I know its way out on this street called Mt. Vernon Rd. Before we moved, I remember a fight I had with this white boy who lived down by Wilbur store named Clifford Hayes and he was trying to bully me because of my skin color. We were only a few feet from each other. I was walking with some friends and heading home.

Clifford said, "Jaynie you know what you are?"

I yelled back, "No what am I." "You are a stupid ass nigger."

All his friends start laughing at me. Clifford started walking away.

Now I am really pissed so I was looking for something to throw at him.

I found a brick. I picked up the brick, and with all my might, I threw it at him. Boy, that puppy flew through the air, and hit Clifford in the back of his head. Clifford grabbed his head and he went down for the count. I didn't leave or run away.

I just stuck around for the fun of it. I really do not know why I stayed. Maybe to make sure he was okay. He got up crying.

"I'm going to tell my momma!"

Good go home and tell yo' momma!

We both went home. About 30 minutes after I got home there was a knock at the door; I went to answer it. This white heavyset woman asks for my mother and she told my mother I threw the brick to hit Clifford. I said; he is a lie. I threw the brick because he called me "a stupid ass nigger." I wasn't going to let him get away with it. Clifford's momma got mad at him for lying. Thank God, I did not get trouble for throwing the brick.

My mother said, "I better not be throwing any more bricks...You hear me Jaynie."

"Yes mam."

My brick throwing days were over. I am surprised my mother did not beat me for throwing the brick. She told us more than once if we run from a fight we will get our asses beat. Well I showed her I didn't run. I stood my ground and threw a brick. I really could have hurt him or possibly killed him. I'm sad, the summer is over and Grandma O is going back home to Metwood, Tennessee. I wished I were going with her; I am still in fifth grade. I continued to see Stan every day before and after school. I am still beating boys up. So now, Tara and I are good friends; too cool. I still don't trust her. I will watch my back. Momma says were moving soon, however, I still do not know when. I hope I get to finish fifth grade here. I still hope Stan can move with us. We will see! I'm still hanging out with Jonessa.

One time in the summer my mother said I could stay all night at Jonessa's house. I was happy and surprised that she even said yes. I headed over to her house early so we could play longer. Jonessa and I were upstairs in her bedroom playing, which was a rarity. I'm just taking advantage of her good mood.

Jade had his friend comes over, and Jonessa had went down stairs to do something.

Jade asked, "Would I let Wilton have sex with me.

I said, "Hell no."

No kids liked Wilton Spinster at all.

The kids at school, especially the boys, are always picking on him. I don't feel a bit sorry for him because he is always picking on other kids, especially me. So now he is getting a taste of his own medicine. Jade was begging me to let Wilton have sex with me and again I said no.

Jade and Wilton tried to hold me down.

I kicked Wilton right in his nuts with all my might, and I hit Jade in the eye with my fist.

I said, "Let me go you son a bitch or I will scream so loud the whole neighborhood will hear me.

They did. I think the reason I did not let Wilton have sex with me because I just didn't like him. I was still getting into trouble for fighting through fourth and fifth, grade. I only hated the boys that teased me. The ones that were nice to me I got along with fine.

There was this nice little white boy named Marc Reinholt he was somewhat chubby, but he was always nice to me. He would pick his nose and eat the stuff that came out of it. The kids use to tease and pick on him for it. I felt sorry for him because I knew what it felt like to be teased, tormented, and bullied. I would always protect him. I would beat up any one who messed with him. I do not really know why I was protecting him, I guess because my brothers and sister were not around for me so I felt I should be around for Marc. I remember when we were in the fourth grade and we were in gym class playing dodge ball. Marc was picking his nose, he pulled out this long stringy greenish color booger, he ate it. He did it in front of some boys that didn't like him. They started pushing him around and I jumped in and told them to leave him alone! I wouldn't move away from him. Our gym teacher sent Marc to the principal and Marc told me later he got a spanking.

I went to school and continued to see Stan on the way home from school and on my way home. I still wished Stan were my father. I bet you Stan would take me places. He wouldn't beat me the way my father did. I would tell Stan my father had whipped me. Stan would just hold me and give me hug and a kiss. He would tell me I'm still his special, good little girl. Occasionally while on school breaks and holidays, we would go and visit Grandma. It would be fun. My cousin Ronal was my mother's sister son. When we would go visit Big Grandma O down south, Ronald and I would have sex in my Grandma O had this old hen house. He would want to go into the hen house and start touching me. I would let him put his thing in me. I do not remember if I liked him touching me, but it happened. This would only happen three times. Again, we received our report cards from our teachers. Back then, the teachers made us take our reports card home. Years later, the teachers would mail our report card's home. I came home with my report card, it had C's and F's, and I knew I was going to get a beating when my parents. read my card. God, how I wish I lived somewhere else. Anyway, I finally made it home after walking as slow as I could. I walked into the kitchen to give my mother my report card and she told me to pull down my pants and lay across the chair. As I was pulling down my pants, she gets the extension cord. Then she just started hitting me on my butt, legs, back, everywhere she could hit me. After she was done, I was so sore I could not even move my arms or legs. I couldn't even lie down. I had to go slow.

My mother said, "Wait till your father gets home."

I knew what meant, another ass beating. I made it to my room and I cried myself to sleep. I dreamt I lived with my grandmother, how I wished that dream was true. Half-hour later, my father is calling me to the dining room. When my father had finished reading my report card, he told me to get the paddle. He told me to pull my pants down and bend over the chair and I did so. He started to beat me and I screamed for him to stop, and I had to go to the bathroom and could not stay in the chair any longer. I fell from the chair and I was moving around trying to get away from him hitting me. Now my father is mad as hell, because I keep thrashing around. My father would place his foot on the top of my head or in the middle of my back, to keep me from moving.

I kept telling him through my screaming and crying, "I have to go poop"! My father would not stop. My nerves were so bad I pooped all over the floor, but he kept right on beating.

My dad would say to me as he is beating me.

"Jaynie' (wack) come home again (wack) with F's on your (wack) motha fuckin report card again (wack) (wack)" and I will beat your ass until your nose fucking bleeds" (wack) (wack) ya

Hear me!"

Yes, daddy "I scream, Yes-daddyyy! … 'I won't do it any more dadddyyyy"!

My fater said, "Clean that shit up off the floor. And get the hell out of my fucking sight!"

"Yes sir."

He hated us to cry in front of him. I was trying to hold it in and not cry in front of him out of fear of being hit again, because of my crying. I finally went to bed. I had two painful, stinging, brutal and bloody ass beatings in one day. I closed my door, and looked at my butt. There were pieces of skin here and there hanging off my butt. I couldn't even feel the welts from the extension cord. However, when I stood in front of mirror you could see them all over by backside. Little did I know I would be getting a lot more ass beating because of my grades! Why should a child be excited about doing better in school when your parents are always telling you are stupid, ignorant, clumsy, and ugly and a big fat cow.

I am very angry and confused. On why my father beat me the way, he did. I was only in the fifth grade for goodness sake. My father never spoke of our beatings. Each child in our household suffered at the hands of my parents. Nevertheless, we never knew what the other child was getting a beating. We never spoke about. We were just glad it wasn't on of us.

(I found out later people down the streets would hear our father beating us, but no one game to help us.) The only thing my sister told me later after she moved out of our house, if my father touched me in any way, please call me. I never did call her. Show me a positive role model. Show me positive, loving, caring, parents. Show me love and understanding and I will show you a child who will make her parents so proud of her. When parents are proud of their children, you can tell by the bright and beautiful smile that shows on their faces when they mention their children's achievements. No matter how much the parent will abuse their child, if she or he doesn't feel love, compassion, or care, in their homes, then the child will show just how the parent feels about him or her. I cleaned the entire poop off the floor, and I went to bed. I couldn't even lay on my back because my butt was raw and bleeding so badly and God knows I did not want to get any blood on the sheets. I should not have given a rat's ass about the sheets. But I thought if I got blood on the sheets my parents would beat me again. I just slept on my stomach. I remember thinking I wished my parents would die from being hit by lightning or a car. I always said I wished God would take them away so I would never see them again.

CHAPTER **3**

OF COURSE, IT did not happen. Maybe possibly they could be ran over by a truck. How I honestly hated them so much. I wished something bad would happen to my parents every day. The next day in school, I could not even sit down at my desk so I sat at the edge of the chair. I would tell the teachers I fell and scratched my butt badly. (Which in a way is true) if they were to ask me why I couldn't sit properly at my desk. Now we are about to move and the excitement is everywhere? I know I can't take Stan with me. Maye is helping my mother get things in order so we can move. The house is a mess and my mother is throwing away stuff we had for so long. I would not have mind keeping some of the stuff I collected, but she called it junk. My mother went through every room of the house.

She said she didn't want to take junk from the old house to put it in the new house. She threw a bunch of clothes away I could not wear anymore, old shoes, and my old dolls. I hope I get new ones. The last day I was to go to school, I stopped by Stan's house as he told me to. When I got there, he is sitting in his chair with his pants undone.

Stan asked me to pull down my pants and underwear and I did. I let him do whatever he wanted to because I was not scared and he was very nice and careful with me.

Stan said, "What I wanted him to do with me, and I told him. Right away, he opened my legs and started to lick me, which I grew to like. Then Stan has me sitting on his lap. He spreads my legs open and now my back is against his chest. Stan put his fingers inside me and he was moving them in and out of me very slowly. Stan asked me if I liked it and I said yes it feels good. He stopped and I said, "I love you Stan". He smiled and told me he loved me too. Do not stop Stan; keep going please.

He kept going for a little while longer and then he took his fingers out of me and he asked me to face him, and I did. He rubbed his penis against me teasing me. He started to kiss me, which he had only done a few times. He put Vaseline all over his penis. He lifted me up on top of him, and it did not hurt at all. It felt good. I think by Stan putting his thing inside me, it stopped hurting when I was about four years old. He took his time in getting me used to his penis, fingers, and most of all, him touching me and me touching him. When he finally pulled his penis out of me, white stuff squirted all over my stomach. I was surprised and I don't know why you would think after years of seeing this happen all most five days a week, I would be used to it. However, I wasn't because you don't know when it's going to come out. Stan called it squirting out. I knew I would get money from Stan whenever I saw him. When I do I am going to buy lots of candy for my friends.

I said to Stan, "I am going to miss you a lot."

He took me into his arms, and I started to cry.

I said, "Stan I don't want to go. .... Stan, why can't you go tell my father you want to keep me.

" Jaynie you know I can't keep you."

I started to cry as the words were coming out of his mouth. I think I cried for a good thirty minutes and Stan just held me and let me cry. He didn't tell me to shut up or I will give you something to cry about. He just let me cry and he told me it will be okay and I could come over to see him any time I wanted. (Well that was a lie) His comment did make me feel much better and Stan said he was going to miss me too.

I should be a good girl, and I will always be his special little girl.

I am crying harder now, I just can't let go of him, and I never want to.

I said, "Well then if you don't want to ask my father, then why don't you go ask my mother.

I know she doesn't want me?"

Stan said, "No Jaynie that wouldn't be a good idea at all. Besides your mother want's you and loves you very much"

"I will still be here if you ever want to come over, I promise. (Again another fricking lie)

After he cleaned me up, he said this is for you. He gave me $20.00 dollars and my eyes got so big. I smiled so much my cheeks hurt.

"Wow thanks Stan." I can't believe I have $20.00.

I wanted to stay with him. Stan was so nice to me, and he showed me more love than either of my parents ever did in my whole life. I didn't want to leave his house, and especially move away from him. Why it is every time I have something all to myself, someone always comes along and takes it away from me? I will always wish Stan were my father.

He told me to be a good girl, and I said I would. I left Stan's house, and went to school. I turned around as I was walking up the sidewalk away from his house, and he was watching me leave. I waved good-bye to Stan and I was still crying, but I kept walking. I am crying like I did when we had to leave our grandmothers house and go back home. It was very emotional for me).

I said good-bye to my neighborhood, good-bye to our old house, and especially good-bye Stan. I will miss you the most of all and think of you every time I am in my old neighborhood. When I come back to our old neighborhood, the first person I am going to see is Stan. I can't wait. I wished I could ask my mother if I could stay here and live with Stan. Please God, do not take Stan away from me. He is the first boyfriend I ever had. I wish I was Stan's age and then I could be with him all the time. Stan made me promise not to say anything about him or about staying at his house. I said okay; I would not.

The funny thing is in the past eight years of being with Stan, I never told a soul. So why would he ask me to keep silent now? As I am heading to Wilbur's store, I stopped crying. When I walked into the store and bought a sack load of candy to take to school. While in school, I just kept thinking about Stan and not seeing him every day. On the way home, I was able to see Stan again. We did the same thing before I went to school. On the way home, my heart was so heavy, and sad. I just played it safe and went to bed thinking of the sensation I was feeling would stay with me forever. Nevertheless, it did until I understood later what Stan and I were really doing. I cried the day we moved. My mother kept asking, what was wrong, and why was I crying so badly? I just shut up because she said she did not want to hear it.

Moving day: Good bye Stan how I will miss you

I am so sad. I want to stay with Stan.

Book Two 1974

IN OUR NEW HOUSE

NEW BEGINNING

THE MIND OF A CHILD.

I'M **11 YEARS old** and in the fifth grade. We had finally moved, and I am finishing the rest of fifth grade at a new school called Menorahs Wright Elementary School. When I first entered this school, the kids acted like they never seen a girl of color before. My teachers were nice and I made some cool friends. Found out later, some of the kids I went to school with also went to my church. Besides, none of us hung out together. I still wished we didn't move until I was done with fifth grade. I'm not sure if I will be able to see Stan. He doesn't even know where we live. In addition, I don't know how to find his house. We moved out to an area I'm not familiar with at all. I wonder if he missed me as much as I missed him? When I see him again I will give him our address so he knows where we live. Our new address is 4117 14th Ave S.E. We were still living in boring Lexington, Iowa. Our new house is big, long, with yellow siding. We had a two-car garage. It was cool except, in the winter time when all of us kids would have to shovel the driveway at 5:00 in the morning so my father and my mother could get out to work. The back door faces our driveway. We had a patio in the back of the house. When you stood in front of the kitchen sink, you can look out the window into the back yard. The back yard is big. My father eventually put in a garden and we still had room to play in the yard. As you walk into our house, you faced the stairs into the basement. You turned right, and you are in the kitchen. Our kitchen was done in yellow. Then you walked into the dining room. To your left is the living room which my mother called the show room. She kept it nice and of course none of us kids were told never go in there. When she was gone, I would play all over the furniture. The living room was done is an off white and the carpet a yellow shag. The front door faced the street. As you walk down the hall, the bathroom is on your right, and right across the bathroom is my bedroom on your left. My parent's room is the next bedroom on your left and my brother's room is the last bedroom on your right.

Downstairs in the basement, my father wanted a room to entertain company so he spits the basement in half. He put up paneling on one side and a laundry room on the other. He fixed the entertainment room up very nice. The carpet was red and black. All the walls was painted in red brick and vanilla squares. If you wanted to, you could actually play checkers on the wall standing. He installed a bar and he had black lights to accent the mirrors behind the bar. There was a stereo to the right of the bar and a TV to the left. He also installed a bathroom in the laundry room for himself. I noticed the neighborhood we moved to was mostly all white, except for about four Black families and one Mexican family in the whole neighborhood. Our next-door neighbors are unquestionably German. One thing I could definitely say, we had a multi-cultural neighborhood. I was walking down the street and I noticed this extremely good-looking tall white guy across the street from our house. His name is Alex Cahulty. I would be outside in the front yard trying to show off, so he would notice me. Understand at this stage in my life, and with all the stuff Stan did to me I had noticed Alex and other men. I am 12 years old, and these thoughts are going through my head. Boy, I thought I knew everything there was to know about sex. What a joke. Hah! I think he is at least in his 30's. Eventually, I found out later he was 13 years older than I was.

When we moved into our new house, Alex was in the middle of building his house and his body was looking good. (I'm thinking, can he kiss well and how would sex be with him. I am saying this to myself. I'm going to find out one day!) Getting use to my new house, and checking out the neighborhood. The kids in the neighborhood were ok, except this dumb white kid named Arthur Mumsby. He is such a jerk. We lived on top of a long steep hill. As I started walking down the hill, my neighbor Arthur opens his stupid mouth.

Arthur yelled, "Jaynie you are an ugly bitch!"

As I turned around to see where he was, (I'm thinking why do kids have to start shit all the time?) I turned around and Arthur is standing on his front porch. I walked back up the hill to his house and I grabbed his shirt.

"If you want to live to see tomorrow you will keep your damn mouth shut." Why are kids so cruel? Arthur didn't say a word. His eyes were huge and you can see fear all in his face. Yes, my skin is dark so what. It doesn't mean I should be called names. I am saying all this out, lout as I started walking back down the hill. I am only in the fifth grade and only eleven years old. My father swore a lot in our house so you pick up many words except you never say them in front of your folks. I felt being around other families, I never heard such swearing in their house as much as I had heard it in mine. I swear to God, I didn't think my father didn't know any other words except, shit, ass, fuck, dammit this and dammit. All the kids in the neighborhood considered Arthur a bully. Whatever he did or said the kids on our block thought he was funny and copied everything he said and did. Not all boys, just the dumb ones. When Arthur called me names, I would beat the crap out of him. Eventually, he stopped calling me names, especially nigger. Sixth grade to me was the same thing as the fifth grade just a higher grade. I also got into fights all the time, and sometimes I got my ass beat, but very rarely. We had this teacher that no one liked. Her name was Mrs. Lindsey. She didn't like me, and I sure didn't like her.

One time I was talking in class to this boy, name Kurt, and he and I were talking about Mrs. Lindsey. She heard us, came over and hit me over the back with a pointer stick. No talking in class, she said. I just sat there a minute, I stood up, grabbed the stick out of her hand, and slapped the stick across her face. I told her if she ever hit me again, I would beat the crap out of her. When she saw the look in my eyes, she knew I was serious. I think I even scared myself with how angry I became. She got so scared she sent me to the principal's office. I said well, I would tell him how an adult hit a child over the back with a pointer stick. I went to the principal's office and I told him what happen and he told me to be nice to her, and I said okay. One of the kids in my class her named was Tynetia Brownhanson. She was trying out for gymnastics so I thought I would try too. She had two other sisters' summer, Yvette, and a little brother, and his name is Zach. They were a nice family. Their mother was nice too. We are practicing every day, and the teacher said I was good. I had the ability to learn different routines, and I was so happy. I ran home to tell my mother. She told me I was too stupid, and clumsy, and I couldn't go out for gymnastics. I cried because I really wanted to join! I told the teacher my mother said no. Tynetia mom name was Anna. I asked her one-day if I could come and live with her if I ran away, and she said no. I asked her why not and she said, my parents would not allow her to let me live in their house with her family.

However, she would let me come over and play with her kids any time I wanted. They would invite me over to have dinner with them, and when they went on picnics, I got to go along. My parents did not care where I was or went, especially my mother. My family only had picnics when we had our yearly family reunion. I wished like hell, the Brownhanson's were my family. They would talk and laugh about what happened at school and hold each other and say I love you. Anna gave her kids hugs and kisses. I even got several of those hugs myself. I would like to say, I liked those hugs more than Anna would ever know. I even told Anna I wished she was my mother and I loved her like she was mine. She said, "I love you too Jaynie." Anna was a kind of mother every kid loved because she treated you with love, and tenderness. It made me cry, because, someone loved me more than my own my mother did. This is why all the kids liked coming over to the Brownhansons house to play all the time.

Anna was a director of the nursing home staff. Anna husband name was Corey. He was a tall man, which rather scared me. I didn't care because he liked all the kids. He would give all of us ride on his back and fly us around on his back as if he was an airplane. He played basketball with us kids, and you knew he always would let us win. It was fun when Corey came home. My mother always made us clean at an early age even before we moved into our new home. Towan and Antwon did their share of cleaning house when they were home, but let me tell you very little. They did a lot of outside work with my father. However, most of the time they were always gone before my mother got up on Saturdays. My job was to clean the basement every Saturday. I would be cleaning more in the future. I learned quickly, if I cleaned the basement on Fridays, I could play on Saturdays.

Along with playing outside, all my friends were white. I definitely remembered my parents telling me repeatedly, they can't stand white people and they do not want any funky ass white kids up in their house. Well when why do we live in an all-white neighborhood. It was somewhat awkward having black friends over to play. The few black kids that did live near me, didn't like me. My friends lived over ten miles away and their parents weren't going to bring them all the way over to my house so we could play. So I had no other choice, but to have the white friends I did like come over to my house and play. I knew I would suffer for it later after my friends left. For disobeying my father, my suffering was getting my ass beat. Obviously, my parents had a problem with color. You just knew when you are in deep shit when you saw the look your parent's gave you. When we were all finished the house would look great, and smell so good, and clean. We would all change and jump in the car, and go to the mall. I really liked the mall because you could buy cheese popcorn, go next door, buy a small cup of melted cheese, pour cheese all over the popcorn, and the two together were awesome.

I remember one time I was begging my mother to go with her to the mall. She told me I couldn't go. I remembered saying why does Antwon get to go? I was always saying that from as long as I can remember. Why can't I? Why can they do go to the mall and I can't? I felt my mother was never fair when it came to us kids. In my own opinion, she shown favoritism, but if you asked her that question she would deny it big time. She gave Antwon, Towan and Maye a lot of freedom, to generally come and go as they pleased. I really had to beg to do anything. I think I got on my mother's nerves a lot so I think she said yes to get me out of her hair also out of her sight. My mother's favorite response was "Because I said so.

" I had cried, and couldn't understand why I couldn't go with my sister, brothers, and my mother, to the mall?

I cried for a long time as they were getting ready to leave. I think my mother was tired of me so she said I could go. Boy, I was happy. I ran to my bedroom to get my coat. As I rounded the corner and looked through the big bay window,

I saw my mother drive away. I mean she just took off. I ran outside in the street to try and catch her, I couldn't. I just stood in the street crying, watching my mother drive down the hill. I don't know how long I stood there crying. After a while, I finally stopped, and walked back to the house and watched TV. When they came home later, I just ignored them. No one asked how I was doing, and I didn't ask about their trip either.

I will never forget the pain of my mother leaving me for as long as I live. When you are a child, your anger does not last long. You just let it go and move on to other things. My family was not the type to ask anything like, how was your day? What did you do today? Did you have fun today? I wished I had more of a close family. I always dreamed of a family that would go places together, and do things together. Maybe play in the yard with us kids; go to movies with us. Possibly go on walks and look at the scenery.

When I would sleep, I would dream of a family like that and I just loved my family in my dreams. They made me laugh and we did everything together. My real family was cold and I felt they were heartless. I don't know of any family that was as cold hearted as mine. The day when my mother drove off the way she did, running to try to catch her, I felt my sister and brothers were laughing in the window watching me run for the car. I bet you anything; they talked about it all the way to the mall. I felt like I was losing my family, and they didn't care about me at all. Not giving me enough time to get my coat was one of the meanest things my mother could ever do to me. I found out later, what my mother did to me then, couldn't compared to what she would do to me later in my life. I felt absolutely no love from my family at all, not even from my parents. When God, gave out hearts, and soul, he skipped my parents.

Finally hitting the sixth grade, my last year of elementary

school. I entered Mc Finely Junior High, and I am so excited. I will be attending the seventh through ninth grade school. I cannot wait. My mother finally told me I was old enough to make my own money. I wanted my own money. I was tired of asking my father for an allowance every week. You could tell he didn't want to give it to me especially, with his facial expressions. I just felt so uncomfortable asking. My mother acted like it was a sin to give me money. I started looking for families that had little kids so I could baby-sit for them. This was how I started making my own money. I am very surprised my mother even let me go. If I wanted to go to the mall, I didn't have to beg my mother anymore. I would just take the bus and be gone for hours. I am too stupid to go out for gymnastics, but not too stupid to take care of someone's child. Does this make sense to you? Because it sure doesn't make sense to me! I remembered so many times when my father was angry with my mother or someone; I wanted to go outside to get away from the yelling.

My father said, "Get yo' ass downstairs… and don't think you going to lay up in your bedroom all day either."

My father made me come downstairs where he was to watch TV. I'm bored out of my mind. I had to watch baseball games. I wished so badly that if I kept making a lot of noise, my father would send me outside, but he didn't. I saw my father out of the corner of my eye, as I came down the stairs. I took a left; there is a black leather couch on my right. The bar was at the end of the house. The stereo, and this God-awful yellow couch with orange and green flowers, faced out to the stairway. There is a green chair, which I'm sitting in. This is where the TV sits. It was summertime, by the way. My father has no shirt on because it's hot inside, and his pants are un-zipped as if they are too tight around his stomach. He is sitting there knowing I can see him, sticks his hands down his pants, and started to play with himself. I hated being by alone with my father. I would try to go upstairs. He told me to sit my ass down. I would try to cover my eyes, but now I realize that is what he wanted. Just the thought of someone in the same room with my father, excited him. (How sick of a mind this man possessed). I missed walking by Stan's house and having him asks me in. My father would play with himself in front of me until I finally left the house for good. I just still missed Stan period. I remember after we moved, I rode my bike clear across town to Stan's house.

When I got there, he had company. I stopped to see Stan to tell him I missed him and wanted to visit him. He told me he had company and I couldn't come in. Stan promised me I could come by and say hi anytime I wanted to. I felt so rejection. I cried and rode my bike over to my friend Jonessa's house. Jonessa and I played at the park. My parents told me to be home by dark; I was home by dark. I don't remember exactly when the incest started with Towan. All I remembered it started soon after we moved into our new house. One day Towan came to me and said,

"Pull down your pants, and lay down on the bed." I did. Towan inserted his penis inside me and he started going up and down on me just like Stan use to do to me. This went on for about five minutes and then he pulled his penis out of me and yucky white stuff went all over my stomach. That stuff had a real strong odor to it. He told me to go wash myself off, and I did. I now knew the smell of sex. I remembered how Stan's penis didn't have a smell or the extra skin as Towan's did. What I noticed between Stan and Towan is Towan didn't do the same things to me as Stan did. I really liked how Stan touched me, there were more feelings involved, and with Towan I just laid there. After a while, I would go to Towan and he would have sex with me. This was to go on for about three years. My God, something is wrong with me! There's blood coming out of me! What do I tell my mother? How do I tell her? I am scared! What do I do? How do I stop it? All I know is my lower stomach hurts very badly. I had to go lay down. I tried to wash the blood out of my underwear, but my mother found them. She asked me when it started. I told my mother, thank God, I didn't get into trouble.

What does starting your period mean? Why didn't my mother tell me about this? Did she think I just knew these things? Eventually, the girls and I in school learned about menstruating from our teacher in sex education class. I am starting to develop breasts and my pubic hair is starting to grow. I hoped I didn't get pregnant by Towan! I heard when brothers and sisters or first cousins have babies together they are born deformed. Saturday nights were becoming more difficult for me. My mother would be on her way to bingo, my brothers would be out with their friends, and Maye had already moved out. Let me tell you about Saturday nights. For some unknown reason my father felt he needed me to wash his back, for him. I was a developing teenage girl washing a grown man's back! I hated it. I knew I would be home alone with my father, which I was dreading. I knew what he was going to say around 8:00 in the evening.

"Jaynie."

Yes, sir I call up from the basement.

"Get up here and wash my back."

Yes sir (This was like clockwork with my father) I guess Saturday was the only night of the week he took a bath. Every Saturday night I had to wash his back, and this would go on for the next several years. I go into the bathroom, and he's naked in the bathtub (of course). My father handed me the soap, a washcloth with the bar of soap in it. Thank goodness, I didn't have to look for the soap. Sometimes I had to find it, but never in front of him under water. I tried not to touch his body. Sometimes, I would accidently touch my father's body and his skin. It felt very slick. I would occasionally drop the soap and then I would have to reach into the soapy water, and search for the soap. Not like my father couldn't find it for himself and handed it to me. Then I would continue washing his back.

All I knew I wanted to get out of there. I am only in the seventh grade when this was going on. Why can't he wash his own fricking back? (I want to tell my father that I don't want to wash your back anymore.) How does a child tell her father she doesn't want to touch him, with the fear of knowing she might get beat? Eventually, I started to resent my father for having to touch him. I felt dirty having to touch the water; let alone him. I didn't mind touching my own bath water but for some odd reason I hated putting my hands in his dirty water. As soon as I was done, I washed my hands in the kitchen sink with dish soap to get my father's bath water off my skin. Eventually, I got the idea to take off from the house an hour before my father was ready take a bath, and not coming back home until about 9:30. I knew he would be gone by then. I would just go out riding my bike. Nowhere in particular, just around my neighborhood.

Growing bored, I would finally pedal back up that damn hill, back to my house. It would be around 9:40 and my father is gone for the whole night playing poker. Cool I got the house to myself. It is very lonely, but it's worth it. I haven't seen Stan since we moved in 1974 and as I said before I still missed him terribly. The way Stan told me, I am a good girl, and he loved me. He was the only person who said he loved me besides some of my other relatives, my grandmothers. When were out, my mother would drive over to Wilbur store which was right across the street from Stan's house to get lunch, and hamburger meat for the rest of the week. I could see Stan's house and he was with his family standing around in front of his house. I would just casually walk slowly past his house. I said hi to Stan and smiled. He smiled at me, and say hi back. I remembered he asked me how I liked my new house. I told him I liked it, but it was too far out to walk back to Wilbur's store. I waited for my mother. Stan didn't even invite me into his house. This is the second time I came over to his house, and he didn't let me visit him. I found out later, he had some kids that were my age, and in the same grade as me. We went to the same school. I remembered asking who those people were in those pictures on the wall, and Stan said they were his kids. I told Stan I was in class with one of his kids and his name was TJ. His sister name was Lera. She was in three grades ahead of me. I liked TJ at first. All the girls liked TJ.

During some holiday, our cousins from Davenport, Mississippi would come and visit. All of us were happy to see our cousins come down from Mississippi. My mother would make room for everyone to be comfortable for a week or two. Rocket, Mazac, Rashaun, and I would say, Rashaun was a little baby at the time, and their sister Da Shanda. I liked our cousins a lot. My father, Tobert and Suan were brothers, and they liked to drink.

When the weekend came, they would get together and get drunk. We knew we could get away with a lot more stuff because their attention was on drinking; not on us. After everyone was finally settled in and both of our parents would go out, I would have sex with my cousins. Not Towan or Antwon had sex with our female cousins. Sometime when we went over to their house, Aunt Tarrasa would let me sleep with Da Shanda. Sometimes Da Shanda and I would play around, but not for long. I liked it, but I don't think she did. This went on for several years at each other's houses. One time when they were visiting, all of us kids were down stairs. Not even thinking about what I was saying.

I said very innocently, "It's funny we all are having sex with each other."

Out of nowhere, Towan hit me in my stomach so hard, he knocked the wind out of me. He hit me with such tremendous force I just doubled over in pain and cried because it hurt so badly, I thought I died.

I said, you wait until my mother gets home, I 'm going to tell on you.

Towan said, "If I did, he would beat the shit out of me." I never told my mother when she came home. I didn't think it was wrong with what I said. I thought all brothers and sisters did. The sex went on with Towan for a year. Towan knew I was not lying so why did he hit me so hard like. He treated me as if I said something so dirty. A few months down the road, we had finished eating dinner and my mother told us kids to go down stairs, and watch TV. And we did. Antwon had track practice and so it was just Towan and I. My mother sent the two of us down stairs to watch TV. It was about 7:00 in the evening and he looked at me and motioned for me to come over and sit on his lap (sounds like one of Stan's suggestions), and I was to face the TV. As if I was watching it,

I said, "What if we were caught?"

Towan said, "We wouldn't get caught because my father is out in the garage, and my mother was in the kitchen doing dishes."

I was very nervous and very scared. Thinking what could happen, I did what he told me to do. I pulled my pants down to my ankles, got on top of him, he put his penis inside me (I don't know whose penis is larger Stan's or Towan's) I'm not even on top of him two minute, and my mother came down stairs, I just froze, I didn't know what to do. Towan said what is wrong, and I just sat there in silence

My mother said, "Get upstairs Jaynie." I flew upstairs.

I don't know what happened, all I knew Towan and I never had sex again. It was nice actually, because Towan never put any feelings into it anyway. I didn't like having sex with him. It felt like Towan just wanted to put his penis in me, do his thing, and leave.

I didn't understand why it was wrong with having sex with your brother! I figured if a child could have sex with your next-door neighbor for eight years, why was it wrong with your brother? Sex with family members were never talked about in school. My parents never said anything to us about it at home.

Now I am hitting the eighth grade and I am 15 years old. I am very tall for a girl my age. I am chasing after boys because I want them to like me, but they would not give me the time of day. I never learned how to approach or manage boys in junior high school. I thought if I had sex with them they would like me better! I was thinking, I could use my body to attract boys and men. While I was walking home from school one night, this older man pulled up next to me and offered me a ride. I was not scared or anything. I didn't want to walk home so I accepted. He asked me my name, and I told him. He asked me my age. Of course, I didn't want to tell him I was only 15. I told him I was 17 almost 18. He asked if I had a boyfriend, I told him no.

He did tell me he thought I was attractive. I did like to hear that from men. He said he was married, but he was not happy. This stranger was rather attractive for his age. I thought he was about 40 something. He asked me if I have seen a penis before? I told him yes, my brother's, and our old neighbor's Stan's. He asked if I would like to touch him, and right away, I knew what he wanted. I played innocent. He then offered me money to touch him, and I said ok. He gave me

$80.00 just to hold his cock and play with it. I did and before we got to my home, he came and he said he had a nice time. He kissed my cheek, and I said thanks. I got out of the car, and went into my house. He left and I never seen him again. What Stan taught me all those years, was coming into focus! I am more comfortable having sex for money; I know how I can make it. I was still trying to find a boyfriend, but no boys liked me. One morning I was walking down the hill to catch the bus, I just happened to notice these two white men moving in to a house. The shorter one had red hair and a moustache. The taller one had curly black hair and a moustache and he looked damn good. What I also noticed there were no women around helping. One particular morning for no good reason at all, I stopped at these guys' house.

My neighbor said,

"Hi and who might you be?"

My name is Jaynie. I live on top of the hill. …. What's your name?"

He's 5'10, 28 years old, I am only 14, and still in boring 8th grade.

"Randy Harmony."

Well hi Randy I just wanted to welcome you to our neighborhood... I have to get going…. Maybe we can talk again some other time ok?

"That's fine Jaynie, and nice to meet you."

I was getting off the bus and starting walking up the hill. I looked over and saw randy in the yard. He walks up to me.

Randy asked me, "Would you like to come over later on tonight?"

What about your roommate?

"He would be gone all night."

I went home and lingered until later that night.

I'm at his house, sitting on his couch,

"Would I like some wine", Randy asked?

Yes.

We sat and drank wine and talked. I was in the 8th grade, I started drinking wine at an early age in my parents' home. I think I was 11 or so. My father had the bar in the basement, and stocked. I started taking sips out of the open bottles. My favorite wine was "Boone's Farm" wine.

Randy leaned over to kiss me, and so I just let the evening flow.

After the evening was over with Randy, I could not wait to have sex with Randy again. He was even better than Stan was. Randy kissed my body all over and he used his mouth as Stan did. The only thing different was when Randy went down on me he would lick me for a long time.

His fingers felt nice, and his kisses are so sweet and very tender. I know I was very young having sex with Randy; I didn't care, neither did he. Don't miss understand me, I really wanted to have sex with Randy. I was very lonely. I didn't like any of the boys at school. Nobody wanted to date me. He didn't push anything on me. Yes, I knew he was older and I should have known better.

Possibly, to Randy, there was a curiosity to find out what it's like to sleep with a different race other than his own. Why I didn't tell anyone because I knew my parents would take Randy from me. My parents were gone again. I even tried to tell my mother where I would be going. Again, my mother said she doesn't care where I was going, and didn't care what time I got home. I sometimes think my parents knew I was into something. They never said anything or maybe they just didn't know how. I was seeing Randy for the next two years, and it was of my own choice. He knew I was under age, but he played it off well. If he would have treated me mean or strange, Randy knew I would tell on him and he would definitely get into a whole lot of trouble. He would have me come over a lot, and I really enjoyed my time with him. I did whatever Randy wanted me to do because I liked him very much. I think I liked him more than he liked me. However, as long as he was good to me I kept going over to his house. Sometimes I would be on the other side of town, I missed the bus, and I didn't have a way home.

I would hitch a ride and most of the men picked me up were a lot older than I was. They would always ask me where I wanted to go. I would make a place so we could end up driving for a while, and the next thing I knew they were touching me my hand. I would tell them I don't think you can afford it. I would let them do anything they wanted; except kissing. I think sex is gross except with Stan and Randy. However, the men I would ride with would have to be much older than myself. They had to remind me of Stan somehow, someway. I would allow these men to go down on me, and sometimes penetrate me with their fingers. Only if they excited me or if I found them attractive would I have sex with them. Before they would take me home, I would have $200.00 sometimes more. This is what I learned from Stan. I knew I could make money with my body. Stan first started out giving me just 1.00, but it changed after a while, and he kept giving me more money. I'm thinking, I can have anything I want for a price. Older men had to pay. I thought I had these older men under control. Boy was I wrong! I was very blind. I knew I was too young to be out hitchhiking, but I didn't really give a damn, what happened. I hated myself and my body, and my parents.

CHAPTER 4

WHAT I DIDN'T realize, this would be my problem for the next thirty-five years of my life. I let the older men touch me, but sex was an iffy. I allowed it, depending on how old they were, meaning if they were Stan's age, also depending on the amount I wanted. I wished I would have known now what I knew back then. I guess I associated my experiences with Stan to the present. I am in junior high school, still noticing the neighbor Alex across the street. He is still working on this house. I wonder what it will look like inside. I'm sure if it looked as good as it did on the outside as the inside, awesome.

One summer day I was on my way to catch the bus to go to school and saw our neighbor Alex across the street. I wanted to make small talk but there was always someone around, my parents were outside doing something with the house. Now I have a chance to talk to him. I am walked really slow so he seen me.

I said, "Alex."

(I noticed he had muscles) and he was working on his deck.

Alex said, "Hi back at you."

I replied, "Bye the way I like how you fixed up your house! How are you?"

Alex replied, "I am fine just working as you can see."

Do you remember my name Alex? I know it has been awhile since I spoke with you.

"I have to be honest I did forget your name."

It's Jaynie.

"Hi Jaynie."

Alex are you all done with your house?

"Yes I am, why would ask?"

Well I was thinking, maybe some time I can see how it looks inside!

"Maybe someday you can."

I have to go. I started walking down the street to catch the bus to go to school. See ya' later Alex!

"Bye Jaynie, have fun in school."

I had many crushes on boys and girls. It was not really crushes if I saw a girl I liked the, I would hang out with her. I really could not make up my mind. One boy I truly had a crush on was John Joneston. His family lived right behind us. They were pretty well off, and so were we. I was jealous because he would talk to the other girls. But we never talked when we were at school. John didn't have any interest in me and we just became friends. It seems to me the men who did not want anything to do with me became my friends. In addition, the ones who didn't like me I had sex with. I could not figure one out if I tried. One of those guy's name was Rusty Tiesmond. I found Rusty good looking. But he knew it too. I called him one time, and we talked for a while and we deiced to meet in the woods behind our high school. The next day after school we did. I was really nervous and scared. However, I wanted to have sex with him so he started to kiss me and he took my pants down and started to put his fingers in me and I let him. We laid down on the ground, and then it was it. It never happened again. I really liked Rusty, but all he wanted was sex and I thought if I did have sex with him, I thought he would like me. Nevertheless, he didn't. I remember one early morning summer I had to clean the house, and my father was washing his truck. I think my mother was grocery shopping.

I was looking through the newspaper and I saw this ad: Wanted skiing companion for the winter if interested call this number. I called the number, and this man answered. We were talking for a while and I saw my father leave the house. The man asked me if I live alone, and I said no. He asked if he could meet me, and I told him sure, but I said my father just left, and I do not know when he will be back. He said he would not stay long and he just wanted to ask me a few questions. I said sure come over. Not more than ten minutes he showed up on his motorcycle. He was very good looking, tall, white and black hair and moustache was thick. I invited this stranger into our house. We are talking and lite laughing and he comes up to my face and kisses me. The next thing I know is we were having sex on the floor in the kitchen. This went on for about five minutes, and then I have never had the experience before. I told him my father should be coming home soon. He left and just as he is going down the hill to the left of the house here comes my father over the hill to the right. After, I tried getting hold of him later on week, but the add was taken out of the newspaper. As you can see, my crushes did not last long. My stupidity did. John Joneston and I became friends at school. However, we also we had an attraction for each other out of school.

When we were in school, he never talked with me, but when he was by himself, he treated me much different. We talked on the phone for hours until it became nighttime and then he would ask me to come over and we would sit out in his back yard, look up at the starts, hug, and kiss each other, which I thought it was nice. He introduced me, to his family. I found them to be very nice. John and I had a secret relationship for about six months. It ended later because he moved out of Lexington Iowa in 1976. I am still in the 8th grade. I missed him for a long time. He was the first real relationship I ever had even if were secretive. Now I am saving money from all of my babysitting jobs. I had asked my mother if I could have a phone installed in my bedroom because we only had one line. Every time I was on the phone my mother would always tell me to get off the phone. My mother said I would have to pay for it so I said ok. Now I have my very first telephone number and it feels good. Independence is a good thing.

After about a couple of month of having my phone a strange man named Charlie Brown I didn't even know would call on my phone and ask to speak to my mother, and so, he would call almost every day. I approached my mother.

I said, "Momma you said I could have this phone in my room for me only.

My mother replied, "It's my house."

But it's my phone. Not hers. What can I say? It's really my father's house. Not hers. My mother always said everything was hers. Several different occasions she would take me to the mall at 7:00 in the evening and she would leave me there until sometimes 9:00. You would think a parent would show more responsibility. I do not know where she went when she would drop me off at the mall. But the good thing is she gave me spending money. In addition, she wasn't even in the mall. Then she would arrive back at where she drops me off at home, and we would go home not speaking a word to each other. When we got home my father would ask us were we been. My mother lied to my father and told him that we went to the mall. I didn't like the feeling or knowing the fact I was helping my mother perpetrate a lie. I can see in my father's eyes that he didn't believe her.

I am hitting the big 9th grade and **I am 15 years-old. I will**

now use my father's first name. My friend Melissa Millstadt and I are on our way to Mc Finley Junior High School. Our first class was in our homeroom class. Melissa and I walked to our class together. This boy Jerry Milton was showing off in front of his friends and he started messing with me. First, it started with smart-ass comments he was throwing at me, I was throwing them right back at him.

He started pushing me into lockers and stuff. I told Terry to bug off and leave me the hell alone, but he just kept pushing me around. I jumped up, I kicked him in the chest, and he went flying backwards into the lockers. Our teacher heard the commotion and he sent Jerry and me to the principal's office. He and I were suspended from school for the next two days. I didn't even start the fight. I had to go back home around 9:00 in the morning. Now what do I do? Where am I going to go? Why can't I be an animal an animal, or something right about now? I was praying to God, neither parents would not be home. Wouldn't that be great? Finally got to the top of the hill I noticed some men were moving something into the house so I am thinking this might just take all day dammit. Wrong again! I get to the back door and they are just finishing up as they were going out I was going in. I went down stairs to see what it was and I was surprised to see a big TV console. My father had just finished pushing it against the wall. I just know I was going get my ass beat again. My father always said if you run away from a fight you would get beat, if you start a fight you would get the shit beat out of you. It seems in my family you can't win for losing.

My father asked, "Why you home from school Jaynie?"

Jerry and I had been suspended from school for fighting, but it was not my fault.

"Get those damn clothes off and get me that damn paddle."

That paddle dad been used on all of us kids. On our entire

butt's, heads, arms, back, or where ever it landed.

And the nasty thing about it, you see skin and blood all over the paddle. I took off my clothes right in front of him. He just sat there and watched with the paddle hanging in his hand. I was so scared I had to run to the bathroom I came back, and he told me to kneel down in front of me and I did. I remember how I kneeled in front of him in second grade when he beat my hands. Well is about to happen again. I know he wants to beat me. I can see it in his face I was already crying in front of him, and he has not even laid a hand on me yet. I did not think it then, but I think it now. My father is a sadomasochist. It sees the more we scream the harder he hits us and the more blood he sees the more it excited him.

Daddy I swear to God it was not my fault.

Terry started it I was just defending myself. I remember you said stand up for ourselves and fight our own battles', what I was doing. If you don't believe me, you can call Melissa she could tell you what happened. I am not lying. For the second time I am actually telling my father the truth. About a hour and a half of sitting in front of my father naked, I had developing breasts and pubic hair, my body was quite noticeable. He told me to get dressed. He didn't even hit me or nothing. As I was heading toward the stairs, I was thanking God, he didn't beat me. While I was heading up the stairs, I was thinking why should I not be able to tell my mother.

"Jaynie!"

Yes, sir.

"If you tell anyone especially yo' momma I will beat the living shit out of you do you understand me?"

Yes, sir.

My father's last comment really shocked the hell out of me. Ever since I could remember, my parents always beat us naked. And they always told each other when we got an ass beating. He would normally tell her everything else and she would do the same with my father, so why not now? My mother came home and you know what I had forgotten all about it the almost ass beating. About this time, I am starting to allow my feelings to come out how I felt towards girls my age. I still had a strong attraction for men.

I was feeling attached to girls all through first grade, elementary, and junior high school. There was this girl at school named Dori Stratton. She looked so much like a boy. I heard she was a lesbian, but I didn't know what a lesbian looked like. Maybe all lesbians look like boys!

Hum … I will have to check out sometime. However, why would a girl want to look like a guy? It made no sense to me. Anyway, I would watch her walk down the hall. She had the prettiest eyes, and I have to say a very nice booty. She didn't carry a purse, but she did have a wallet in her back pocket. I wanted to get to know her. Do I approach her without sounding stupid? I am feeling a weird feeling inside my stomach when I see her. It is like a tingling sensation. I can't explain it any better than. I have always wondered if I had the strength to approach Dori. She always walked around very cocky. I think is what attracted me to her. Her hair was short right above the neckline. She wore jeans all the time she never wore a dress as long as I knew her. I made sure I saw her every day. I would think, how do or will I approach her. She is so beautiful I just love her walk. She is about 5'8 and is 16. I will just have to wait and see what happens. I watch her walk by me and I felt good inside. When she said hello, I felt giddy inside. I wonder if she can see it. Even though I knew, she knows nothing about me or even had a clue. I had a major attraction to her. I had to realize I will have to talk to her in time.

I couldn't wait to take a shower with the other girls. I always liked watching girls running naked through the shower room. Of course, I felt fat and ugly. Thanks to both my parents for their constant support of my self-esteem, and confidence. I really had this attraction for this one guy name Robert Lyght in junior high. My mother played bingo every Friday and Saturday night until 1:00 in the morning, and my father of course played poker every weekend. When my father left the house I would call Robert and invite him over, we would have sex in my bedroom. Then he would leave. He was nice, but he was not like Stan for sure. He treated me more like how Towan treated me. There was no feeling in it at all. This continued for a while. I just decided to stop seeing him. After a while, I started to become depressed. I didn't want to do anything or go anywhere. Food was my comfort zone. I couldn't do anything right in my parent's eyes. I was a burden to my sister. Maye would rather hang out with my cousins Jessie and Tonda. I guess they had more in common with my sister then I did. I was a burden to Antwon and Towan. I didn't know how to play football or basketball. I just wanted to belong and to be accepted. Finally, it was getting to hard to fit in anywhere. I concluded I just wanted a way out. I tried to commit suicide four times before the age of 15. My parents never knew about it. I felt they didn't mind if I lived or died. I know you think oh come on but trust me it is true. Many times, I thought suicide would be the answer. Something would not let me do it. I would start to got scared, and call the hospital. What would happen if you did this or. I swallowed a handful of my mother pills, I got scared, and I made myself puke. One time I did trying cutting my wrist, but fricking knife was sharp.

Why did my sister and brothers hate me so much? I have done nothing to them. I know little sisters can be a pain sometimes, but so can big brothers, and sister. When I was around the house I was a bother to everyone. When I am away from the house, my family seems better off. I really don't want to live I hate my life, my family, and I hate me! Death seemed such a nice place to be. I know death would be a lot better than the house I lived in with my family. I have caused nothing but shame, pain, humiliation and I am only 16. How does a 16-year-old cause much devastation? Why was I even born? Why didn't my mother get an abortion? She always said to me when she was angry with herself. I wish I could have taken Jeffery's place many times growing up. My family doesn't want me any way. I just want my parents to love me and be proud of me. If I could run away, I would. However, I would not know where to run.

Part of 9th and 10th grade was very scary time for me. I thought if I dated men were older I would be more mature. Little did I know I was completely wrong? I thought the young guys in high school liked me for me, but they didn't. Is why I decided to date older men. Older men were more mature and we would have great sex, sometimes we would have dinner, and sometimes-older men would buy me stuff. I was attracted to men who were 30-55 years old. I was dating this one man in particular Jerry Richards, I think he was married whenever, I asked him he said he wasn't. I just believed it. But he really was. I was just naïve. He was a traveling salesman and he was good looking. I only saw him when he was in town. When he was in town, he would call me from his hotel I would meet him, we would have sex then I would go home. It became boring very fast. It seemed the only time I see Jerry was when he wanted to have sex. I wanted more. He said he didn't want a relationship with any one. I pulled away. I missed Jerry for a while, but I eventually got over it.

Wow, I am **16 years- old** and in the 10th grade. Maye is living by herself across town. Towan found an apartment with Meloney, (I will call her Mel, for short). They lived right across the street from the school I went to. Now I can stop by and say hi to Mel. The only one left in the house with me is Antwon. He is busy with gymnastics. I don't have anyone to talk with except my friends down the street. I feel I am becoming terribly depressed, lonely, and abandoned. I definitely don't want to go to school. If I didn't go to school, the school would call my parents. My father would beat my ass so bad he would break a bone in my body, or my neck. Therefore, I have no choice but to stay in school. If I could quit and die at the same day, I would be so happy. Let me tell ya' life is so sad. My family isn't proud of me. They don't care if I failed. Why should I be excited about the 10th grade? When I would leave for school, I would tell my mother that I was leaving, and she told me that she doesn't care. I wonder, when I am not home, at home does it make my mother happy? When I am, home does it make my mother angry? Does she hate the sight of me?

Does she wish I should have died instead of my twin brother Jeffery! They are very proud of my sister and brothers' accomplishments throughout their junior and senior years. Before Towan had moved out of our house, Towan had a job for over several years. I felt jealous I didn't have a job. So when he would get off work in the morning from working third shift. He would be dog-tired. I would be getting ready for school and he would be crawling into bed. Towan would have already cashed his check. Being the good sister I was, I just helped Towan spend some of his money while I was in junior and senior high; I use to take ten dollars at a time out of Towan's wallet. If Towan knew I was stealing money out of his wallet, Towan would have beaten the crap out of me. I took money from Towan's for a few months he never noticed it. Boy, he was tired! (Hmmm). For some unknown reason I decided to do the same thing to my father. Call me stupid. Was I looking for a death wish! One time when my father would come home, have dinner, go down stairs, and watch

TV. At some time while he was watching T.V. he would get up take off his pants and lay them on the couch. I would come down stairs with him watch TV acting as if I was enjoying the show. I would be down stairs for a good two hours. I would wait until he was asleep and then I would go into his wallet. I would be shaking like a leaf, until I got the money back upstairs. The next day I would go to Wilbur's store and buy lots of candy, on my way to school. The following night he would come home furious and calling us all down stairs and asking my mother, Antwon, and me who took his twenty dollars. We all just stood there looking like we don't know. No one admitted. I knew I wasn't going to tell on myself.

My father said, if he finds the one who took the money they are going to wish they never been born. Call me stupid! I did it again the next night. The next day I bought candy, note pads, pencils, whatever I wanted to buy. Again, my father asked us again and again no one admitted.

I guess I was taking his money because I resented everything he represents in being a so-called father. I also felt in my mind I was punishing him, for all the times he didn't give us an allowance growing up. If we wanted one, we had to beg for it. Almost like Robin Hood taking from the rich (my father) giving to the poor me. I only did it for about two months because the fear of being caught was always in the back of my mind. However, I never did and he never even had a clue about who was doing this to him. You would think he would fake sleep to catch who was taking his money. Thank God, he didn't if he did, I knew I would not be sitting down for a while. On the other hand, he would have broken my bones or death. I never heard my family say they were proud of me. I really needed to hear from my family. I guess you can say I made my own praise. Good news! My Grandma O is coming to visit for the summer again. I cannot wait to see her. Grandma was and will always be a very strong independent woman to me. When we would get in trouble, she would spank us with a switch. Then she would say I love you and you should have known better. I really love my grandma. I love her more than I love my own mother. Actually, I don't love either of my parents at all. The more I try to love them and gain their love back, the more they pushed me away. I think our love for each other stopped for the two of us when 1963. I remember so many times my parents would be fighting, and,

My father said, "I should kill you, and daughter of yours.... is what I should do, you fucking bitch!"

I would be in the bed listening to all this because our rooms were right next to each other. Then I would hear my mother crying and,

My mother said, "Sylvet she is your daughter and he is your son."

"The fuck she ain't. I don't know what you were doing when they were born."

Why does my father hate me so much? Is it something I have done? Why would he want to kill me? Most importantly, why does he want to kill my mother? If he is unhappy with us, why does he not leave? No one is telling him he has to stay! Many times, I would get dressed and lay in my clothes just waiting to make an exit out my bedroom window. However, after a while, I would fall asleep and the house would be quiet. Maybe is when I should have been scared.

Who knows what I would have done or tried to do if he walked into my room and tried to kill me in the dark? Maybe it is something my mother has done to him in the past. Whatever she did; it is haunting him and still in the present is why he is threatening to kill me? Who knows when it comes to my father and his stupid anger! I knew my father always kept a gun in the bedroom closet. One-night my father came home drunk and he was mad he lost a lot of money playing poker. He came home and took it out on my mother. I don't know what was exactly said, but I heard the gun shot. The next day when my parents left, I went into their room and looked for the bullet. There was the bullet lodged in the wall not far from the ceiling, on my mother's side of the bed.

However, she put a picture of the hole to cover it up; I don't even think my brothers and sister knew. If my father were unhappy, why would he want to shoot my mother? At the time, I didn't know parents would want to shoot each other. Growing up in my house was extremely volatile. Actually, I always had the fear one-time my father would actually carry out with his threats of shooting us. There were some good times, mostly bad times in our household. You never knew when my father was mad. He would beat you for the stupidest thing.

Or my father would have a bad day at work and if he would take it out on one of us kids. One of the ways he would make us suffer was to have us crawl on the floor on our hands and knees and pick up stuff on the floor. The one thing I most hated about my father was when he would sit between my legs. I would have to scratch the dandruff out of his hair. All the dandruff would fall all over my lap. Then I would have to take hair grease and grease his whole head. I couldn't wait for to be over. I just hated touching my father in any way. When he was in one of his moods, my father would tell us to wash and wax both cars. He would walk behind us to make sure we did it right? By the way, my father was in public. You would never know this man was a perfectionist. I felt like there were eggshells everywhere, morning, noon, or night we stepped on all of them. When my father was angry, he didn't talk in a normal voice. He would yell us to get the point across that he was mad. He was the man in the house I mean master of the house and we were his slaves. When we be watched his TV it would piss him off. If you were watching a good movie, he came down stairs and he would change the channel. He didn't care if you were watching it or not. It was his TV, his house, his rules.

My father would first look in the TV Guide to see what he wanted to watch. He would tell one of us kids to turn the channel. It really made all the kids upset. You learned very early you don't talk back to your parents. If you wanted to go flying across the room, picking yourself up off the floor.

I knew my day of moving out on my own would be coming eventually. Alex, our across the street neighbor, is looking better when I see him. I kept checking him out. When I'm mowing the lawn, when I 'am playing in the front yard, when I 'am walking to catch the bus, and on my way home from school. I what reason will I come up with to see him? I could think of many reasons to visit Alex; I just didn't want the reasons to sound stupid or childish. I wanted him to think I at least had some brains. Finally, I am in 11th grade and 17 years of age. Just one more year and I'm done with school. Thank God. I answered an ad in the paper for after school and summer childcare, and I got the job. The Cresants had a little girl named Laurel. She was five years old. They also had two twin boys named Davis and Michael. They were three. The family is nice. The mother was from Africa. Her name was Constance. Constance's husband is a white man his name is Willis. Finally, I had a chance to go over to Alex's house. It's Saturday night in the month of February and its cold. Not bad. I was so nervous. I was sweating profusely. The way I was sweating, I didn't even notice it was winter outside. The moon was out and full of excitement. My mother is on her way to bingo as usual, and my father is getting ready to go play poker.

I left the house around 8:00 in the evening. I won't have to wash my father's back tonight. I rode around on my bike, and watched for his car to pass. When it did, I peddled back up the hill to Alex's house. I am getting nervous. I don't know why. I have butterflies in my stomach and my hands are sweating. It's not as if Alex was my boyfriend or anything like. I guess I am afraid of rejection. I have experienced rejection so much in my life. I' am rather use to it, but not really. I imagined what Alex and I would do. I can't wait to go over to his house. While I was still in the 9th grade, I stopped chasing the stupid guy's in junior high. Then in the remainder of 9th grade, I started chasing older men. Older men are more mature than the boys in junior high are. I guess when I finally had sex with Randy was the decisive factor. I have been thinking about having sex with Alex for a very long time. Ever since, we moved into the neighborhood five years ago. What if my parents come home early, and see me leaving Alex's house! Oh, what do I say? How would I explain it?

Right now, I do not care. If I get a beating later, it would be worth it. I remember putting on one of my mother's is tight revealing shirts. I hoped he noticed it. I finally got the courage up to go over to his house. I am over there less than 30 seconds. It seems like hours before I got to the door. I am standing at his door and it is darker than dark outside. The streetlights are working right. It just seems so dark I am scared as hell! What if he's not home? I saw his living room light on. I go to leave, but I am too damn scared to move. I am talking under my breath to myself. Come on Jaynie, what is there to be scared of? He's not going to hurt you! I raised my head to look up. I finally knocked on the door. I heard him coming down the stairs. All I remember is when he opened the door my heart stopped. He invited me into his home. I know he knows why I am here. He's not making it obvious and neither am I.

Hi Alex,

"I just thought I would stop by and take you up on rain check." One reason I just wanted to be nosey to see if the house was finished.

Alex answered." I remember somewhat. It's been many years.

Cool "It would be nice to see how you completed you house."

Welcome come in and look around. He stepped aside and I walked up the stairs into his home. Alex is 31 years old. He is 6'0 tall, sandy blond hair, and has bluish green eyes.

Alex wore glasses, however, would look better without them. His skin was soft, and tanned from working outside with no shirt on. The khaki pants Alex was wearing; I have to say Alex's body is looking very good. Everything was in the right place. He followed behind me. He showed me around the house and I'm impressed. We are sitting on the floor talking about, his house, my going to high school, my family and his family. Unexpected Alex said, "Would you like to get high

Jaynie, would you like to get high?

Sure.

He is rolling a joint right in front of me and he gave it to me to light it. The first time I got high was a few years ago at our new house in the garage with my sister Maye and my brother Towan. I remembered coughing at first and I remember they were laughing at me. I got upset, went into the house, and started eating everything in sight. I never smoked it again until night with Alex. We are talking about stupid things.

We were laughing our asses off. My mouth is somewhat dry; I asked for a pop. Instead, he offers me wine. Alex and I are lying parallel to each other. He leaned over to kiss me. I let him. I kiss him back. I am hungry for his kisses. I'm starving for affection, starving for his touch. I want him to kiss me longer and never stop. I'm stoned and intoxicated. I forgot to tell Alex when I drink wine I get horny. I said without hesitation, Where's your bedroom?

Alex shoots a look at me and he is smiling.

Alex said "Down the hall and to the right. … Do you want to see it?

Yes, I would.

Alex got up off the floor, offered his hand to me, and he started walking down the hall. I followed him holding hands. We walked into his bedroom. His bed is unmade. The light is on. His room is off white with tan carpet. His room was a total mess. I didn't care. By then I just want him in bed! He started to undress me. 3I let him. As I begin to remove his shirt, I am kissing his lips his neck, his chest, and everywhere he would allow me to kiss. We are lying in bed naked with each other.

I said to Alex, "What if I get pregnant?"

We will name it Alex.

We didn't use a condom stupid us. To be honest I don't know why. We continued and I just really got into the romantic side of sex with Alex. The kind of sex I have been searching for so long. Alex touched me all over with his mouth. He took his tongue, and started to rub my nipples, my shoulders. He started to go down toward my stomach, which butterflies are going crazy. Goddess, he is hot and good with his mouth, and ever so gentle with his tongue. Not biting hard, but biting enough I don't want him to stop. Hi biting was not too soft, but just right. I like this kind of kissing and touching a lot. After about four and half hour, we finally lay next to each other in bed and I am very relaxed.

It's getting rather late Alex; I should be going home.

I didn't want to let him go at all let me tell ya.

"What time is it.?"

"It's 1:00 in the morning."

After fooling around with Alex awhile longer I finally got up to head home. I decided to head to Brownhanson so I can have a cover in case my mother was home. I rode my bike to their house, there were no lights on so I peddled back home. While lying in bed an hour later, I couldn't stop thinking about Alex. I would find any reason to look at his house. I would be outside doing cartwheels in the front yard in a swimming suit so he would see me.

I wanted to have sex with Alex again. I'll see what happens. About a week later, I went over to see Alex one night I wanted to have sex with him again. He opened the door and he saw it was me.

Alex said, "Jaynie you are a very sweet young lady. . . But we should not let this happen again."

"Did I do something wrong?"

"Not at all you did everything right. It is just you are rather too young for me.

You are 17 years old and I am 31

You soon you will be an adult and you should be dating guy's your own age.

I am just looking at Alex with my mouth open, wondering what the fuck just happened.

Alex said, good night Jaynie. As he closed the door, I left his house crying.

I am 17 years old. I am thinking and hoping that we could have sex again. A week after playing with Alex, I noticed my period was late. Oh my God! What the hell am I going to do now? I waited about two more weeks. Then I knew I was pregnant. I'm 17 when I realized I was pregnant. Alex was the last man I slept with. It has been a long time since I had sex with anyone. I was so afraid I didn't know what I should do. I knew I couldn't tell my parents. I knew I couldn't trust Maye, not with her big mouth, she would go right to my mother. Instead,

I told my brother Towan. I begged him not to tell anyone. He was the only one I knew would keep my secret. I thought it was only fair since I kept his. He said he would not tell on me. He did keep his promise. Towan admitted to me later he had suffered my mother's rath. He took many ass beatings for me, and he still kept my secret. I didn't tell anyone not even Alex. I was in high school in the 11th grade and pregnant. Thank God, it was not any one from school. At school I would be studying in a book, I would just fall asleep, within a few minutes of laying my head down. I would wake up in a cold sweat. My body was developing a child in my stomach. Wow, is all I could say. As Jennifer grew inside I became more nervous, scared and more confuse. I couldn't even be happy about her coming into the world. How would I be able to tell my parents? They don't even love or care for me. On the other hand, they don't want me around. They wished I would get out of their sight.

I'm just a big stupid cow, and I will never amount to anything. No one likes cows. The fear they instilled in all of us kids early in life was the one thing I never forgot. The strongest reason why I never told my parents, I was afraid they would have beaten me for getting pregnant.

And I was ashamed. In July, Grandma Odemesse was visiting us. I was I was already five months pregnant. I desperately wanted to tell her. I was scared and I knew she would tell my parents. I was afraid I would be beaten severely and possible lose my baby. I never told her. God, I wish I had. I felt bad I couldn't share my news with my grandmother. I knew and felt she would not be ashamed of me. She is the only woman I truly loved in my family besides my grandmother's sisters. When I was home, I hardly ate anything. I was so hungry. I was afraid if I started eating at the house my mother would realize I was eating more than I should. When I was away from home, I would eat like a horse. Twice a week I would go to a Sub King Sandwich shop in downtown Iowa, and they had the best sub sandwiches you have ever tasted. Before I was pregnant, I could only eat one. When I was pregnant, I was able to eat a foot long with no

problem. My only transportation was my bike, bus, or my feet. I had to walk everywhere. The one thing I craved most was a full glass of ice and 1/2 cup of water. All I would want to do is crunch, crunch, crunch.

I am in about the fifth month of my pregnancy. My mother started asking questions about me to Maye. Maye didn't know. I'm being teased in school. I would wear baggy pants and big shirts so it would not be noticeable. How did they know or suspect that I was pregnant? Was this beyond me? I never told a soul at school. I finally got tired of the students teasing me about being pregnant and I couldn't take it anymore. So I dropped out of school. My mother is dying of curiosity. All she can do is wonder. I thought about telling my mother that I was pregnant.

Then I thought about all of the things she said to me. So I kept my mouth shut. Finally, my mother couldn't stand it anymore. She told Maye to take me to see our family doctor Dr. Harrisberg.

While driving in the car I said.

"I am pregnant. I think about five to six months along."

I looked in the review mirror and my mother followed behind us. We arrived at Dr. Harrisberg office and he asks me to lie on the table. I started to cry and I told him I was.

He touched my stomach a couple of times and he took me into his office where my mother was waiting. Dr. Harrisberg guessed I was seven months pregnant.

"You're getting an abortion."

No I'm not. …. Abortions are very sad. They kill the baby.

I just could not/would not do that to a child. … The thought of having an abortion would make me want to take my own life, if I took the life of a child.

My mother kept pushing abortion, and I was trying my best to fight her. My mother sat in silence after what I said.

Jaynie, you are so stupid. Why don't you use those damn brains that you were born with? What were you be thinking? What about the Corevine's pride?

What about it? … It never did me any good.

I looked dead in her eyes. Corevine's pride or not, I am not having an abortion! Who cares about the stupid pride! I sure in the hell don't. All I knew, I am having this baby. I don't care if you like it or not. That was the first time I ever talked back to my mother. We left the office. There was so much silence you could hear a pin drop. I carried Jennifer in my rib cage.

I hardly showed at all thank God. How would have my mother handled it if I were showing and walking like a penguin. Boy, I think she would have had a cow! She would be so upset with me. My mother would be beside herself. In addition, the shame on her face would make it obvious that she had been embarrassed of me.

I decided on the name Jennifer Patrice Corevine. Isn't that a pretty name?

"You will be putting her up for adoption."

No I won't …. You just watch me. I'm keeping her. The day I went to Dr. Harrisberg was on Wednesday October 31 1979. A couple of days later I am down stairs watching TV. All of a sudden, I felt this pushing sensation. I was not sure what was happening with my body. I just knew that I wasn't feeling good at all. I just played it safe and went to bed, thinking that sensation I was feeling would eventually go away. But it didn't. I fell asleep for about two hours. I woke up again; I felt this pushing sensation in my stomach. I looked at the clock and it was 12:00 am. I am up every few minutes pushing. I would take catnaps and that helped for a short time. After a while, I thought I had to go to the bathroom and poop bad, but I didn't have to. I was extremely thirsty.

I was drinking water like it was going out of style. The more water I was drank the more I had to push. About 2:00 in the morning, I am trying to find somewhere I could lay down so I could go to sleep. I went to the living room to go to the living room, and laid the floor. Again, I had to go to the bathroom and poop, but I didn't have too. I am realized I'm pushing every three minutes. When I was not pushing, I was able to sleep for a few minutes. My mother gets up, comes to my room.

"What's wrong?"

I honestly don't know.

My mother gives me a couple of aspirin, told me to go lay down, and I did.

I heard my father say "What is wrong with Jaynie?"

My mother just told him "I was not feeling good."

I am up and down all through the night. After an hour of taking aspirin, I threw it up. Few hours later. 6:30 a. m. arrives and Sylvet is leaving for work. My mother is about to leave.

"Jaynie if anything happens call me at work."

Okay.

I was very scared. I didn't know what was happening to me. My mother knew and she could have helped me but she didn't! Why didn't my mother stay home with me? She left at 6:40. My body is feeling weird, and I still don't know what is happening to me. All I knew is I'm sleepy. I'm too tired to get out of bed to call Maye. Or anyone to help me. I tried one more time to get out of bed. The pushing sensation would not let me stand up. I am crying and extremely petrified. I was leaning against the bed rest, which felt comfortable for a while. It clicked I was about to have a baby. I kept on pushing, every time with all my might. The baby started to come down. The baby would go back up inside me. Finally, I said God, you have to help me I can't do it alone. All of a sudden, I felt my body split and it didn't hurt at all. At 6:50 a. m. Friday November 2, 1979, I delivered a baby girl. I cut the umbilical cord and held her in my arms. I honestly didn't know what to do with a newborn. I just only knew to hold her next to my chest.

Her eyes were open. Her eyes were a beautiful blue like the sky in the summer time. She was staring right at me, as if she could actually see me. I got a towel and wrapped her in it. I called my mother at work and told her I just had a baby girl. There was no reply from my mother at all. She hung up and called Dr. Harrisberg.

CHAPTER **5**

SOMEONE CALLED THE fire department and ambulance. Jennifer and I we're taken to the hospital and there I delivered the placenta. Because my water didn't break it had to be drained out of me. There was a lot of water. I told the nurse I had to go to work. The nurse said I would be staying in the hospital for a couple of days. I called the Cresants and told them I will not be in today. Constance and my brother Towan come to see me in the hospital. I started to cry because I was so happy to see either of them or of anyone for that matter. Towan took pics of Jennifer and me. You would think my mother and my sister would have come and see me.

Neither my mother nor Maye came. Now you understand how I feel about my mother. Why I can't stand, or love my mother for how she had treated me. My mother abandoned me when I really needed her the most. My mother and Maye never came to see me until they had to pick me up from the hospital. My mother does not give a rat's ass about me. So why, I ask myself, why would my mother want to come and see her grandchild or me. I was so scared and wanted my mother there so badly. The doctor came in my room.

Jaynie what is the name of the father, so we can place his name on the birth certificate? . . . Also we would have the announcement in the newspaper.

I told him I didn't know who the father was.

I lied, because I was afraid my parents would see my name in the papers, and I didn't want Alex's name in the paper either. In addition, I was ashamed and scared.

If you don't tell me, we will just print it in the newspaper.

Could I please talk to the father first before I give out his name? I don't want to get him any trouble.

Sure, that would be fine. I'll be back tomorrow and talk with you further.

Fine is all I could say before I started to cry.

After he left I just laid in bed, cried, and wondered how I was going to tell Alex he has a daughter named Jennifer Patrice Corevine. She weighed seven pounds seven 1/2 ounces. Born at 6:50 a.m. On Nov 2, 1979. Knowing the way, he lived, I knew he would be disappointed. Like my parents will be when they find out everything.

Later on evening, I called Alex.

How are you Alex?

I am kind of busy Jaynie what do you need?

Well I have something to tell you and I don't know how to say it.

What is it Jaynie.

"Well Alex, (I took a deep breath.)

I just called to tell you I delivered a baby girl this morning at home by myself, alone!"

All of a sudden, I heard this click. He hung up on me. Now I am mad I called him back.

Listen you son of a bitch. Don't you ever hang up on me again. I am not asking you for \a damn thing. You have a child in this world so deal with it."

Jaynie, I can't afford to take care of a child. I am just getting started in building my business. I don't have the time or the money to take care of a child."

I am not asking you to and I don't want anything from you. I can do it by myself. We don't need anything from you or anybody else. I have to go. I hung up the phone crying.

The doctor came in the next day and I gave him Alex's name. I told him all my fears and he said our names would not be in the paper.

Jennifer is now in a foster home waiting for me to pick her up, to start our life together. When my mother and Maye picked me up from the hospital, she told me not to say anything. I am to go straight to my room. I walked right to my room. I walked with my eyes down. I was so afraid. I thought my father was going to ask me where I have been. I walked fast to my room. When I walked into my room the walls were clean my bed was made, hmmm! Three months have gone by now, and I have not seen or held my baby. I miss her so much. I am still trying to find a place for Jennifer and me. Again, my mother told me I have to put Jennifer up for adoption. I'm still trying to fight her with all my strength. I came home from work, Sylvet is sitting at the dinner table, and he asked me what this hospital bill was about

(First, who gave him permission to open my mail). He looked at me, I couldn't say anything. I thought of my God, he is going to beat me again. Unbelievably his calmness shocked me.

"Who's the father Jaynie?"

"I didn't know!" I lied.

Sylvet gave me that look and he asked me again.

It was Alex Cahulty, our next-door neighbor. Sylvet got up, went outside got in his truck, and drove off. I thought he was going to go over to Alex's house but he didn't. I was about to call Alex and warn him. My mother made me hang up the phone. I found out later Sylvet had gone to Maye's apartment. Maye told me that he asked her if she knew about my pregnancy and she said yes. She told me that he started to cry. Wow, that was deep for me. I have never heard or ever see my father cry. My guess the reason why he left is because he felt hurt. On the other hand, maybe my because I couldn't come to him to tell him I was pregnant. Who knows? How can I come to my parents and tell them I'm pregnant, knowing they might beat the shit out of me? There was no, if there is a problem of any kind, you can always come to us. In my family, it was fear, threats, control, beating, intimidation, secrets and violence.

My father has feeling after all! I was very touched by his emotions I'm not sure, when he came home. The next day went like this. My mother says,

"Jaynie you putting that baby up for adoption!"

No I'm not., I am keeping my baby.

How do I stand up to a bully of a mother? The next day Sylvet was already home when I got home from work. Sylvet told me to sit down. He looked at me.

"I don't care if you keep her but you ain't living under my roof."

Fine with me."

Then in a few days, I am talking to a social worker and his name is Leo Hiker. He works for Christian Social Services. When I was speaking with Leo; he was very kind and really understanding. His voice was very soothing. I had told Leo I wanted to keep and raise my baby. Leo told me if I could show him I can be responsible, and could care for Jennifer. He saw absolutely no reason why I couldn't keep Jennifer. Leo gave me ideas about getting my own place, and I would have to do to get on AFDC temporally. I am back at the Cresants babysitting. I wanted to see, and visit with Jennifer. My social worker and the foster parents arranged for me to be with daughter, for the day. Understand, I have not seen her in three months. I'm really excited. On Thursday morning, there is a knock at the door and Leo has Jennifer in his arms. I was so happy to see her I couldn't wait to hold her and kiss her. I took her out of his arms and he left. After the kids were done, admiring Jennifer the baby one of the boys took a picture of me holding Jennifer and I was smiling big time. The first time I actually smiled for the camera and looked good. She fell asleep while I was holding her, I laid her down on her blanket.

For the whole day, all she did is eat, sleep, and poop. I couldn't wake her up. By this time, it was time for the foster parents to pick her up. I cried big time when she left. I am thinking I can't wait to hold her in my arms again. This was really cool and, very kind of the Cresants. They were going to give my baby clothes, baby bottles, and a stroller, everything I needed for Jennifer. I also found a place for Jennifer and I to live. The woman I would be living with also has a baby boy about Jennifer age. We would share the house together and we would have our own room. I am so excited I can't wait to tell Leo. He told me the foster parents would be gone for the holidays, and they would be back on Jan 3 1980. He said I could pick her up in his office sometime in the afternoon. At one-point, my mother came to me and said she knew of a woman who wants to adopt Jennifer and I said no way! Even if I was contemplating adoption I would be damned if I would adopt her to anyone who knew my mother. I went so far as to call the army reserves to join the army with Jennifer. They said I could bring my child with me so I am thinking I will join the army and keep her with me. If I could have passed the knowledge test year in 1980, I would not be writing this book. January 3rd 1980 finally arrives. **I am 18 years-old.** I go to my social worker's office, which is downtown. I am all excited.

"Hi Leo how are you…Happy New Year"

As I walked into his office with this great big smile on my face, as I closed the door.

Leo said, "I have some bad news."

What Leo was about to tell me would change my whole

life forever. How I felt about, my parents, adults, and authority figures and trust no one ever again.)

"Jaynie, you can't have Jennifer!"

What! Why? Haven't I shown you responsibility?

Leo just sat there in his chair behind is desk with his hands crossed over each other.

You told me I had to have a place to live, and all the necessities to take care of my baby. I have that babysitting job that you brought her over to that time. I can bring her with me to work. Just silence. I have been waiting for this moment even before she was born. I hoped and I prayed I would be a good mother to her. I know I don't want to abandon my daughter, like my mother did to me.

"What the fuck does that mean, I can't" Finally, this motherfucker's mouthy starts moving.

I can't hear any words, no sound, I am crying to hard.

"I just think you are way too immature, naïve, and not responsible enough to care for a child on your own Jaynie. You're but a child yourself."

I said, "What the hell Leo I am 17 soon to be 18 in February 14ᵗʰ dam it.

How old do you have to be?

Now I just want to die again. I want my fricking baby. It is not fair.

I did everything was requested of me

You told me just two weeks ago just the opposite and also you said I would be able to take her home with me.

We're you lying to me Leo? ….. Why would you tell me this now?

Wait a minute. What's really going on here?

Did my mother talk to you?

Leo couldn't even look at me. Busted!

What did she say to you Leo. . .? Did she threaten you in

some way?

Leo please talk to me! Please don't do this to me.

Don't be like my mother." My mother does not want me to keep her at all. Please be on my side.

I just want to know, please tell me!"

Leo would not look at me. He just kept looking at his hands. Leo never even answered not one of my questions. He didn't have to I already knew the answer. I finally was beaten. Leo, Lyle, my family, my mother. I flew out of his office crying. I cried all the way home. I couldn't see straight, walk straight. I finally got home, Walked in the house.

"What's wrong with you gal?"

I wanted to yell at her, (Why you never cared before.) "That is funny she never asked what was wrong with me, before. Now is the first time she ever asked what was wrong with me, in 17 years.

I opened my mouth to say something, and all this stuff just started pouring out.

"What did you say to my social worker…. Why did you talk to him. . . What business was it of yours…? Why would you care if I kept my child or not . . .? You can't stand me anyways; you don't love me…. You never wanted me…. I can't tell you how many times I remember you saying to me if abortions were legal you would have had one!"

Now I am able to stand on my own, and show love to someone, which you never did, now you want to take that away from me. Why don't you just mind your own business and stay the hell out of my life!

"If you tried and kept that kid, I will claim that you are an unfit mother…. I would have the courts take her away from you for good."

I would had fought you all the way!

In actuality, I was very much afraid of my mother. Not

knowing if what she said is really true or what she could do to me. You would do to me your own daughter. I realize I was naive and very sheltered. I thought could my mother really that to me? Does she hate me that much?

Could she be that much of a bitch to hurt me that badly? Would she really do to me? She would enjoy embarrassing, and hurting me. I just stopped talking about it, and moved on.

After all this shit, I decide to go back to school, but a different high school. A couple of weeks later I was looking through her dresser to find a shirt to wear to school. As I was, looking around, I saw this white card. I picked it up to read it. Leo Hiker Christian Social Services phone number etc. I went back to Leo asked him again if he was threatened by my mother? Again, he never answered me. What I didn't realize there was absolutely nothing she could say or do to me. When you reach eighteen years of age, you are an adult. However, at time I believed her. If I knew now what I should have known back, then I would have said I would like to see you try to say I was an unfit mother. My mother knew I had led a very protective, sheltered, smothering life in the Corevine household. If I only known about life outside of our house. Leo contacted me months later. He reminded me that he was working on getting the adoption papers, ready for Alex, and me to sign. Alex has not seen Jennifer. He doesn't know what she looks like. Or how big she is. Who am kidding? He doesn't want her. On top of that he doesn't even care. Why would he care what she looks like? He is pretending as if nothing ever happened between us at all.

Leo have you seen Jennifer?

"No. Not since, he allowed me to visit me at the Cresants house. I've been really busy."

I was thinking who am I kidding? Leo doesn't want me to keep her. On top of, he does not even care about my feelings. I wanted to call Alex, but I knew how wouldn't have treated me. Well no matter he now has a child in this world. Eventually he is going deal with it. I am hurting so bad inside right now, I beg to die right now. That's way the pain would not hurt me anymore. In just two days, I will be signing away the one thing I could love unconditionally.

Someone who could love me back and she would say "I love you mommy". That day has finally arrived, and I am trembling so bad you can see my hands shaking. I told the Cresants I will not be at work today, but I will see them to-morrow I think. Alex and I arrived at the same time, but not together. I see him and I can't look at him in his face. I hate him so much right now.

I have so much rage right now toward Alex its best he just signs those papers, and leave. I don't know what I would have done if he spoke to me? I just want to die at that every mo-ment. I don't want to sign any damn papers. I just want to take my baby and go away from here anywhere and away from everyone. Please God, help me. Don't let my mother win this fight. Please! Alex signs the papers first, and then he leaves. Good riddance I hope you are hit by a car you fricking bas-tard. Then it is my turn. I'm crying, so hard I can't see what I am doing. Leo feels awful, and so do I. He told me to take my time. I started to sign my name; I felt this intense awful pain in my stomach. As if I were being shot at point blank range right through my stomach.

When I signed those adoptions papers, it took me over an hour to sign my name. When I did sign my name a part of me died. I don't say anything at all, to Leo. I just ran out of his of-fice. I finally went home and (I will now use both first names for my parents). Othea never even asked me what is wrong like she did last time, when I walked into the house. My eyes were red and puffy. Othea does not give a holy fuck about me or my feelings. She got what she wanted. She was to fricking embarrassed because I had a child and I brought our last name shame. Well if she wants to talk shame, well let me add in my unwanted opinion. Sylvet had an affair with Jonessa my best friend's mother Dianna for over 15 years. Even at the age of 15 they were still having an affair. Hell everyone knew about; it. I remembered Sylvet would go as far as have me call her on the phone, and ask me to ask for Dianna. Othea let's talk shame. You knew this relationship was going on for years, and everyone in the streets knew it too. Who shamed whom?

Yet you are too stupid to leave because of your stupid ass pride. You continue to allow it to happen. You jeopardize your life and ours as well, that is shame! If I were in your shoes Othea, I would be embarrassed as hell. I would have left his ass a fricking long time ago. So be very careful as to who is calling the cotton white. Regardless, if my kids were just babies at the same time or not. You allowed Sylvet to beat my hands in elementary school for having sex in the bathroom with Brian Kipps until my hands were so red I couldn't even bend them. You don't even tell me what I did wrong. You didn't even derive a conclusion and realize I was being molested. I have to wash your husband's back because you were never around. You make me sick just thinking about you. Othea you have no room to talk. You are two timing, committing adulterous, hypocrite, and sneaky snake. Want to have your cake, and eat it too bitch. You have an affair with a man named Charlie Brown.

A white man on top of that, you can't stand white people. You had him call on my phone asking for you. I pay the phone bill because it is in my name. Yet it's your house. This whole situation is so unfair and totally fricked up. You never offer to help me pay the bill. Then you took me to the mall, and dropped me off, so you could spend time with the man you are having an affair. You had me lie to Sylvet so you would not get in trouble, and get your ass beat. You also had sex with one our cousins in their bed when we were visiting in Tennessee. You want to talk about shame. You and Sylvet had threesomes in our house on 10th avenue. These women were white, and you continued to claim you can't stand white people. You knew the one thing would make me so happy. You ruined the only thing I truly loved away from me. Well guess what Othea and Sylvet you will never have a grandchild from me ever. I made a solemn promise to God, myself and that was, I will never give my parents grandchildren.

Jennifer, the adoption, the delivery, would never mention again. It was just like when Jeffery died nobody ever talked about him again. No one even spoke his name. I knew I needed help. Slowly I was forgiving Leo. I am letting Leo help me emotionally. Slowly we are working together, to help me heal from this tragedy, of placing Jennifer up for adoption. It is really hard because when I talked about it, or try to talk about it, I felt like a bullet went through my stomach repeatedly. I would just cry uncontrollably. With my social worker Leo Hiker, I eventually had joined a support group with other women who had children, for adoption. The support group started sometime in January 1980. Leo (social worker) felt I needed a lot support to see what other women had gone through. To know I am not the only one suffering. I also, talk to a therapist I never even heard of a therapist; let alone to talk to one. I was a stranger to that process!

No way could I tell someone I don't know what has been happening in my family. I knew she would tell Othea. Then Othea would tell Sylvet and I would get a beating worse than ever before. This group was learning how to be more assertive and not be afraid to ask for what we wanted and needed. All I needed was for my parents to say it's okay. Jaynie, we still love you no matter what. That was just a daydream. Who am I fooling? I am telling the group how my mother treats me. They suggested I write a letter. I thought great I'll try it. It couldn't hurt, right. I wrote a two-page letter asking Othea why she treated me the way she did. (God, how I wish I had kept that letter). Why I felt Othea hates me so much? Why Othea felt I shamed her and my family, after I had the baby. So when the group ended I left and went home feeling good inside. I walked through the house and I found Othea in the bedroom. I told Othea that I wrote a letter, just for her. She took the letter and went to my bedroom.

I don't know where, or when, or if Othea even read it because I went to my room. I had to use the bathroom, as I was sitting on the toilet; I glanced at the trashcan. Looked inside and there was the letter I had given her. I took the letter out of the garbage can. This time I didn't confront Othea. I just ripped the letter to shreds. Maybe Othea read it and felt she didn't need to read it again. Maybe she never read it at all. All I can say, I reached out again to Othea again I was blown out of the water. We never discussed the letter. I started back to school after I had Jennifer. I had a talk with my social worker Leo and a school counselor at another school. They both told me I needed to finish school if I want to get a better job in the future. Therefore, that is what I did. I felt a shame to return to my old school. Afraid everyone knew I had a child, and would tease and pick on me like what happen when I was pregnant. I transferred to a different high school called Kenney High School. I am 19. Years-old.

I took a job being a nanny in a little suburb called Hiawatha located outside of Lexington Ia. I had been out of school for at least one year. I answered an ad in the paper for a nanny. This would be the second time I would be working with another white family. To be honest I felt uncomfortable.

I was feeling uncomfortable at school also. For some reason, the kids at my new high school were laughing, and taunting me, and I didn't know why. I found out later why, and I took care of situation. One white girl who is a skank in particular kept laughing, talking about me, as were walking out of chemistry class. She was ahead of me calling me names and talking shit to her friends about me having a child. I heard her say very loud, "At least I didn't give birth to a bastard child." I took my chemistry book and threw it as hard as I could at her. I hit her in the back of the head. She grabbed the back of her head and she went down. That action took all my anger away for day. I just kept walking, and smiled as I walked past the bitch. I bet you she will not talk shit about anyone else again.

I had to see the principle named Mr. Alvin Skidoffe. After telling him what happened he didn't suspend me. The girl was bothering me. Mr. Skidoffe and I got along really good. He was 6'1, and skinny as a beanstalk and very nice and funny. When he saw me, he would always call me Core. I always called him Skid. We never called each other by our first names. Mr. Skidoffe would be the only person I would miss at school. I just couldn't take it anymore. Again, I dropped out of school. Not caring if I never graduated, or not. The people I was babysitting for were acting weird. They would stay to themselves with the kids. They would shut me out. I was feeling edgy at the family's house. Battling my mother over the phone almost every day, and arguing with the mother of the house, only made matters worse. Eventually I moved back home. I also transferred to another high school. There was no mother and daughter bond, or relationship with my mother. Othea and I avoided each other like the plague.

Dealing with school, my goal was to achieve my diploma and graduate. The high school was called Kurkwade Adult College. Again, I transferred my credits to Kurkwade. My

GPA was bad. It was under 1.00 and you needed 2.00 just to graduate. Sylvet always said I was too stupid to graduate. Too ignorant to get a job so why worry about school. On the weekends, my parents were never around and I felt alone. I was becoming very depressed. I started going to the bars. I am **19 years old** so why not. I can drink now! Hmm. I would go to the bars for the sole purpose of seeking out affection and possibly relationships. I was going to the homes with a different man every Friday and Saturday night. Othea knew what I was doing and Othea never said a damn thing to me. I knew Othea was not stupid. I honestly felt she really didn't give a damn about me. One time I went to this bar called Gatsby is which was located on 1st Ave across the bridge. I love that bar. Anyway, I met this nice tall man. I forgot his name along with all the unknown men I have met. We went down stairs, we had sex on the couch. About two hours later Sylvet came home, and we hurried, and got dressed. Sylvet stumbles down the stairs.

We just sit on the couch as if we were watching TV. I introduce this guy to Sylvet. Eventually Sylvet said hi and goodnight. Sylvet heads off to bed. My guy also leaves a little after, and I never heard from him. Like all the rest. In the morning, Othea is in the kitchen. I come up from falling asleep in the basement. As I head to my room Othea stopped me.

"Don't you ever bring any men back up in my house again Jaynie. Do you hear me?"

Fine no problem.

I have such a strong hatred for Othea.

From now on I will just have sex at their house ok…. That way you don't have to be ashamed of me. Othea just didn't care about me You would think by now I would have realized; you can't find healthy nurturing relationships especially in bars. The relationships have to come to you. You can't go to them. You can't tell a 20-year-old, who just wants to be held, and have affection. I am still not done with school. I went to class every day and studied hard. Guess what I did it. I accomplished something. Finally, I was able to graduate. I reached for something and I got it. What were you saying Sylvet, about me being too stupid to graduate? Wow my self-esteem. Myself confidences were higher than they ever had been, in my whole life. I was so proud of me. I was truly happy to be finally marching down the aisle. 19 years- old and it is a very special day for me. I finally received my high school diploma. I begged both parents to come. Only Othea came with the pleading of my brother Towan. Sylvet was too busy playing poker. I did better at this school then all the other schools I have attended. Now I am done with school.

"Come Monday you're going to go out and start looking for a job…. You ain't going to be living in my house for free…. You will be paying rent to live in my house."!

Yes, sir.

You remember my friends the Brownhansons down the street right? Anna told me they needed a part-time laundry aide at the Lexington 4th Ave Care Center, where she is a Director of Nursing. She suggested to me I apply, for the po-sition. Monday morning, I went looking for a job. I went to where Anna worked. Guess what she hired me. I really love woman. It paid to know someone in the health care profes-sion. I finally started a real job. I hoped to find an apartment and get the hell out of my parent's jail. Living with my parents for the last several years has been a total living hell. I couldn't go anywhere. I had to come home straight from school. I had to clean the house, and do the dishes. I truly felt like I was living in a jail. Secretively, I started buying stuff on sale for my apartment. I hadn't found one yet. For the past two years, I stored everything downstairs. Towels, sheets, kitchen utensils.

You name it; I bought it. I am working part-time saving money. I was only making $5. 00 an hour, and I was taking home $240. 00 every two weeks. I am looking in the newspaper for an apartment. I called this couple who were renting out an upstairs apartment for $150. 00 a month. All utilities included. Free washer and dryer down stairs, I thought hey, I couldn't beat that. I went to look it over., I was very happy with it so I took it. I didn't tell my parents. I was afraid they would say I could not have it. After graduation, I said I was living in jail practically, except I was not cooking. Sylvet treated me as if I was his damn slave. I still can't go anywhere; I am 20 years old now. My parents are still treating me as if I were still a child. The only exception of leaving the house was to go to work was the only time I could leave the house.

Sylvet called me to wash his back like usual on a Saturday night. Thank God, Othea stayed home night for some reason. I stood up for myself to Othea, and said,

I didn't want to wash Sylvet's back anymore. For God's sake, I am 19 years old and his daughter!

You would think Sylvet would have had a clue. I didn't want to see my father naked ever again. For the first time Othea stood up for me. Othea went in to wash Sylvet's back

I heard Sylvet asks, "Where's Jaynie?

That's when shit hit the fan and the roof.

Jaynie don't need to be seeing you naked Sylvet.... On top of all she does not need, to wash your back no more.

I can imagine Sylvet is looking at her with shame and anger.

Jaynie is a grown woman... Sylvet you a grown man now, act like one.

I was happy Othea washed his back instead of me.

He came out of the bathroom yelling. He started calling me names, yelling this and, but I didn't let him scare me.

Sylvet, Jaynie is done washing your back and I mean that.

The words Othea used to protect me against Sylvet felt nice I might add. I never had to wash Sylvet back or see him naked ever again. At that moment, I wanted to hug and kiss Othea and tell her thank you for stepping in for me. However, I know she would not accept it. Why didn't Othea stand up for me when Sylvet beating the skin off my ass? Oh hell, off all our asses. For the first time she finally came to my defense. I will always have that memory. All of us kids had to wash his back, and all moved out of the house, and I was the last one to wash Sylvet back and the last one to move out of the house.

Othea was not home as much and I felt like I was the wife, and Sylvet was the husband. Even after, Othea came to my defense against Sylvet about washing his back, he still tried to make me do it. Othea left to play her bingo. Sylvet would start in again using threats against me.

Sylvet said, "If you don't do as you're fucking told, and wash my back when I tell you to, get the fuck out of my house"

Fine.

I got on my bike and took off to the Anna house. They weren't home. I waited unit I saw his car go by. Then I headed back home. I didn't want to have to keep going through shit every weekend so I figured when she left, I left. I never washed his back again. I just kept saving my money to move. I just couldn't take it anymore. All the mental and psychological abuse was weakening me. I was trying my best not to come home anymore because of how he treated me. So finally, in the summer of **July 1981** That elderly couple contacted me, and told me I could have the apartment. Oh my gosh, I was so elated I couldn't control my excitement. I called Anna that same day. I asked Anna if she could pick me up and help me move into my new apartment. Anna said she would stop off tomorrow after work. I hung around the house all that day.

I had the day off. I just watched TV. I didn't have the mental strength to stand up to Sylvet to tell him I was moving. I had been watching for Anna Station Wagon to come up the hill all day. When she came to the door, I let her in. As she came in Sylvet asked who she was and what she was doing here. I told him. Boy shit really hit the fan again.

Sylvet didn't intimidate Anna, thank God. She told me once we get to the basement don't stop to talk to my dad and I didn't.

I'm Jaynie's friend, and boss, and I am helping her move to her new apartment."

You could hear him yelling all the way down the street. Sylvet was going off at the mouth, about me moving out because he didn't have anyone to control and dominate anymore except for Othea.

Anna and me are loading up my things in her Station Wagon, I am crying really hard, and the car is finally loaded up. I am leaving to get into the car, Sylvet yells,

Sylvet yells, You're to fucking stupid to live on your own, once you leave you're not coming back. You hear me?"

Don't worry I won't.

Finally, I am free. I was happy. If it were not for Anna helping me, and not letting Sylvet scare her, I would still be living with my parents in my jail cell. Sylvet didn't want me to move out period. Sylvet wanted me there to yell at, to do all the house work, lawn work, watch him play with himself, everything.

Sylvet said, "You will never make it on your own…. You need us…. You will be crawling back.

No I don't need you. I will never come back. I knew that, that would never happen.

Sylvet replied, "You'll be back in a month you just watch, and when you do you ain't moving back in my motha fucking house…. Get the fuck out and don't come back."

As I gather my last load, and close the door for the last time, I am saying to myself, there is no fricking way I will every move back to this God, awful jail, I hate both of you. Out loud I said, Don't worry I won't ever come back, and I will never ever step foot in your jail cell again, it will be a fricking cold day in hell. I was still crying and Anna just held me and told me I was going to make it. Sylvet was angry because I wanted to live on my own. Little did I know Anna was right. I guess my parents had something different in mind for my future. I said yeah right. I am feeling everything Sylvet said about me was true, and Anna said only if you let them be true.

I moved out two weeks after I graduated, and I'm 19 years-old. I have to be honest and say this was the best two weeks of my life. I had it to do all over again. I would have moved out sooner. I was not happy emotionally, physically, or psychologically, living in my parent's house. To be completely honest I was so afraid of failing.

Sylvet always said I would never make it on my own. Sylvet had me thinking and believing that I needed them to survive. I am finally living on my own. It feels fricking awesome. Those words stayed with me all my adult years of living on my own. Not once did I ever-go back, not even to visit. The day I moved out was the last time I saw my parents. Maye told me later they didn't like it, but I didn't care. I was now living on my own. I knew I had to work Monday morning so I unpacked all weekend and God, was it hot outside. Hey I I didn't let the heat stop me from being in such a wonderful mood.

The world could end and I would be happy. I put everything away within the next couple of weeks. Everything is unpacked. I have to get use to really being on my own. I just stayed by myself for several months. I would clean when

I wanted to clean, cook what, and when I wanted to cook, played my music as loud as I wanted to, or sleep where I wanted. I finally believed my apartment was my own, my parents couldn't take it away from me. It was my first apartment for the next four years. My address is 1220 2nd Ave. SE, Lexington Iowa I loved my address. Thank God, I am now taking care of me and surviving on my own. No parents around, it feels so damn good to finally have my own independence. I moved out only working part time, which eventually turned into fulltime. I was able to walk to work, which was just around the corner. How cool was that. I would walk to work and home for lunch, and spend time with Anna.

I decided I wanted a pet. Never had one of my own, so this would be a new experience for me. I called and asked my property owner if I could have a pet and he said I couldn't have a dog, or cat.

The only thing I could think of was to have a bird. I have never had one before, but I always wanted one. I looked in the paper for a cockatiel. I found one, they were moving out of town, and they didn't want to take the bird with them. I bought him, for $100. 00, and I couldn't wait for the owner to bring the bird to my apartment. I had been in my apartment for a while. Somehow, I ran into my curly haired old lover Randy Harmony who lived down the street from us, on 14th avenue. I told him I had my own apartment, and he should come by and see me sometime. Months later, it is mildly warm outside. I just came out of from taking a bath, and I hear a knock at my door. I didn't have time to put my clothes on so I just answered the door in a towel. I was not really thinking about anything. I opened the door. It's Randy. I was in shock, and I am like wow.

"Hi Randy, what are you doing here?"

I was in the neighborhood. He took a few steps into my

living room, and started touching me. I told him to stop, but he was much stronger then I was. He tore my towel off, and started doing what we had done together in the past. I truly tried to get him to stop. He pinned me on my couch, and he raped me. I was crying, and begging him to stop. He didn't. After he raped me, he told me he would be back later. I told him if he came back, I would do my best to kill him. I was crying, I told him to leave, and never come back. I was going to call the cops. How would I explain what this man did to me? do I explain what this man did to me? I didn't see what he was driving, and I didn't watch him leave. I even know if that is his real last name. I was only wearing a towel. I just let it go. I moved on. I had to wait a few weeks for my bird. A woman arrived with the bird. I let her in and we talked for a little bit. She handed over Amba to me. The woman had named him Amba and I liked his name so I kept it. Plus, he was already two years old. She left and it was just Amba and me. I left him alone for two weeks, until he was ready for me to hold him. After, we were inseparable. I took him everywhere with me. I never thought about Amba flying away.

It never crossed my mind. (Boy how naive I was). I would come home and play with Amba. He was a real cool bird. After I felt Amba was comfortable with me, I started going out with friends occasionally. I started hanging with a RN named Lacey Thorton, who worked with me. She was nice and attractive. We had exchanged phone numbers to hook up sometime. We had two things in common was work and dancing. On nights Lacey had off we decided we would go to a country bar or to the Gatsby to go dancing. The more we went out together the more I liked her. This woman was a divorcee with two children, but she looked so good, yum yum. One time after going to a bar Lacey go drunk and I guess I took advantage of the situation. I kissed her in the car. She told me I was never to do again and I apologized. She was the first straight woman I had ever kissed. Our getting together became less and less. I guess I made her uncomfortable. I felt bad. Amba was so cool. I would be eating some food and he would fly to my plate. He would take some food with his feet to eat. I thought that was a nice trick. I was happy Amba trusted me enough to eat with me. It was funny when he would try to hold cooked spaghetti. I liked having Amba around. However, I becoming very bored. I wanted to socialize and see people. I decided to go to this bar called "Al's Hangout" and I saw my sister-n-law with my brother Towan. I hung out with Melody and we talked and danced. She was a petite woman. She was a cool sister-in-law. I liked Melody. I would say she was a good supporting friend.

After a while, Mel and my brother started having problems and my brother would start beating up Mel the way Sylvet beat up on Othea. The vicious cycle of abuse was starting all over again, in Towan's family. That is why I started to despise Towan even more. That is also, why I also pulled away from my family. When I finally moved on my own, I came to realize I didn't like the fact Towan would beat Mel up. Then turned around and have affairs behind her back. Towan had the attitude he can do whatever he wanted.

What a creep. Mel only stood up for who she loved, and wanting the father of her children to take responsibility for his children. The more she fought for Towan the worse he treated her. They have two boys Cameron, and Khristan. I really love my nephews. My brother Towan was quite the busy boy. He knew what my father had done to my mother in the past, and I can remember Towan saying, if, and when he got married, he would never treat his wife like. Yeah right! Towan is a splitting image of Sylvet. Adultery was running rampant in the mid 60's, 70's, and 80's. One time I saw a picture of Othea, Sylvet and a white woman. Sylvet was sitting in the back, the woman was in the middle, and Othea was in front kind of leaning against her, with her arms draped around her neck. There were some naked pictures too of this same woman in the pictures with my parents. Sylvet brought that kind of sexual promiscuity in our house early on. Towan had numerous affairs. While he was still married to Mel. With some of those affairs, he had children. As far as monogamy goes, Towan does not even know the meaning of the word. Yet these women wanted him and thought he was all and a bag of chips, but he truly isn't. Towan is a typical man who just couldn't keep his dick in his pants. I think he has pussy envy. If he could get pussy to go from a convenience store, he would be buying it 24/7. Mel and Towan eventually split up years later. I have to say for an abusive relationship Mel gave it her all. From the black eyes, busted lips, being pushed down the stairs when she was pregnant with Cameron. (I write this because I saw Towan on many several occasions be abusive to Mel) if I could have stopped my brother from abusing Mel trust me I would have. However, I know if I did interfere he would start whaling on me. I wondered if Towan could he have fought two women? Probably so. Who knows, but I would have done my best to hurt him or kill him. Ha, who am I kidding? Towan is very tall for one, and very strong. I am not just talking to hear my mouth run. I have seen Towan evil side, not pretty. I saw it when he was making me have sex with him.

CHAPTER 6

MY BROTHER HAS had a lot of bent up anger! To the abuse Mel suffered behind closed doors, we don't know about. Through the domestic violence. I saw him push Mel down a flight of stairs because she wanted something to eat for her and Cameron. He grew tired of her asking. Thank Goodness she is still living and doing well. I knew what Towan was doing was wrong. I was not strong enough to stop him especially not on my own. I still remember when he punched me in my stomach when I was younger. Sometimes, when I think about it I can still feel the pain. Knowing Towan and his temper, he probably would have hit me again this time much harder.

Women everywhere who think they should give it their all to save their marriage, or relationships, and keep their man, or woman I commend you. However, don't stay if your life is being threatened, or if your life is in jeopardy. Realize the partner you are with is not going to, or is not making the effort to change. Leave them behind, and move forward. The months following went like clockwork. My first year at my job and I am 22. I really like. One reason I get to work with all women at the center that's very nice. I get to work and see Lacy. I am feeling I want to be with women very badly. I fantasize about kissing, holding, touching, women. Feeling their skin under my hand, as I glide my hand over their beautiful bodies. I don't know why I guess because of how I felt with the help of Stan. If it wasn't for Stan and the molestation. Would I have the craving I have for women? I wish I would have had that opportunity on my own. I will never know the answer. After I had Jennifer., I stopped seeking out relationships with men, I decided to become celibate. Could I really do without men. Do I really need sex with men to feel wanted? Would having a man really complete me? I decided this after I moved out of my parent's home in 1981. Even though I felt these strong urges, and desires even, before I was pregnant with Jennifer, I went to this adult bookstore down town and bought a vibrator shaped like a penis. I used it. I learned how to masturbate to really see if I could give enjoyment and pleasure to myself. And I did. If I am going to become celibate. Then I have to learn to enjoy touching and giving my body sexual gratification and stimulation.

While I was going through this transition mentally and physically I normally would notice men, but instead I would be looking at women. The desire to be with a lesbian was becoming more intense. I enjoyed looking at women when I walked down the street. Instead of always looking at men. I just watched women, studied them, learned about the way they moved. I just became a woman that is a lover of women. I liked looking at women's lips, mouth, eyes, and hair, their chest, their booties, how they walk, how tall and short women are. If they are big, or small. I don't have to look at men anymore, which feels good. That gives me a big sense of pride. Knowing I am finally following my heart, and desires to pursue my happiness, which meant a lot to me. I truly wanted to be around lesbians. Just to look at women made my stomach flip. I got in trouble a lot at work with Anna. I kept getting caught talking to the elderly residents and not doing what I am supposed to be doing, which was laundry. I didn't mind her telling me I have to work more and talk less. I just hated doing the laundry. However, I really did enjoy my job. The sheets were full of piss, and feces, and I was not about to touch it with my hands. I wore rubber gloves all the time when I have to pick up, or touch the laundry. I had to work with two other women. One of my co-workers was a talk black woman by the name of Rosolyn Bidwill. She knew I liked women. That didn't seem to bother her or our friendship. I thought she was just to cool. She didn't take shit from nobody. I would see her out at A's Hangout. We would hang and talk for a while. Then she would go her way and I would go mine. Rosolyn She and I didn't like the other woman who was working with us.

Her name was Betty Wickett and she is this scraggly looking, wiry haired, green toothed, foul breath, dirty clothes wearing bitch. We just could not stand her teeth, and her breath was terrible. You try to be nice to her and she tells you fuck off. Screw trying to be nice. She was extremely heavy and she smelled as if she never bathed. When it was summer and the temperature read 90 degrees you could just imagine how hot the laundry room was with two big dryers. We would have the fan blowing and funky sweaty Betty would stand right in front of the fan while she was folding sheets. Her arms would be flying, and that funk would hit you so hard and so fast, you would need to go outside and get some air. One day I gave Betty a birthday gift. When she opened it she was so angry. Hey Betty, we tried to be subtle with you, and you didn't get the hint. So now it's time to be bold. I gave her some toothpaste, brush, washcloth, deodorant, soap, and some Comet. If the soap will not cut through shit, I know Comet will. She went, and told Anna. Betty you're lucky it was Jaynie told you instead of me. I have been at the center for three years It is now 1982 there is talk in the air we might be losing our jobs. **I'm 20 years-old.** I hope not because this is the only experience I have except for childcare. Nevertheless, you know how bunches of women are when they work together; gossip,

gossip. I am at work Anna comes into the laundry room while were folding. Anna asked us to come to her office when we had some time. I looked at her face and she looked like she had some bad news to tell us, but she just turned around and left. About noon, all of us went to her office and she told us they are going to have to let some employees go. Some will work part-time. I was one who started last and the first to go part-time. Funky sweaty Betty was there the longest. Then there was Rosolyn. Eventually it came down to sweaty Betty working the only full-time position days and Rosolyn worked nights. And wouldn't know it.

My part-time shift was in the morning working with sweaty Betty. I am working and Betty's body odor is so bad. Common sense would tell you, not to stand in front of a fan. I tried to tolerate sweaty Betty, but this job is not worth smelling Betty every day. I went to Anna's office. I told my dearest friend, my boss Anna I'm quitting. I told her why. She tried to talk me out of it. I still quit. I hugged her, cried in her arms again, and said good-bye. I left, crying my eyes out. I know she felt bad that I was leaving. Shit she practically raised me. She helped me move out of my parent's. I think I thanked her at least 100 times. I did notice one thing which I feel bad about. I never invited her over to my apartment. I wish I would have. I know she would have loved it. I have an apartment and no job does make sense? I have been hanging out at "Al's Hangout" so much that I became very bored. I don't know where any of the gay bars are dammit. I called a cab company and he told me where there was a gay bar. Yippee. Eventually I will get the notion to go to the 2nd City down town. You know the coolest thing was. The bar was just ten blocks down the street from my house. Doesn't that beat all? For now, I have to find a job. I am walking home from "Al's Hangout" feeling really down. I don't know what I was going to do about money? I will be damned if I was going to ask my parents for help. There were times when I desperately needed money, food, necessities, but I refused to ask my parents for help. I could hear Sylvet in my head. "Hell fucking no, I am not going to help that bitch! Let her ass fucking ass starve for all I care. I can hear the words so loud and clearly! She wanted to move out so dam bad; now let her. I told you she would need us." I would not give them the satisfaction. If I had to survive, I will. I needed a place to live, and I didn't want to lose my apartment. I would literally have no place to go. I would become homeless. I just couldn't let that happen. My mind was just reeling right now. I knew I should buy some food in case I don't find a job right away. I had walked past this building that had a help wanted signed in the window. For some reason I didn't feel comfortable so I didn't stop in.

I walked home with groceries in hand. I put everything away. I decided what the hell. It was very cold that day. Winter was in full blast. I decided to walk back to the place with the help wanted sign. I went in and I saw women in dresses, skirts, and teddies. I am thinking what the hell is this place? I only heard what went on in these kind of places. I had never even thought to step into a place like this. However, all I know is I needed and wanted a job desperately. Because I didn't want to hitch hike and or end up killing myself. In addition, I really did love and care for myself. I know I could do better.

This man said to me, "Can I help you?" I turned around and there was this short curly blond haired man with red cheeks and no taller than 5'7 standing behind me.

Would you like to fill out an application?

Sure, that couldn't hurt. As I was filling out the application, I had asked him his name and he said it was Tyler. I told him my name was Jaynie and I asked Tyler,

What is this place?

"It's an adult massage parlor."

What would I be doing if I get the job?

You would be giving massages to men in private rooms.

Oh okay.

With a look of surprise and bewilderment on my face.

Terry replied, "They climax, pay you, get dressed and leave.

How do the men pick the women they want?

"The women you saw when you walked in are the women men can choose from. …. They pay for the cost of the session and the room is included. The model goes back with the client to an empty room. …The client pays to see you topless, bottomless, or totally nude. The more he wants to see the body the more it cost him."

There isn't any sex in the room right?

"No, if there was were sex going on the models will be fired then prosecuted." If the client is an undercover cop, he busts her. She is going to jail. That part scared the fuck out of me. I have never been to jail, never want to go to jail, and I wouldn't be a good inmate in jail."

Terry said, "If the client is an undercover cop, he busts her. She is going to jail…. Besides every session you do you must have a tape recorder in there with you at all times…. In case something does happen you have proof to back up your story. If you were to go to court our lawyers would be there to defend you as long as you know you are innocent."

I can accept that. This job won't be so bad after. At least I will have money.

How much do you make an hour? I'm thinking cash!

"As much as want to, if the clients pick you through the night. ….. Are you interested in working for "Clues Modeling?"

Yes, sure, I could try it, what harm could it do? I was hired and started later that evening. I started there at the age of 21.

Terry asked if I would be willing to travel to other locations and I said yes. I left went home and got ready slowly. I came back in a nice pair of pants.

"The models needed to wear clothes that were more revealing."

I had to walk back home in the cold, and laughing at myself. I came and came back an hour later. This time I wore a dress. My first night and boy was I nervous. I was the only black woman on duty my first night. Terry had me train with another model. Her name was Elsa. I sat in on one of her sessions. She was very attractive and I was to just sit back and watch and learn from her. I am thinking this could be interesting, another woman hum,

I had a smile on my face. The next thing I knew her client was asking to have me join them in their session He offered to give the two of us $100. 00 each. I said fine. Elsa said no. She said she didn't feel comfortable. Damn this stupid woman, all the money we just past up. I am guessing she is very straight woman. However, I convinced her nothing was going too happened except what is supposed to happen. She agreed and we both made $100. 00 for practically nothing. The session was for 1/2 hour. All three of us just laid in bed and watch some porno movie to get the client excited. The client got hard she and I masturbated him. He climaxes. You give them a towel to clean themselves off. They leave a tip and then they go. Sometimes depending what day, you could make bogoos of cash. My thoughts, are I will try to be calm as possible and not let it show, I am overly excited. Being my first night and all I made over $400.00 and I was so damn happy. I have money again yes! After my first night, and every night after, it got easier and easier. It also became easier for me to prostitute myself for money. I always try to be careful. You never know if the client was actually an undercover cop or not. I never told anyone. I was lucky. Very lucky. Eventually my boss said he liked how I treated the customers with respect, and asked if I would travel to different locations. To help bring in more clientele. I said sure. I always wanted to travel. However, inside I really just want a real eight-hour job. I traveled to, Indianapolis, Kokomo, Muncie Indiana, Danville IL, Waterloo, Cedar Rapids, Burlington Iowa, and Janesville WI. All the cities I traveled, I would stay sometimes two to three weeks at a time. Sometimes, I would stay a month. No longer than that. Indianapolis I enjoyed the most just because was where I had my first lesbian experience. I was traveling back and forth between all the cities, I hardly had any time at my apartment in Lexington, and I missed Amba.

Before I took off on my first trip, to Indiana, I asked one of the models her named Charlotte if she would like to watch my bird. I told her all about Amba. She said no problem she could handle it. I said he likes to talk especially when the sun comes up. I let her watch him. I had been working with the agency for over eight months, I felt I could trust Charlotte. Little did I know I would never see my bird Amba again. Within the time I was working for the parlor, I started having dreams about a big shiny penis chasing me. I couldn't understand why? There was no face to this penis and the excitement was over whelming. I would have dreams about being touched and penetrated by this shiny penis and it felt really good. This was happening during my travels and it started getting worse. I was trying so hard to shut it out. Along with the bad dreams, I was also having the strong desire to check out the gay bars in Indiana. I honestly felt like I was a fish out of water, gasping. The first week I arrived in Indianapolis It was very nice outside for a Thursday afternoon in the month of July in 1985. I was picked up at the bus station and the woman's' name was Pamela. She took me around town. I was able to see the all the downtown sights of Indianapolis, which I found very intriguing. Maybe I just might move here; who knows. When we went to the location, on the way there, Pamela preceded to warn me about Heidi.

"Jaynie, I want you to know I am trying to help."

I give her a nod with my head, but inside I am thinking, what the fuck is she getting at. Well there is this fucking dyke that works at the location and I can't stand her.

So what!

"She likes women and I think it's sick. Gay radar came in my head. I played stupid to see what else she had to say. …. Her name is Heidi and if I had my way, she would have been gone a long time ago. I just feel Heidi being a lesbian I feel really uncomfortable just being around her."

Pamela is the type of woman who would lie to make herself look good even though you know she is lying.

Pamela, thanks for giving me. I will be sure to keep on the lookout for the lesbian named Heidi. I am thinking I am going to be working with this backstabbing two-faced little cunt for the next month. Well is just great. I will make sure they don't schedule me to work with her. When I got there for a few hours, I was told and warned by other women Pamela was a troublemaking instigator. She showed me where all the rooms, bathroom, office and the safe.

I was looking at the schedule and guess what I saw. I' am on the schedule to work with Heidi Saturday morning. We both had All day Saturday morning all day and night. Awesome. This is too good to be true. What I have noticed there are not a lot of black women working in the parlor circuit.

I think was somewhat sad. I think black women are just as attractive as white women are. I noticed white men prefer black women to white women. Now me I have no preference. I like all women of color. Friday finally arrives, I had to work the night shift, with this other woman named Condey. I ordered Chinese food, and watched movies until the men started coming in. The night was long, and I left night after we closed about 3:00 in the morning. You had your typical crowd from the bar show up who wanted sex. They knew that kind of stuff did not happen here, not yet. I went home with about $525. 00. That was nice. I went to my hotel room, took a shower and went to sleep. I was so excited about tomorrow morning I couldn't sleep. As Saturday morning creeps into my window, I got up, and I start to get ready. Our shift started at 10 a.m. I took myself to "Eat While its Hot" for breakfast. I wonder who comes up with names for restaurants. I brought my things with me and a change of clothes in case she decides to take me out with her. I arrive at the location. We switch shifts. It was just Heidi and me. Yeah baby, can you tell I am excited? Heidi is about 5'8 with brunette curly hair, brown eyes and a nice complexion. She has a gap between her teeth, but I think it becomes her. She is wearing a rap around skirt, stocking and black high heel shoes. I have on a blue body suit with a rap around skirt, and stockings with blue high heel shoes. I am nervous as hell and so I finally got the nerves up to speak to her. It is around 12:00 in the afternoon.

Kinda dead right now, huh Heidi?

"Yes it is. What's your name again?"

Jaynie.

Heidi have you worked for the agency long?

"No not long only about five months…. What about you?"

I worked for "Clues Modeling" going on nine months now!

Heidi do you like this kind of work?

"No, not really, but it pays the bills and puts food on the table."

I know is right girl, I hear ya!

Heidi can I ask you something? Please be honest with me with your answer.

"No problem, what's up?

Well first of all let me say I think you are a very nice person, and I have nothing against you at all. …. I am sure you will guess who told me when you hear my question.

"Just wondering does this question include Pamela?"

Yes, it does. Damn your good Heidi! How did you know it was her?

"Jaynie do you have a problem with my life style. . . Actuality this is none of your fucking business. If you do have a problem, fucking deal with it. If it is too much for you there is the door. There's the street see ya!"

Woah! Hold up Heidi I am on your side…Please don't jump down my throat not just yet okay! I ust told you I like you as a person… I have nothing against you being a lesbian. …. I am actually happy to meet a lesbian. I couldn't wait to meet, and see you …. I'm happy you are a lesbian. I've always wanted to see what it was to kiss a woman. I couldn't wait to meet; and see to what you looked like.

"What do you think about me now Jaynie?"

I think you are very attractive. I've always wanted to know what it was like to kiss another woman. I kissed girls in school, but had never kissed an adult woman. Only one time when I worked at a care center. She was a nurse and when I kissed her, she told me never to do that again.

"You are joking right?"

No Heidi, I am very serious. ….. . I wanted to know what it's like to kiss a woman, touch and caress a woman and make love to another woman. … and I want that woman to be you Heidi!? If that is something that would interest, you? I want to know what a woman's skin feels like under my hands.

"You want me to be the one you kiss first, am I right?"

Yes, if you don't mind me being inexperienced?

"Jaynie, what are you trying to say to me?"

Looking right into her eyes I took her had. I said Heidi I want to make love with you, I want to do everything I fantasized about doing with another woman.

Heidi just sat there, with her hand in mine.

I know this is bold. I just want to kiss a woman so badly I can't stand it."

"Okay, Jaynie we can do this together. …. When."

My heart skipped a beat. I started sweating from her word when.

Heidi how long have you been out as a bi-sexual? …. What was it made you want to be a lover of both sexes?

"Well, I just always knew I liked women. I just followed my heart. I have been out as a bi-sexual for over ten years. However, I love men too. But if I find a lover I stay true to that lover may it be male/female …. I did the society thing. I dated a man and I got pregnant…. He split, and didn't want the baby or me. …. I have been taking care of my son on my own for about ten years. …. "What about you Jaynie?"

Well I have liked men all my life. …I had always liked girls since I was in elementary, you know kids crushes. …. But going after my desires I would say since 1980.

Do you ever regret having your son?

"Yes, for a while when he was an infant, but it got easier as he gotten older."

Would you ever merry a man down the road?

"To be honest it would depend if he would except that I am bi-sexual." Smiling.

Ha ha she's funny. I thought at least she has good humor. I felt like sharing with Heidi. I started telling Heidi a little bit about myself and my past. I had a baby. I placed her up for adoption, and that it was very difficult to give her up. I felt and believed my mother blackmailed me.

As I was talking, she kissed me right on my lips and I melted.

"I said put the sign up for lunch and let's go exploring, for a while! .... What do you think Heidi?"

"I think you are correct on that note."

We put the sign up "out for lunch" and we would return." We went back to the waterbed room. I was extremely nervous, and my hands were shaking, and my knees were made of butter.

My heart is racing. I am so scared. I put my fears aside because I really wanted and needed to experience these feeling as if I never wanted anyone as much as I wanted Heidi. If I never sleep with a bi-sexual or a lesbian again, at least I can say I did it once. Heidi takes off my skirt as she kisses my body. I allowed her to remove my body suit and as Heidi pulled it down she kissed my body everywhere she saw skin. I was so excited I could have died. I started to undress Heidi and I followed her lead until we hit the bed. I started at her toes, kissed each one of them, and started working my way up her body. Heidi skin was salty, and so soft to the touch of my tongue. I didn't want this day to end at all. I let my hands caress her breasts, and my nails titillated her nipples. I opened her legs, and allowed my fingers to trace her lips with her inner wetness. I let my fingers find her (boss) bush of sheer sweetness. I let my fingers go as far as they could go. I love the internal deepness she possesses. Heidi pussy was so wet and it felt so good on my skin. I just moved my fingers around her wetness, and I found her clit. I let my fingers and thumb do the talking as I traced my tongue over her stomach. I worked my way up to her nipples I was looking at them, and they were beautiful, and so pink. Heidi's skin was so white I licked around her nipples, and sucked on them, played with them as I sucked on her nipples until they were hard. I blew cool air on them to keep them erect. I kept my hands down in the warmth of her wetness as I played with her clit. My other hand was massaging her other breast while I worked my mouth on the other. I just kept sucking on her beast as if I were a baby.

Finally working my way to her neck and then to the hunger of her mouth. As I was kissing Heidi I laid my body on top of hers' and spread my legs over hers. My clit was right on top of hers and I started moving on top of her thigh in a rhythmic motion, as we moved together. Kissing each other and playing with her wetness. I just let go, I started moaning as I climaxed all over her legs. Her mouth was so warm, and sweet. I worked my way backward down her body as I removed my fingers from her bush. I wanted to play hide and suck again. I started to kiss her legs, and I moved up to her inner thighs. I could smell her pussy, which was calling my name. Falling into her boss is so sweet and tasty.

I put my face right next to her lips and blew on them and Heidi pushed her hips toward me so I pulled back, its seems just when I would get real close to her pussy Heidi would come towards me. So I teased her for a long time. I took my tongue, and just barely touched her clit. I did that, for a while until I couldn't take it anymore. I lay completely on my stomach. I spread her legs open with my arms wrapped around her legs. I parted her hair with my tongue, and I finally found the jungle of boss delight. I put my tongue inside of her pussy as far as my tongue would go, and I just drank her. I didn't stop. I just drank, and drank. The nectar I found within her body was sweet, and very tasty. I have never tasted anything so good, so sweet, in my whole life until I went down on a woman. Heidi tasted so good I didn't want to ever stop. If I just had to have sex all day with Heidi, I would see no problem with at all. Then she made me come back up. She laid me on my back and she started to kiss my body. I was already wet from making love to her. I longed to feel her fingers inside me. I have thought about this day for many years and now it's finally coming true. She started kissing my neck and working her way down to my breast. Her mouth felt so good around my breasts I thought I died and gone to heaven. She slowly worked her way down to my stomach and I felt a sensation that I had never felt before. She had entered me and my body just went totally crazy. I started moving with her fingers and it was fricking awesome. She started teasing me with her tongue as I did to her. I felt her tongue part my hair. I felt this hot feeling. I felt her tongue lick me. I just laid back, and enjoyed the ride. My body had never felt kind of sensation before. I wanted this lunch break to keep going, and never stop. The feelings Heidi gave me I graved for more.

I felt like my body is on a wave on erotica. I just go higher, and higher. I don't care how far, or how fast she was going all I knew is I wanted to just keep riding. After several hours later, we laid in bed cuddling each other.

"Are you sure never slept with a woman before Jaynie?"

Yes, as I smiled. Heidi I am sure. You are my first woman and bi-sexual I ever touched and kiss before. ...Why do you ask? ...Didn't you like it?

"I just find it hard to believe with all the stuff we did together you have never did this before with a woman.

Well Heidi just believe me when I say it's true. ... I hope we can make love many more time if you are up to it.

After about another hour of cuddling, we finally got dress and we had shared intimacy for at least three hours.

Do you think we should open up Heidi? Or should we just stay out to lunch all day?

We both thought about answer. We both said "maybe"

at the same time. We started to laugh. Heidi did say it was a really nice thought. I really could have made love again to Heidi, but I am hoping I will be able to do it again maybe later on tonight. Customers started coming in around 5:00 in the evening. Since Heidi was the acting manager. Heidi told me we could run our sessions anyway, we wanted as long as the tapes kept rolling. I agreed. My thoughts and emotions are on my depression about my family, and the shiny penis was still chancing me. The thoughts of killing my self was still in my mind. But I never told Heidi. She would think I was a nut case.

My first session was with a man about 6'0 and weighed about 300 pounds. I took him to the table room and I did the normal session. After that session was over and while the tape recorder was going he laid $600. 00 dollars on the table. I looked at him and he pointed to his penis, which I might add was huge, I should say very thick. We spoke with our bodies not with words. I started pointing here, and there. He was big, but because of his weight, he was very erect. The thought of making love with Heidi not more than an hour ago was still in my mind.

I knew I had to behave myself. I had to control my voice because the recorder was still recording. I put Heidi in my mind, and gave him a nice hot session with my hands and tits, and my pussy. He eats my pussy well. He was licking me in slow motion. I came so hard, and he just kept drinking me. He finally got dressed. He was about to leave and he gives me another $150. 00 and told me he had a really good time. I said cool thank you. I wish Stan had never touched me ever. I was just about to go in the next session when this flash back hit me. Reality had finally hit me. I finally saw who the shiny penis belongs too. It was Stan' dick! Why is this in my mind? Why would Stan's penis chase me? Stan told me the stuff we did together was okay, so I thought. I went to the bathroom, and cried. I really don't know what I just did.

Why was it coming back to me now? Right at moment. I understood why I had flash back, and why they were coming at a rapid pace. I had accepted from Mr. Fat Jack. Was it because there was sex, and money involved? I was doing the same thing with Stan. Because every day he gave me money after he had sex with me. The association goes hand in hand. I couldn't get that flashback out of my head, and they just kept coming that night on. I also had sex with only six guys before my shift was over. I made $1000.00 that night. I hated it because it made me think of Stan. An hour before my shift ended Heidi pulled me aside and said we had to stop making money, keep it cool and I said ok. Not wondering why, I now realize why. It was because of me being black I was getting a lot more customers than she was. I was doing customers almost every half hour. That must have bothered Heidi.

She is sitting out there with those men and they are all waiting to see me. I would not have minded if she took some of them off my hands. By the way, I didn't have sex with all of them. I only had sex with the men turned me on. Alternatively, the only ones I found attractive, which was maybe six of them. Our shift ended at 11:00 o'clock, and Heidi asked if I would like to go to a lesbian bar called "Wooyung 20", and I said sure. (In my head I am thinking yes). I get to go to my first gay bar. I got my stuff together and we called a cab. Went to my hotel room took a shower together, and it was hot and erotic. She let me go down on her in the shower. It was wild. I thought for a second I was about to drown, which would have been fine with me. I let her dry my body with her tongue. Heidi just started to lick my body all over. I just said, said you go girl just lick me clean, and she did. Her tongue was nice and long. After having sex again, we finally got dressed, and went to Wooyung 20 bar. She took my hand, and we walked into the bar together. I was on cloud number 2001. Ummmm. I noticed this gorgeous, hot looking, beautiful black woman. I would have loved to hook up with her. I am looking around, and I noticed how cool the Wooyung looked. The bar had several different bars in one. In addition, every bar you walked into was playing different music. When we walked into an eatery. There were are tables to sit at, and any kind of food you wanted. This bar was so amazing. Heidi asked if I wanted something to drink? I told her yes, her.

I just smiling big time. Then I told her a beer. As Heidi left a woman who I didn't know approached me, asked if Heidi was my girlfriend? I said no she just a friend of mine. This woman asked me to dance and I said sure.

While we were dancing Heidi came on to the dance floor, and I took one look at Heidi and she left the dance floor. I took one look at Heidi and she left the dance floor without saying a word to me. I went to talk to Heidi. I had to search for her I found her and she said she couldn't talk with me. and I said why not. She would not tell me so I left her alone. I came back a few minutes later, asked Heidi if she would like to dance? She said yes, we danced for a while until this very large woman approached us and called Heidi a fucking bitch. She looked at me and was about to call me a name and I told her to think about what she is going to call me. She just walked away. Later on same woman was arguing with Heidi. I didn't understand why until later. They were lovers. You want to know what is really funny? I never even asked Heidi if she had a lover. It never dawned on me. I'm really pissed. She could have told me. Now ain't that a bitch! The night was ending and Heidi took me to where she lived. I was happy because I still wanted to spend time with her. I don't care if was her lover, or not, I liked Heidi and I was not ready to let go yet. I spent the next four weeks with her, and plus working at "Mid Air Modeling". I met her son, and I finally met Heidi's girlfriend Ethel Mooresso. After my meeting her we all started spending time together. All three of us went to the bar a lot, and danced and shot pool together, and was really cool. I felt somewhat bad once I gotten to know Ethel, she was pretty nice actually nice. Ethel was losing her hair at a very fast rate, and was the only thing I found unattractive about her. I also felt bad because they were lovers, but they were having problems. I felt I was the one causing them. In all honesty it was Heidi causing the problem and I was along for the ride. If Heidi had been honest with me when we first met. None of this shit would have happened. Heidi knew, I was new to this scene and she played me, unbeknownst to me, and I allowed her. As long as she didn't care; than I don't. Eventually I would change my way of thinking. When the four weeks were up it was so hard to say good bye. It was also nice to know I would be going home to my apartment. I'm looking forward to seeing my bird Amba. I really missed him. I said good-bye to the girls at work and I let Heidi take me to the bus station, and gave her lots of hugs and kisses.

I knew I would be back in about a month and I couldn't wait to see her again. I hopped on the bus and I am crying as I watched her wave good-bye as we pulled away from the curb, and I waved good-bye to her one more time. I wiped my eyes, I couldn't see any more. It has only been a nine months since I left my old job. **I still 21 years-old**. I stopped crying after a while and looked forward to going home and sleeping in my own bed. I laid my head back and cried myself to sleep. When I woke up finally I was home back in my home town. I had left Sunday at 8:00 in the morning. It was a 12-hour ride. I arrived in Iowa around 8:30 in the evening and I am excited from the trip. Thinking about Heidi and the fact I was home.

You know, I am not that tired. Hum what to do? I called my friend Chad to pick me up from the bus station., He gave me a ride a home.

"Girl, you be looking too good!"

Thanks Chad. Hey, I have a question …. Where are all the gay bars around here? …. There's more than one right?

"Oh Yeah."

Where are the women's bars?

"They're really boring not much excitement …I think you would a good time at "The Ware House" The music is booming, you will be dancing and looking at women all night."

Well smart ass that is one of the reasons why I want to go so I can look at the women …. well let's go." Later on that night, we made a date to go to my first gay bar in Lexington. I have to say it is not like the Wooyung 20 in Indianapolis. The Warehouse was dark and the dance floor had black and white tile on it. I couldn't see in the bar because it was so dark. There was a clear through plastic divider between the dancers and the watchers.

Not one woman asked me to dance, how disappointing. I will not be coming back here again. I wasn't impressed with the Warehouse at all. I guess as you walk in the place, you think you went from day to night in a matter of seconds. The bar itself was not bad; I just felt bad cause there was not Heidi and no Wooyung 20. I had first walked up to the divider because I saw some women dancing together. I went to the bar and bought a drink. I noticed women at the bar.

But not one woman asked what my name was. All these women did is stared at me with a look of, who is she? Maybe women in this town are afraid of talking with you because they don't know what to say. Chad and I take off, he took me home, and I got ready for bed. Unpacked my clothes took a shower and went to bed. Normally when I come home,

Amba just starts talking up a storm because he knows it's me; I'm missing his voice. Monday finally arrives, and I go to the parlor to pick up Amba and talk with Charlotte and the other girls for a while. I started calling Amba name and whistling for him like I always do. I did that for him, so when I come home he does not get overly excited when he sees me. However, I didn't see Amba.

Where's Charlotte?

"She's in the back."

I went back there and she was acting like a total bitch.

Hey Charlotte what's up …. Where is Amba?

"That fucking bird would not shut up, for nothing. …… He was really pissing me off. …. I couldn't sleep, he whistled at everyone walked in."

Charlotte, I told you he was a talker. You said was no problem. Now I am getting pissed. I only had my bird for one year!

Where the fuck is my bird, Charlotte?

"I gave him to some man who wanted him"

You gave my bird away to some stranger without never even asking my permission you stupid bitch?

"Jaynie you were here to deal with it?"

Why didn't you ask our manager where I was? …. . Did you even pick up the fucking phone to leave a message on my answering machine? ….. Or maybe call the location where I was working?

"No, I didn't, and plus I forgot your phone number." I said that was a crock of shit.

Well your stupid ass bitch. You didn't think to wait until I got back or give him to one of the other girls to give yourself a break. ….. You know what, let's go.

"Hey where are you taking me? …. Hey get your fucking hands off me!"

Charlotte you can act a fool if you want to, …. but for

right now you are walking out of here with me.

If you keep acting ignorant I will open a can of whup ass! You can't imagine how much you would hurt when I am done with you. You understand me? It's you. Now you decide.

You can best assure I won't be killing you or anything like that. Now move your dumb ass! She put her shit in check, and we left the building. We went about a block up the street to Wanna Pet store in absolute silence. Charlotte tried to apologize to me, I told her, shut the fuck up. I didn't want to hear anything she had to say to me. There's nothing she could say, she fucked up and, she knows it. Now she will have to pay for a new bird of my choice. Why do people have to be so cold hearted, as to give away someone pet without the owner's permission? I could never do to anybody. I have been thinking what kind of bird I want if anything ever happened to Amba, since stupid bitch gave mine away.

We get there and I went to look at the type of bird the store had. I saw some I really liked. I have

to say the price was pretty expensive but I didn't care.

Charlotte said very loudly, trying to embarrass me no doubt. I don't have any money to buy you a fucking bird! … Besides if you want another bird you should be buying it, not me!"

I approached her and said very politely; in my cold yo ass is mine voice!

You work last night didn't you Charlotte?

"Yeah, that money is for my kid's food this morning when I get home. …. My old man demands all money as soon as I walk into the house. …. That's why I can't buy you a bird. …. . You understand don't you Jaynie? I would if I could. I swear to you, I just can't."

Charlotte, now I'm fuming, and I am about ready to slap the white right off her face. I took her by her dirty shirt collar.

You should have thought about before you gave my bird away. .... Here's what's going down.

First I saw what you feed your kids, and you won't need much cash to buy Cheerio's ... and two all your old man does is drugs. Maybe it's time for him kick the habit. .... . Right now, you will replace my bird .... And that is all I have to say; do we understand each other?

Charlotte didn't say jack, just looking at me with tears rolling down her cheeks. The end of the story I got my new bird. A miniature Beebe Parrot the exact colors on a mountain dew can. Hey that's what I will call him. Mountain Dew (Dew for short). Mountain Dew cost stupid bitch $200. 00 dollars. I saw Charlotte after the bird incident about a month later, and you know she has not said jack to me; she's very lucky she didn't. I was asked me if I wanted to go to Muncie, Indiana for two weeks?

CHAPTER **7**

I KNEW MY apartment would be in safe hands. Lacey said no problem, I gave her my key, a hug and a good bye and left. Lacy is the woman I kissed, and she said I was never to do that again. I bonded with Dew right off the back. As I was on the bus, I remember I forgot my vibrator. I thought to myself when I get home I will use it. Knowing my apartment was safe I left feeling good and I arrived in Muncie about 6:00 evening on a Thursday. Had a cab take me to Halies Massage Parlor. After I checked in with the manager of the parlor, I left and got a room right around the corner. The place looked decent enough. I was just glad to be in Muncie. I had to work that night and Friday afternoon, evening and all day on Saturday. I had Saturday night off. Something told me to be careful when I had my days off until I checked out the city, and the people. The men were looking sad. I mean sad. You would think by their reaction of me they never seen a black woman before. During my first couple of days there I tried calling Heidi. They said she was too busy to talk on the phone. I hung up and I never called her again. I left several messages. She knows I am in town so if she wants to talk she can call me, fuck it. Thank God, Saturday here. After my shift ended I got ready and took myself to dinner and a movie. I had been hearing about a movie called Rocky Horror Picture show. It was playing so I went to see it. How was I to know people really dressed up for this movie as the characters?

I didn't, and I got wet dam it, really wet. I was happy

the movie was over. I called a cab. The driver took me to my first gay and lesbian bar in Muncie. The bar was called Let's Have One, which was down town the street from the theater. It looked really nice, but the dance floor was very small. But there's plenty of seating. I got a booth, sat down and ordered a drink. After about an hour of sitting by myself. In walks this nice looking couple. They headed toward my table. They asked if they could join me and I said sure if you like. They sat and we started talking. After about an hour of chitchat Larry and Charity invited me back to their house to get high with them. I said sure. I can never pass up a free high. As we were leaving the bar, I am walking in between Larry and Charity. This woman comes out and yells,

"She too much of a woman for the two of you!" Whatever that meant?

"You're just mad because we approached her, before you did.

I could see by the look on that woman's face that she was boiling mad. I didn't know what I was doing, but in a way I did. We arrive at Larry's house and we sit on the couch, and Larry goes upstairs to change. He comes back in some short shorts. He sits down next to me, and I found out the Charity is bisexual, and Larry is straight I thought cool. I can have both of best worlds. We smoke a joint, and Charity suggested we go upstairs, and Larry followed up behind us. They both undressed me, and started kissing my body all over the. I knew what I was getting into as soon as Charity told me she was bisexual. Larry lays me down on the bed, and Charity lies next to me and Larry starts to touch both of us as Charity starts kissing me. I should tell you at the time, I was still 21, Charity was 42, and Larry 55 years-old. Wow I am about to experience my first ménage a trois. That is French for 3some. They both were touching me in ways I never felt before. It felt good too. Larry asked both of us to sit on top of him, I was nervous let me tell ya. I sat on his penis. Charity sat on his face, and I have to say I was getting into it after a while. I was kissing Charity with hunger. Charity's body is rocking at 42. Larry asked us to switch and so we did. I Charity said,

"We should work on Larry as she kissing me."

Okay.

After about three hours of Larry paying all his attention to me. Charity said,

"Larry I want to go home!"

Bye.

"Aren't you going to give me a ride home?"

Charity just take a cab will ya, and go home.

"Larry, you're an asshole."

I just lay there in bed listening to the two of them and I am thinking what did I get myself into. I spent the next two weeks with Larry at his house while I stayed in Muncie. I checked out of the hotel, which was good because I did not feel comfortable there. It was fun with Larry he has a Ph. D. in Anthropology. He is a retired professor of Anthropology at Agate University in Muncie. The last weekend I was to stay with Larry I finally convinced him to go out to a dance at the bar we met at in Muncie.

He said yes, I practically begged him to go.

It is as if he did not want to share me with anyone. He didn't want me to go anywhere. If it was not for my job, I would be at his house (24/7) and I could not handle. At one point, he even tried to get me to quit my job. He even wanted me to live with him. I just kept telling him I could not do to that. I felt like Larry was becoming my keeper. Besides, I have an apartment, and my bird waiting for me. Yes, he had good ideas, but he was acting more like a partner than just a friend to me. We finally go out together we walk into the bar, and he is trying to take my hand like were together. I kept trying to keep my distance from him in case I met a woman. I am woman shopping for me not Larry. That was my purpose of going to the bar with him. He asked me to find someone so we could have a threesome together. Please like I would find a woman for him to involve us in a three some. That's just not going to happen.

We were dancing together and I felt kind of embarrassed because here is this 55-year-old man, dancing with me. You would think he was old enough to be Sylvet. All I wanted to do was get the hell out of there with Larry. We finally left about two hours after we got there. We got home, I am totally. Larry wants to do is have sex all the time. I like to have sex too, but four times a day tends to get a little boring. I reached my limitations of sex; his request was becoming too peculiar, very strange. It is as if Larry felt he finally met a woman would join in his taboo desires! Not!

"Larry asked me to pee in his mouth and he even went as far as asking me to shit in his mouth?

I just looked at Larry and said, "What the fuck Larry! Are you some fucking freak?... Asking me to do some freaky shit like that!... Really! .. . Man, you're killing me. Don't ask me anymore.

Sunday came and went. Larry drove me to the bus stop. I can't believe my eyes, Larry started to cry. He is telling me he is going to miss me. I will miss him too, but not much.

I have only known this man for two weeks so it is not as if I fell madly in love with him. The bus pulled out, I was waving good-bye to Larry one more time. I had to go to Kokomo, Indiana for a week. I had a real boring ass time in Kokomo Indiana I couldn't tell who was a lesbian or not. The women there were very butch, and I mean butch. I didn't know my way around the town. I didn't have a car so I hung close to the shop. Finally, the end of my work week. I am hopping on the bus going home thank God. I left Indiana about 7:00 in the morning. I rolled into Iowa some hours later. I called Lacey to pick me up at the bus station, but there was no answer.

So I caught the city bus and went home. I was so horny from thinking about Heidi and Larry. I decided to use my vibrator. I took a nice hot shower, and I went to bed to get my vibrator it was not there. I know I always kept it in my top dresser drawer. I looked in every drawer, under my bed, mattress everywhere, no vibrator. Where could it be? I'm thinking maybe Lacey borrowed it. When I dialed the number out of order and the new number was unlisted.

Then I decided to call my old job thinking she was on duty. They said she quit last week. That bitch stole my dick. If I didn't mention this to you before I will say it now the dick vibrator was operated by electricity and it had two speeds hi and low. Wherever you are Lacey, I hope you are enjoying your new dick because honey is the best dick you will ever have. Stealing my only vibrator, searching through my stuff, and I thought I could trust her. The nerve of her! If you can't trust your own friends than who the hell can you trust? No body.

I was home for a month and felt good. I told my manager I wanted to eat some home cooked meals and see some of my friends. I just wanted to hang out at home and not do a damn thing, except work my shift. I had to work nights at the location. I started secretly prostituting myself to make sure I had money to take care of myself. I just used two fake names instead of my own. When someone would call and ask if any women would go out with them I would tell them about one of my friend named Scottie. She would love to go out with you. She really likes to have a good time. But I also told them she does not get of work until 11:00 at night. They said that would be fine. I gave them my home address and I would be home in time enough to change. Then there would be a knock at my door and would be them. They would ask me who Jaynie was, and I told them she was my roommate and she would not be home for a while.

They would come in and I would make them take their clothes off in the living room in case they were cops. However, none of them was. I don't know why I started selling myself again. I just thought it was one-time deal like the way Heidi and I did at the massage parlor in Indianapolis. Why is it following me all the way back home? I was prostituting myself at the age of 11 years-old. With help from Stan. I was doing it earlier with Stan, but I didn't know what prostitution was at three years-old. He and Annie had something set up between them. In order for her to allow him to molest me. That bastard showed me I could make money with my body. Stan gave me money every day and that was my start. While on this path of destruction to hell, I met this good-looking guy by the name of Lowell. He living in a half-way house for armed robbery, and I didn't think anything about his crime at all. The only thing I thought about the fact he was Italian and very tall and nicely built. He had shoulder length jet-black curly hair. I would go visit him. After a while, I noticed Lowell started becoming possessive of me. He wasn't even my boyfriend. He was trying to tell me where I can go, and I what I can and cannot do. I told him to go fuck himself. He is nothing to me, but a play toy friend that's it. I decided I didn't want to see him anymore so I stopped. Two-week later the motherfucker stole my ten-speed bike and so I called the cops and I described my bike to them and I got it back. Over a year goes by with me working at the massage parlor and me leading a double life. Then out of the blue, all of a sudden, my landlord started asking questions like

"Who are those men come out of your apartment?" I could not say anything. What could I say. I just acted stupid and said,

Oh those guys they're just friends of mine. No big thang! .... Why do you want to come up and check, around?

"Yes."

I don't know how I started having sex with my landlord for money, but somehow it happened.

I was seeing, married men, single men, my landlord. One man was a bus driver for Lexington transit, I would see him once a week. He gave me $200. 00 a week.

My landlord only hooked up with me once a month. I only got $150. 00 a month. This was cool with me. He was paying my rent so let him. I never slept or had sex with young men.

These men were always in their 50 and up. I guess because Stan was in his late forties when he was molesting me at the age of three and up so I related with the age group.

After just being by myself for five days and making money at work and at home, I was in a good mood. I called Melody and asked if I could come over and visit. She said no problem so I left. I had about $150. 00 in my pocket so and I stupidly took all my money with me. Why I do not know. I got there and knocked. When she opened the door her eyes were healing from being hit in the face. I asked Mel what happened. Like I really didn't know. Yeah, right. I asked Mel if she would like to go out on the town, my treat. Mel said sure. I hung out with her and Cameron until Towan came home. We decided to go to the Great Gatsby's around 9:00 that evening because we wanted to get good seats. Before we arrived at the bar, Mel asked if I wanted to get high, and I said sure why not. Man Mel could get the good shit to smoke. Before we hit the bar, I was high. We get to the bar and I stoned. We are dancing and laughing together and I always thought when Mel and I were together we always seem to put whatever bothering us behind us. We would just talk about anything and everything except our private lives, nothing depressing. This nice looking man asked Mel to dance and she said yes. I am watching them dance and when they were done, I heard him ask Mel if she was married? She said yes; he thanked her for the dance and he left. When the gorgeous man left, I turned to Mel, and I said, why didn't you want to go there?

Do you think Towan doing the same for you? Not! I am drinking screwdrivers, and I am feeling good. The night is coming to end and Mel drops me off at home. I made myself go upstairs to bed. I am going up stairs I start unbuttoning my shirt, unlacing my shoes, by the time I hit the bed I was out usually. I took my pants off in bed, and I take the money out of my pocket. I didn't his time because I was intoxicated. At 3:00 in the morning, there is a knock at my door. I answer, and it is stupid boy Lowell. You would think he would take a clue, but I guess he's not smart. I think men can dish it out, but they can't take it.

What the fuck do you want Lowell? (God, my head hurts from too many screwdrivers, and smoking weed.)

"I just wanted to come to say hi to you."

You do realize its 3:00 in the fricking morning.

I was being absolute bitch and I didn't give a shit. It was late, my head hurt and I was dead tired.

"Don't be like Jan, I don't want to fight with you."

First my name is Jaynie, well come in and if you come up stairs you are to sleep, If you have something else in mind, then leave right now and let me go back to bed!

"That's alright with me. I'm tired too."

Lowell followed me upstairs and we went to bed. He tries to starts feeling up on me.

Don't even think about it asshole. If you try it again you are out of here.

"I miss you Jaynie. I just want to make love to you." I just ignored him, and I started drifting off to sleep. I woke up again I felt the bed moving. I found Lowell lying on the floor.

What the fuck are you doing Lowell? .... . Are you really trying to piss me off?

"Nothing Jaynie. My back hurts so I thought I would just lie on the floor for a while."

I went back to sleep. I didn't think anything of it and the next thing I know he said,

"I'm leaving because I'm ignoring me"

Goodbye as I drift back to sleep. I wasn't even a few minutes and something just hit me like a ton of bricks. I flew up really fast not thinking about my headache .... I found my pants on the floor and I checked the pockets. That son of a bitch stole over $95. 00 from me. I got dressed, and I knew he was not too far ahead of me. I could not find the bastard anywhere.

He was probably lurking in between the houses. I just went back to bed. The next morning, I went to his half way house. They said he didn't come back last night.

As the month rolled on I forgot all about it. In the following few months I am playing softball on a straight softball team. I had bought an aluminum bat. About a week later, Lowell showed back up at my door. I know he is thinking maybe he can steal from me again. I allowed him ahead of me, and he is sitting on the couch in my living room and I was being nice. I offer him some water and as he starts drinking.

Where is my fucking money? Really Lowell, stealing from me?

"I didn't take any money from you!" Don't accuse me of something I didn't do

He is trying to fuck with my mind.

Then why, we're you in bed one minute, and down on the floor next to my pants?

"I told you my back was hurting." It's was just my imagination, that after you got what you wanted, your back felt much better and you took off right?

We are both still in my living room and Lowell sitting on the couch. I was facing my closet.

I get my bat I walked up to him with my bat in my hand. How much money do you have in your pockets? He takes out $74. 00 and some change. Out of nowhere, I hit him in the leg he starts crying drop's the money on the floor and I pick it up. I said this is for you stealing from me. I'm keeping it. You get the fuck out of my house. If you ever come over here I promise I will fuck you up, and then call the cops.

Lowell starting to limp towards me, he's speaking very low. Like its ok Jan. I will take care of you. I won't hurt you.

I started backing away from him, raised the bat over my head, and said stay the fuck away from me Lowell, I'm warning you. If you don't leave now, I will hit you upside your head with this baseball bat, I swear.

Lowell is still coming towards me, I swung the bat, and I smacked him in the arm. He screamed,

"You fucking cunt. I am going to beat the fuck out of you."

Try it motherfucker. I'll kill you. …. Leave while you can still walk. …. Don't ever back here again. He called me a fucking bitch again and left. I never saw him again.

I was asked by my office manager asked me if I wanted to spend two weeks in Danville, Illinois and two weeks in Cedar Rapids, IA. I said sure. I asked my brother Antwan to watch my place and he said no problem. I took the bus to Danville to the massage location and, the location was in a trailer was really weird. The women there were so ugly I wouldn't even want to sleep with them. There was this client who came every week. He always requested small model so they could walk on his face while he masturbated. It was the same model all the time. Clients preferred it. There was this heavy woman who got paid $300. 00 to let this ugly man fucked her between the tits, and let me tell you they were big. My time in Danville was short. I couldn't wait to get out of there. I hopped the bus to Cedar Rapids had an okay time there. I didn't know where the gay bars were. I didn't know a lot of people there except for the models. None of the models spoke about going to out to the gay bars. I didn't bring it up.

I did like working in the location of First Avenue. There was so much traffic, and few shops to shop at to buy gifts and things. And right down the street from the massage parlor was an adult theater. When I got back home to Lexington, I was extremely tired of traveling**. I am 22 years-old** and I had to get my courage to quit. They didn't want me to. I said the traveling is starting to really bore me. So is this job. I hugged my boss good-bye and I left. You want to know what is funny out of all the money I made. All I have to show for it is I still have my a roof over my head, food to eat. My clothes, shoes, make up, and fake jewelry and my mountain dew (bird).

Wow is all I can say. Isn't that sad? No money saved in the bank. Not one dime. However, on the flipside I never went to my parents for help, and I never had to move back home. I still my independence, and my freedom. Keeping my freedom was very important to me. The desire to be around womyn became stronger than ever. Now it's time for me to hang out in the bars in Lexington. I just didn't know where they were at and the only way I remembered how to find them was to call the cab company. What ever happened to Dori Stratton? I always thought she was a lesbian and maybe she might be at the bar. I have not seen her since I transferred to Klenmore

High School in 1980. I am not sure if she is stilling living in Lexington or if she moved away. I decided to go to the bar called 2nd City Tavern by myself. As I approach the bar I am extremely nervous, but I took a deep breath, and walked in. The bar was located right down town in Lexington. As you walked in front of the bar there is a big bay window facing 2nd street. What is so cool about the bar is they have a pool table. The bathrooms were located in the back. I walked up to the bar, and asked for a drink. It was a Saturday afternoon and there was a pool tournament going on so I asked the bartender her name is Carmon I asked if could join in, and she said sure. I saw a platform in the back of the bar I asked Cameron what platform was for. Carmon said sometimes on the weekends they have drag shows (drag shows are female impersonators and preforming front of an audience) I thought hey I have to see this. Then I asked her when is the next show, and Carmon she said tonight.

I would be here. She said it starts promptly at 10:00 p. m, which gives enough time to get ready later on that night. I am thinking I do not know the first thing about pool.

Today is my lucky day. My turn is up to play pool. I am scared as hell. I had to play against a womon who I might add is very good. I told her I am not that good. They offered me the opportunity to play slop, which means make it take it.

The game started, and I wasn't doing too badly if I say-so myself. I won, the other womon was too cocky. She lost by scratching on the eight ball. Which was good for me because I was able to stay in the pool game until it ended. The pot was $30. 00 to the first, and second place winner won 15.00. I game in fourth place. Hey I did it. After the pool tournament was over I met some nice womyn. All of us just hung around and talked. I didn't know them well enough to ask what they had planned, for later. I just went home and thought about the drag show later night. Looking for work never left my head.

The show will be starting in an hour. I was really excited about going to the bar. I wonder if Dori would be there? If she would even remember me? I start walking to the bar. and you can hear the music a block away. What I thought was cool about the "2nd City" was it was right across from this really good Chinese restaurant called the "Dragon Inn" I get to the bar. The place is packed, and I had to sit toward the back of the bar, which was fine with me. This way I can watch all the womyn. The show started and some of the drag queens were good. A few needed to go back and practice. I really liked two gay men, one was named Howard. The other was a black guy by the name of Don. They both just cracked me up. Their mannerisms were so femme. Don would imitate Dianone Warrick. Howard would twirl the button and dance. The show was nice and somewhat funny. The drag queens just killed me with laughter. The bar had mostly men in it I didn't see a lot of womyn. I was told they don't hang out at "2nd City." Instead they hang out at a place called the "Lavender Womyn Bar." After the show was over I decided to go back home because I didn't know where the "Lavender Womyn Bar" was located, and besides it was after 1:00 in the morning. I was still prostituting with the old men I had met on my own, and along with the men I met at the massage parlor. I knew I need more income. If I wanted to survive period.

Who's knows how long will these me will want keep seeing me down the road. But some reason I couldn't stop taking their money. One minute I think I am not going to see these men again. They call me I haven't had any money for a while. Trust me when the men call I am so happy they called. One day I was reading the classified section and I read this, "Would you like to get paid to style hair?" I said hell yeah. "Want people to learn how to do hair and get paid in the process, "Young's School of Cosmetology College" Get paid $200. 00 dollars every two weeks while learning to style hair. The school was located in the heart of down town Lexington. **I'm 23 years old.**

I am thinking hey cool. I would be able to pay rent, and still be able to see my clients. I went and signed up. These people were talking so fast I didn't understand them at all. They were talking about taking out a student loan to attend school. Which I knew nothing about. I wanted to ask questions, but I felt stupid. I let the school speak. The next thing I knew, I'm at the bank taking out a student loan to attend college. I if I knew then what I know now about student loans trust me I would not have applied for one period. I would have survived the way I had been doing. I got all the paper work done, and I started school.

Every time I turned around people were talking about all of us gay people. They were calling me a dyke and my gay friends queers. I would say out loud I rather be gay then straight. Who wants to suck dick; not me? All of us gay people laughed. I wanted to be a dyke so I dressed like one. I got rid of my purse. I bought a wallet, I started wearing men's clothing, and hats. I could actually pass as a man. I had done just for the fun of it. I started to get this attitude at school either you like me for who I am or if not KMA (kiss my ass). You have to have attitude. If you don't, stuck up people would walk all over ya. The people who couldn't accept my lesbianism stayed away. The ones who could, we got along well, which was fine by me.

I had long hair before I started, but within three months, my long hair was gone. I meant gone! I let students cut on it. I liked it better short anyway. It was the instructors made it difficult. I saw homophobia, racism, and extreme favoritism. I hated being there. I needed the money. The men I was seeing came in so I cut their hair. They would give me cash for seeing them the night before. Plus, all students can receive tips. I was taking care of myself. I was doing what I had to do to survive. What Stan taught me, I think I'm doing good. (Or am I)? I didn't turn to my parents for help. I stayed in school as long as I could. There was income coming in. I didn't to get behind in my rent. By going to school, I was able buy food, necessities. That's why I stayed even though I really hated being there. One strange afternoon Sylvet decided to pay me a visit at my apartment. I said come in and we go to the living room. He sits down and he looks at me. He had the nerve to asks me. What do you do in bed with a woman? I looked at my father and said. What do you do in bed with my mother? That was none of my got damn business. I came back with right back at ya. My father pissed and left. After that scene, my he never came over again.

I decided to go to "Al's Hangout" and show off my new dew. I did not expect to see Sylvet, but he was there. He was heading toward and I caught up with him. I tapped him on the shoulder,

Hi Sylvet, do you like my new haircut? My hair was so short you could not even crab it with your fingertips. I meant my hair is short. Like almost bald. He was about to say hi, as he turns his head his mouth open. He took one look at me. My father turned his back like he didn't know who the fuck I was. I just walked away hurt. We were both in the bar. My father totally ignored me. As the bar was closing I followed my father to the parking lot.

Dad, what's wrong? Dad my father turned around quickly and said to me,

"Stay the fuck away from me Jaynie! I can't believe you cut off your hair. Don't come near! ... I don't have a faggot for a daughter. You are not my daughter.

You just don't know how crushed I was. I stood there with tears in my eyes. I fired back with, you will never see me again. For your information, with my hands on my hips, lesbians are females, and faggot refers to gay men. My father his hand up to hit me. I told him that as soon as your hand hits my body I will have your ass in jail. If you think I'm lying, try me. I won't let you hit me like you hit Othea. He lowered his hand and walked away adding stay the fuck away from me Jaynie. I mean it. Of course, I respected his wishes. I didn't want to see my father ever again. After that scene in "Al's Hangout" parking lot, my father and I would never speak again until 20 years later. About six months after I started school Towan was laid off from his job. Towan was on unemployment. Towan knew I was in college, and had financial assistance. One morning in June 1983, Towan came over to my apartment. I was surprised to see him.

Towan asked if he could borrow 600.00. Like a fool, I thought if I helped him maybe, he might love me the way a brother should love a sister. In addition, I wanted to help Mel and the boys. I gave him the money. Instead, he just he just used me as he did when we were living at home.

Towan gave me all kinds of excuses. Like the one he needed to buy clothes and food for the baby. I didn't think to say no. I didn't want my nephews to starve. I know all the money I gave him would not reach Mel. I didn't know how to say no. Towan promised to give me back the money in a couple of months. It turned in to years. One thing I can say about Towan, nothing is important or comes first in Towan's life, except for Towan. If one of his cars needed repairs, that came first. But if the baby's needed some food, he would bitch, and bitch how he never had any money for himself. He is very selfish, just like Sylvet. Towan always worried about his fricking image. I guess he didn't think that maybe I needed the money to live on. No, he just thought of himself. I knew deep down inside I would never see the money from Towan again. I never gave that much money away again, to anyone. I would do anything in the world for my family. I am going to cosmetology school every day. I'm thinking how fed up I am of this school also of "Al's Hangout". I decided to go to Watering Hole. I called the cab company for directions. The night air felt cool on my face. I decided to ride my bike. I did not know what to expect. As I am riding my bike to the bar, I wonder if anyone would like a womon of color. It was be a sad day if not one womon asks to dance? That would totally suck. However, I needed to go**. I am 23 years-old** and I need, to be around women. Let me tell you I felt like a fish out of water. I was not sure if I was wearing the right clothes. I finally got there. I looked into the bar, the floor and the railings are wood. The bar itself is nice. Bar stools, are next to the bar on your left and I face the mirror along the wall. The dance floor is to my back.

The bar is big. You're not able to tell from the outside. I am listening to the "SOS band." I heard this song before. It's one of my favorite songs, and I am ready to dance. I have not even been in the bar two minutes, as I'm looking around I see women's heads turn to look at me. They go back to what they were doing. I walked up to the bar and I ordered a beer. I lean against the railing the railing, trying not to look too obvious, too late. I stood out like a sore thumb. Wish someone would ask me to dance, no one did. All of a sudden, Dori comes into my head. I start looking around the bar to see if I can see her. There are so many women to look at. I started to walk around the bar. I saw tall, short, small, large, Black, White, Hispanic, Bi-racial, and I felt like I have gone to heaven. All these women looked so good. I just felt so good! I do not care if no one asked me to dance. I'm just happy being around all these beautiful lesbians. So many women, so little time, to see and meet them all. I happened to notice this one woman. I thought she looked familiar. So I walked up to her and I was about to say something, and she turned around and it wasn't Dori. I turned around and walked away. I just watched women dance, and I stayed for a while. I left around 12:30 at night. Not one women spoke to me.

My fears came true. Maybe they thought I was a guy. My hair was so short. I said to myself I'm coming back here again. I felt like I was at "Let's Have One bar" in Muncie, Indiana all over again. I went to school all week, and couldn't wait for school to be over. I told Richard about my first night at the "Lavender Womyn Bar". He said cool. I thought oh well. Friday I stayed home and cleaned so I could play Saturday. I called Don and Howard to say hi. I wanted to know if they were going to the "Ware House Bar" tonight? They were. They asked if I was going out? I told him, I think I'll pass. As usual, I let them talk me into going. Again all men. Hardly no womyn.

Where are all the lesbians? The "Watering Hole Bar" that's where! After a while, I walked home. It was so hot. I wasn't tired at all. I was almost home and I took a detour to this cool bar called the "Made Rite Bar & Grill" where they eat pea-nuts, and throw the shells on the floor. I felt like playing some pool. I saw this guy playing pool by himself. I approached the table. I asked him.

Would like to challenge me to a game of pool? ..... The guy looked up at me and smiled,

"Sure, are you good or do we have to play slop?"

No. But I am getting better. What's your name?

"Marcus Gladdenson."

Nice to meet you. My name is Jaynie. I'll rack em up'

"Okay, while you rack the balls, I am going to get some-thing to drink. Jaynie, would you like anything?"

Sure I'll have a screwdriver. Thanks.

Man this guy is nice looking. He is about 5'8 curly blond afros, about 190 pound. He looks like he is in his early 40's.

Your break Marcus.

As he was breaking, I was looking at his ass. I was saying um um um; I want that tonight. Boy I am lonely. After we played several games of pool, pleasant conversation, and I can't tell you how many drinks I had.

"Do you need a ride home?"

No thanks, I just live right down the street.

"I don't mind. I wouldn't want anything to happen to you."

This man is flirting with me, like he had been doing all night.

Okay Marcus you can give me a ride home.

I'm feeling very giddy. Shit, I cannot believe Marcus bought me all those dam screw drivers. Dammit I just knew I'm going to have a big headache in the morning.

We pull up in front of my house. Marcus keeps talking. It feels like he does not want me to leave. I invited him in. We walked up to my house and up the stairs. We're sitting in my living room.

Marcus do you care for something to drink?

"No, thank you. I had fun playing pool with you Jaynie. … Maybe we can play again sometime?"

He is looking at me like he wants something.

Okay, what's up Marcus?

"I don't have a lot of money, but how much would it cost to make love to you?"

I thought you son of a bitch. I never even had any of that shit in mind with him. Since he thinks, I sell pussy, well then, he will have to pay for it. 250 either you got it or you don't.

He slaps 250 dollars in my hand. I have a look of shock on my face. Now I just want him gone. I was not sure if he was an undercover cop. And at that moment I really didn't care. I Marcus undress in my living room. As I undressed in my bedroom, he comes in butt naked. I'm horney, lonely and need some loving. I let him take control and he is very gentle. He starts kissing my body all over. (Why can't he be a woman?) He takes his fingers and starts to caress my body and all other parts needed to be touched. I felt this soft wetness as he is licking my clit with his tongue. I just lying back enjoying it.

After a while Marcus comes up, he lies on top of me. He penetrated me, and he felt really good inside me. He just keeps looking at me and I feel bad I took his money. He shouldn't have asked how much. I wasn't wearing anything revealing. Just a pair of pants and a nice shirt. That was all. After several hours we both fell asleep. He got up at 5:00 in the morning to go to work. I hugged him good-bye. He asked if he could see me again? I said sure, and gave him my phone number. He called two days later.

"Hi Jaynie, Are you busy?"

No, just studying for school, what's up?

"May I come over?"

Sure you can.

We hung up, 20 minutes Marcus is at my door. I go to shake his hand to say hi and he puts $250. 00 in my hand.

What's this for?

"It's for today. I brought the same as last time. I want to make love to you again."

Marcus I don't want your money.

"No keep it Jaynie you deserve it. and besides I don't mind giving you money."

Okay if you want me to.

He thinks I am a prostitute. Let him think it.

After that afternoon, I was starting to get kinda serious with Marcus. He was nice to hang around. He was funny, kind, and very giving. I am feeling, I don't want to keep taking money from him. I was seeing him almost every day. Marcus didn't tell me until weeks later he had 3 kids by another woman. He wasn't married to her. I thought, this is just great. Why don't I ask people, if they're in a relationship or not up from before I get involved? Dammit.....

When will I ever learn? I did not want to stop seeing Marcus. He didn't want to stop me as well. Marcus just smiled took me into his arms and kissed me. I continued to see Marcus for the next five months. I really liked him. Regardless of his relationship, and his three kids.

I talked with Marcus told him how I felt about him. He just smiled, took me into his arms and kissed me and took me to bed. After a few more months of goodness with Marcus, I started to notice Marcus was becoming a jealous lover.

I answered an ad in the newspaper. I called the number and a woman by the name of Minnette Melrose answered. We chatted a little bit about the job, and all it details. She asked if I wanted to come in for an interview, and I said yes. I am now **24 years old**. I got up, put on some nice clothes, and went to my interview. I got there early, and filled out an application. I asked for Minnette and I waited for about two minutes. Minnette was the assistant manager. For "The Coalition to Lower Utilities Rates for the "Citizen of Lexington Network".

Out walks this tall white woman. About 5'8. She looked pretty young, I guessed early 30's. Her face looked smooth, and her eyes were blue. She shakes my hand and leads me to her office. I am sitting in her office, I am getting excited, and I do not know why.

We were chit chatting. I asked her point blank (I swear she looked just like a lesbian with her short hair). I am not trying to stereotype you at all. Minnette are you a lesbian? She hesitated a second or two.

"Umm yes."

I thought to myself yes, I knew it. Can I call out lesbians or what?

I said wonderful.

"Why."

I just wondered. Then I said I'm bi-sexual. I want to make a choice. It's hard. I always been with men all my whole life. One not by my own choosing. I told her about Stan and what he did to me. I have only been out since 1980. In addition, I have yet to meet any lesbians in Lexington. You are the first. I no longer feel alone. I told her right now, I attend Leaonna Cosmetology College and I have to let them know I am quitting school. I had one more month to go before I graduate. Minnette hired me and I started on Monday at 2:00 in the afternoon 1983 After the interview, I asked if she would like to come over to my apartment and hang out, drink some beer and smoke? Minnette said sure. (Boy I was a cocky little shit wasn't I?) At around 6:00 in the evening she was at my door. That girl is punctual I can tell you that.

I was extremely nervous. I let her in, and we sat in my living room. We just smoked and shared our pasts. Damn the stuff Mel gave me is so good. One minute Minnette is sitting to my right. The next thing she turns around; she straddles my lap. She is now sitting directly in front on my lap. She kissed me lightly at first. I'm thinking, oh kiss me again and again. I don't say anything, her lips on her face are so soft, plump, pink. Her lips remind me of strawberries and her breath smells yummy. This time I kissed her back. Minnette gets up off me, takes my hand, and leads me into my bedroom. I told her I have only slept with one lesbian. Which I enjoyed immensely. I'm not that experienced. I just love being with womyn. She looked at me and took off my clothes. I took off hers. She gently laid me down on the bed. She placed her beautiful body on top of mine. In my head, I am thinking, Marcus please don't call.

All these thoughts about Heidi flood back into my mind. As my mind was wondering Minnette started to kiss my body with her tongue. Sucking here, there, and everywhere a tongue can possibly go. I lost track on where she was until I felt her tongue go deep into my boss. (Bush of sheer sweetness). Her tongue darting in and out of me. I climaxed all over the place. Then she put her attention on my clit and she took her fingers guided them inside me. I help her go further by using my hips. I already knew I am multi-orgasmic. Minnette was hitting spot every time.

Minnette honey you got to stop!

"Why," as she sucking my clit."

Please Minnette you have to stop.I reached down, and pulled her to my face. I have wanted to make love to a woman ever since my first time experience in Indiana. That woman is going to be you. You are my first experience here and I want to do to you what you are doing to me and then some. I want to taste, smell and most of all; I want to drink you. I took her face into my hands and pulled her to my mouth. I kissed her long and passionately. Hungrily trying to quench my thirst. I want to hear the sounds I longed to hear for such a long time. I laid her on her back. I was actually lost in lesbian erotica, for what seemed like hours. Whatever she did to me, I did to her even slower took twice as long. The words I longed so desperately to hear was, "oh Jaynie don't stop." After were just lying bed cuddling with each.

CHAPTER **8**

I STARTED SEEING Minnette every day before and after work. After three weeks of seeing each other, I told Minnette I was becoming very attracted to her.

I should tell you Minnette, I never had a lover that was a female!

"That's good cause I have not had one in a while."

I guess it was settled. We became lovers, and it wasn't a problem for either one of us. Minnette and I went out a couple of times. We went to the "Ware House" together. I had only been at the bar with my male gay friends. It was nice being there with my girlfriend. We just danced so well together. We were both tall and I was a little bit taller than Minnette, I didn't care. Our bodies were as one.

I could not wait to get her home, and we both could make love to each other. I went to school Monday morning, and told them I am dropping out of school. I signed some papers, said good-bye to my friends and left. I made sure I also gave gay Richard a hug good-bye. I get home later that evening. Marcus came over and he started in on me.

"Jaynie, why haven't you been home? .... . I've been calling you, and you return calls"

Marcus, are you my keeper? .... Is there a written law I must stay home to get your phone calls?"

"Jaynie, who have you been hanging out with?"

Someone I like and care about very much. Is it a problem?

"Whoever it it it's too much."

Marcus you should know by now, and your opinion doesn't matter much right now or ever. .... Why in the heck are trying to get on my nerves? What I do and where I go is my business. .... You're the one who is having his cake and eating it to. I don't say anything about it to you at all. ..... . I let you come over and fuck me and then you go home to your little make shift family. You have some fucking nerve asking me questions like that. .... I should be the one asking you questions.

I really want to see Minnette. Since I met Marcus, I stayed away from the "Watering Hole" I have not stop wanting to hang around Minnette.

I never told Marcus how I felt about womyn. I don't know what he would think if I told him. I wasn't ready to take that chance.

I decided to tell him, to finally get it over with. I set up a time to have a chat with Marcus. He came over a week later.

Marcus there is something I've been meaning to talk to you about!

Jiminy he's looking at me. I feel he's looking right through me.

"Yes what is it Jaynie?"

His attention is all on me, and I can see it.

I have been seeing a womon by the name of Minnette Wilcaster for a while. (My hands are sweating so badly)

"Okay, now you told me, you can stop seeing her. I don't want to share you with anyone, especially a fucking woman."

What the fuck are you talking about Marcus? .... "You and I are not committed to each other.

"You heard me!"

Marcus, I am not going to stop seeing Minnette. .... I really like spending time with her.

"You are leaving me, for a lesbian?"

Yes, but understand I really liked you. That's it just like. …
. Look Marcus, it's my life. If I want to be with a womon or
whomever, it's my choice.

Marcus left my apartment. I think he was crying. He
would not look at me. He left my house hurt, and angry. A
week or so later, I had to go to work, I thought I would stop
by at Marcus's job to apologize to him. I asked again, if we
could be friends. He didn't want to talk with me. I left. I still
had an hour to kill. I hung around down town. Finally, 2:00
O'clock rolled around and I was off to work. I got to work
thinking I was going to be working with Minnette. Boy was I
wrong! I found out I had to ride with a bunch of strangers. To
a certain side of town. We were called Canvassers. Minnette
would be off somewhere else. The ride would take an hour or
so. When we reached our location, we would start canvass-
ing. We would jump out with our clipboards, canvass up, and
down the street. Knocking on doors, asking for donation money, sign a sheet asking if the city to lower utilities, and lower
the cable cost. After my first night, I knew job would not be
lasting long. As I became acquainted with Minnette, I noticed
she was a workaholic. She smoked too much weed for my
taste. Don't get me wrong I smoke weed too. I'm not judging
anyone. I am just saying Minnette, smoked weed all the time,
every day. Her smoking was starting to cause problems in our
relationship. It was a Friday evening. I rode my bike over to
her house. Again she is smoking weed.

Minnette lets go dancing.

"No, I'm tired."

I am out of here; I had enough of your shit. … Minnette.
…. . All you want to do is sleep and work and smoke weed.
…. I'll see ya' around.

"Go leave little girl. I know you couldn't handle it!"

I slam the door behind me. I was so angry. I decided to go

down to the "Watering Hole" and shoot some pool. I think I needed to vent my anger! You know what I mean? Also it was Friday and I sure didn't want to go back home. (I just love my bike. Can you tell?) I took my bike down to the Watering Hole, and thank Goddess it was warm out. I walked into the bar and I looked around. It wasn't busy. I ordered a drink and went to my favorite spot to lean against the rail. I looked around and it was dead. I looked at my watch and it was only going on 8:15 p. m. The bar didn't start getting busy until around 10:00. I decided to leave and go to" 2nd City". There were some womyn playing pool. I just stood there and watched the womyn shoot. I looked over by the platform, and they were getting ready to put on another drag show.

My time went by fast, and I looked at my watch and it read 9:30. I hopped back on my sweet dependable 10 speed, and went back to the "Watering Hole". I bought a drink, and leaned against the rail. I figure I stood in the same spot someone had to notice me. I hoped. I was just about to take a drink, and I looked a crossed the dance floor. I could not believe my eyes! There was Dori Stratton, she was playing pools. I walked up very casually, and put some quarters up. I was hoping she would recognize me. She didn't. I just stood back, and watched her. She was playing with a womon I never seen before. I have to say, I never seen Dori shoot pool, she's really good. She won the table. I'm next to cool. Dori walked up to me.

"What kind of game do you want to play? Me with my no pool-playing ass look up and I said.

Make it take it. (Call pockets).

Finally, after months of looking, for her she right in front of me.

By the way my name is Jaynie, I use to go to school with you.… I tell her this as she is shaking my hand. … Isn't your name Dori Stratton?

"Yes it is."

Wow, too cool. What a small world. I have been hoping to run into you since 1980.

"Thank you, is pretty nice to hear, a woman has been waiting and searching for me for over three years." It is 1983

I asked her if she remembers seeing me in school, and she said kind of. We were playing pool and talking. Dori said introduced me to her lover Cookie. I shook her hand and said hi (as I am thinking to myself she may be your lover now, but not for long). (Again with the cockiness. I was so naïve at time). We talked about everything under the sun, and I noticed Cookie was getting very mad at Dori. I don't care because I had been waiting for this encounter, for a long time. We played several games of pool that night. She won the first three, and I won the last one. I was happy I beat her ass in pool. Also I am proud to say I am doing better at pool. A song came on I really liked.

Dori would you like to dance?

"Yeah, but let me see what's wrong with Cookie".

Dori goes and talks to Cookie. Before you know it Cookie gets up and leaves the bar in a huff. I am happy I finally get to dance with Dori all night long. We just kept laughing about school and people we knew in general. I admitted to her I had a crush on her since high school. I just smiling like a Cheshire Cat.

We looked back on high school and laughed. I still had a big crush on her. This time I am an adult. We danced all night. We even slowly danced together a couple of times.

I liked the way she moved her body to the beat. She felt really good moving next to mine. I just felt so good finally talking to someone in the bar instead of standing by myself. The bar just called last call, damn! Dori and I exchanged phone numbers. After that night of finally finding Dori, we talked every day to each other. I knew Cookie was very upset and extremely jealous. Eventually Dori and Cookie broke up because of my friendship with Dori. If I knew more about relationships back then, I would have left Dori and Cookie alone. I was just **25 years-old** at time and very naive to lesbianism and relationships. I did not care if I hurt the other womon. I went after what I wanted. I only had two short relationships since I came out in 1980. Had not contact with the Gay Community except in gay bars.

After talking and hanging out with Dori, I really wanted to kiss her and I did. Right on the lips. Her mouth was so soft, and sweet. Before long, we were hanging out at the bars just chillin. We held hands, kissed, slow danced, talked, laughed at whatever came to mind. I am going to the "Watering Hole", more and more with Dori. I am really falling for this womom. I have been waiting, for so long. I felt like we have been together for ages. It felt so right. By this time Dori would come over to my house. Dori and Cookie lived together. It was easier, for Dori to come to my place rather than me going to hers.

"Jaynie would you like to go with me to one of my favorite places in Lexington?"

Sure. (I'm thinking oh yes. Take me where you want me to go.)

We drove up in her little green Nova. She really loved that car. She took me behind Adams University, which was actually located six blocks from my house. I never knew this place even existed.

It was past 7:00 in the evening, in December, 1983 it was so cold. I didn't feel the cold while we were together. (I wondered if Dori ever brought other womyn or lovers here.). She turned off her car and we just sat and look over the city. The lights were so beautiful and glittery. We were just making small talk and Dori leans over and kissed me. I'm shocked and surprised she kissed me before I kissed her that night. Boy, I thought I worked fast! She fooled me! Hum, she is a tasty sweet treat. I know I was extremely excited. I have been waiting for her to kiss me, for over two months now. Since the night I kissed her. I didn't want to appear too pushy. Dori looked at me and kisses me again. She was the second womon kissed me in Lexington. Her favorite song comes on the radio. She wants to dance.

She took my hand, we get out of the car, and we slow danced to her song in the frigid cold and in the snow. It was very cold; but very beautiful. Dori wanted to dance. On a whim we went to the "Ware House". What is with the Ware House. It's such a men's bar. Ugh.

We walk into the bar. It was dark. As you walk in there is a window you pay the cover charge. Dori, and I go in holding hands. I'm still in awe with what just happened in the car.

"Jaynie would you care for a beer? …. Jaynie, Jaynie?"

What! I am sorry I didn't hear your question!

"You want a beer?"

Oh yeah. I need one. Thanks.

It's Friday night, I forgot there was a show tonight. We go grabbed a place to sit. The bar is packed. I never knew this building use to be a real warehouse; too cool. I was looking around. I saw to gay men kissing, and several womyn couples slow dancing together. Drag queens were trying to dance in high heel shoes. I'm in heaven. If there was a bomb, I know I probably would not hear it. All of a sudden I hear a voice calling someone a fucking bitch. I looked up, and Cookie is walking straight towards us. (Oh my goodness; does she not get the hint?) Do we have to go through this bullshit all over again? I mean really (I'm thinking this in my head!) I got up to move and Dori, grabbed me. Dori is to my right, and Cookie is yelling at Dori. Dori and I are both watching Cookie make a fool out of herself! I guess she's a little bitter. Dori asked me to dance and I said sure. We both walk past Cookie as she steps aside, and we go to the dance floor. We're looking into each other's eyes; I was getting excited just by watching Dori.

Out of the corner of my eye, I saw Cookie leaving the bar. I sort of felt sorry for her. We danced together, having such a great time. We kissed back and forth. Finally, the drag show is over, the bar is about to close. I don't want this night to end. Dori asked, if I would like to come over to her house? I am thinking, oh hell yeah. We head over to her house, and Hasus Elionsita is playing "Lady, Lady Lady". This is one of her favorite songs. She lights candles and offers me a beer. I am nervous thinking, what is this womon up to? (As if I really do not know). The lights are off; the candles are burning. I just froze. We start slow dancing again this time she undresses me, I let her. I know my body is shaking.

I wondered if Dori is as nervous as I am. I don't want her to stop so I started to help her. She finally gets me undressed. and she finally gets me undressed and then I start to I undress her. Dori's body is so beautiful and her curves are just right. I just wanted to kiss her all over her body. We kissed each other as we walk backward to her bedroom. She laid me down and starts kissing me all over my body. Shoulders, neck, stomach, arms, everywhere you could imagine. By now, I am so excited. I can barely contain myself. She takes my legs and opens them and she is going to my BOSS, with the help of her fingers. I just laid there and enjoy the ride Dori is giving me. I roll on top her and do the same thing to her. Longer and longer, I never wanted to stop. My fingers and my tongue find her BOSS. I'm in total blissfulness or it's heaven?

We finally end up lying in each other's arms. Our legs are intertwined. We eventually fall asleep in each other's arms.

I felt so good in her arms and it felt good having her for a lover, which I have waited for so long. I am hanging with Dori. Mostly going to the bars. Dori likes to drink a lot. We're having a good time in the next several months that we shared. One day Dori introduced me to her ex-lover names Roda Mayert. I'm not really thinking anything to be honest. After a while, Dori starts hanging out with her ex-girlfriend Roda, and two kids. The whole family is taking up Dori's time and I see less and less of Dori. I was jealous and would argue and yell at each other over Roda. We fought so much we eventually break up down the road.

Boy doesn't that beat all. I took Dori from Cookie and Roda came back into Doris' life. Ain't a bitch? How does cliché go, what goes around, comes around! I like this one. Carma's a bitch. You know what happens when an ex-lover appears. I will miss Dori. I think we would have had a nice time together if she could have slowed down on her drinking, could have kept Rhoda out of our lives. The other thing that was saw was that we were only together six months! I was invited out to a bar called "Sweet Dancing Club" located in Crowns Town, About 30 minutes from Lexington. This bar is big, and the dance floor is huge and the music was feelin' fine. I am dancing and I saw a womon watching me. After I was done dancing, I walked up to her, asked her name, which was Beth Moorish. She was attractive in her own way. Her personality was kind and she was 5'5 maybe 5'6. I really was not attracted to womyn were shorter than I was. Beth has sexy lips that went with her mouth. I just want to eat em up! After the night of dancing mostly with Beth. We decided to hook up. We exchanged phone numbers. I am working odd jobs to stay afloat. I am spending time with Beth, almost every weekend. I would sometimes stay at her house and vice versa. I am thinking, hey I have all this money and I want to get the hell out of here. Crowns Town was looking better and better every time I would go up there. I was invited to Jonessa's wedding. Jonessa was my childhood friend. Her mom and my father had an affair throughout my childhood. I cannot believe she is getting married. I thought she would definitely come out as a lesbian. I went to her wedding however. I stayed in the back. I left before the wedding was over. For some reason I was crying uncontrollably. I didn't want to see any people that I knew.

I surely didn't want to answer all the questions, that I knew people had. I had made up my mind I am moving to Crowns Town, Iowa. I asked Antwan to help me move along with Beth. Antwan met Beth and I think there meeting went well. Antwan showed up with my father's truck. If my father knew why Antwan wanted to use it. My father would had said no. I told my landlord I was moving. One good thing, I was never behind on rent. I never had to pay a deposit. The apartment was in the same shape when I moved in. I had been there for four years. He told me he would miss me. I said its time for me to move on. I have been packing all week and I am ready to get the hell out of this dead town. Beth pitched in to help me pack. We kissed, packed kissed and packed.

A couple of times we made love in bed. Sunday was finally here, it is 1984. Antwan is outside in the truck. All the days for it to rain, it would be today. I have found a nice place to live. We drove to 533 East Locust Street. We unload the truck, gave my big brother a tight hug cried a little kissed him good-bye. I am I living in Crowns Towns with my bird Mountain Dew. **I am the big 26 years-old**. This is a very much a parting town. You see students everywhere. Bikes galore. Students party here until 4:00 a.m. in the morning. If you do not hear music blasting, then you hear fights breaking out down the street. I have only been here one week, and I already miss my apartment. Going from a quiet town to a University town is something to adjust to. Beth comes over, and wants to go downtown. We walked down the street holding hands. Winter is finally over. I am happy about that. I like where I was living in the summertime it is very pretty. It feels good having a lover again. Beth found me a job thank Goddess. I am working here and there, as I did in Lexington. Beth and I decided to go out tonight. We had not been out for a such a long time. I started to think maybe Beth wanted to live as a hermit. Were at "The? Mark". We walked through and Beth introduces me to a womon by the name of Andria Malunnie and this womon is extremely attractive, very tall, and taller than me. I might add very yummie. After a while, being with Beth. She just started to change. I noticed it even before I moved to Crows Town.

Before I moved, Beth and I would go out almost every weekend. We enjoyed being around her friends. Now she just wants to stay home. I think, okay no big deal. We had been together about five months and I felt like it had been years. Beth and I have discussed in the past about having a threesome. We never pursued it. There was a mutual agreement if one of us left the room for any reason than the other partner would follow. I agreed. A mutual friend of ours, Jill Boythrod was having difficulties with her lover. She needed someone to talk with. Jill called and asked if she could come over to Beth's house. Beth said yes. Jill, Beth and I are sitting on the couch and Jill is crying. I do not know how it exactly started. Somehow, all three of us started kissing each other. We were on our way to the bedroom all three of us. We are taking off our clothes and everybody is kissing everybody. Next thing we were all lying in bed. Touching and kissing each other. I start to smell smoke. I asked Beth if she had anything on the stove. She leaves to check. I just kept right on with Jill, and Beth came back to join us. I guess she didn't like what see saw so she left and started drinking. Sometime later Beth is drunk, and passed out I think. I never got up to check. Jill is going down on me and my body is making sounds Beth has never heard before. Beth comes back to the room. I said go away, I don't want you to see me like this. Beth left.

I had to admit for as short as Jill was she had fingers that were magic, and a deadly tongue. I really enjoyed going down on Jill. She tastes so good. After hours of sharing intimacy with Jill. We finally emerge from the bedroom, and Beth is still passed out on the couch. I give Jill a hug good-bye. Beth and I got into it. She was angry I didn't leave the room when she did. I honestly forgot about the agreement we made three months ago. When there is a womon lying next to you in bed, she's naked, and skin so soft it glows, it's really hard to member anything at moment especially damn agreement. The whole time I was with Jill, I really felt more close to Jill than my own lover. Bethea started drinking again and I went back to my apartment for the first time in the several months. I think the threesome is what caused our relationship to deteriorate and long with my behavior with Andria. Somehow, I ran back into Andria again down the road. She was the one I described at the bar "The? Mark". She was taller than I was and very attractive. I have been hanging out with Andria at the bar, at parties. I thought she was a cool woman to hang out with. I am sitting at home and this tall Amazon womon is on my mind. In the next, several of months Beth and I were fighting constantly. I stayed away from her more and more. As far as Jill, we never hooked up again, but Goddess I wanted to. We just remained platonic.

Andria and I start hanging out more and more because Bethea and I are constantly fighting about her jealousy. I was tired of always staying home with Beth. She hardly wanted to go out anymore and she was trying to keep me locked in her small little apartment. I decided to stay at my place at night. Earlier in our relationship, Beth was talking about how she wanted to get a place together,

Beth really? .... Are you kidding me? .... Not the way we have been going at each other. Beth is now getting extremely jealous of Andria,

"Why do you always have to hang out with Andria all the time?"

She's my friend, Beth. .... Do you have a problem with that?

"Jaynie you are always with her. You never hang out with me anymore. .... We never watch

T.V, or listen to music."

Beth do you want me to be around you all the time, 24 hours a day 7 days a week? . . .

"I want to spend time with you too Jaynie."

Beth, if you have a problem with my friendship with Andria, you have to deal with it. I am not going to stop hanging out with her because you have a jealousy problem. After weeks of fighting and arguing, we started making headway and starting getting along. Beth introduced me to womyn's music, womyn literature, lesbian poems, short stories, and self-help books of all kinds. My favorite quarterly magazine called "Lesbian life Common life." I liked the music these womyn had produced. Their music was so peaceful and so beautiful. The books were interesting and a good read. One day, Beth invited Andria over for dinner. Andria came over around 6:00 in the evening. I thought Beth and I were going to make dinner together. Instead Andria helped me prepare dinner while Beth sat in the living room pouting and getting drunk. I decided this is going to be a fun dinner. Andria and I were dipping chicken in flour to make fried chicken. Andria and I decided to have a flour fight. When we were done, flour was everywhere, all over everything. We were white as sheep. We didn't care, boy we had such a good time. Playing around and cooking together was great. Dinner was very good. Beth said,

"Jaynie, I am really tired. I am going to lay down for a while. Do you want to join me?"

No, go ahead, relax. I'll be there after a while. Beth looked at me like "no come now." My look was "no not right now honey.

Beth went to bed. Andria and I were in the living room sitting on the couch. We were listing to Lana Sand, a lesbian musical artist. I decidee to burn some candles and incense. The mood was right to kiss Andria if I really wanted to. However, I did not. Eventually, Andria is about to leave. I gave her a hug and a kiss good-bye. Beth came out of the bedroom, and right away started in on me about Andria.

"I wished it was "Ferin" I was listening to on her CD, instead of Andria!"

Beth, if you hadn't gotten so damn drunk, you could have listened to "Ferin's" music with me and Andria. You said you were tired, remember.

"I just want you and I to be as close as you and Andria have become. That's all Jaynie".

Beth at this rate, what you're doing with all your drinking, is pushing me farther away from you, let me tell ya. You are not gaining any brownie points with me.

We went to bed with no hugs or kisses. I was with Andria almost every day and I saw less of Beth. The whole time I was hanging with Andria, we were just friends. I can honestly say I was faithful to Beth.

Andria and I hung out for six months, platonically. In that time span, Beth and I broke up. The final reason why I left is Beth asked if I wanted to go to the "Michigan Womyn's Music

Festival" for seven days. It is nothing but womyn. Of course, I said yes. We got into an argument, and tells me she doesn't want me to go. After several days she apologizes, and tells me she wants me to go. I felt as if I was on a roller coaster. I made the decision not to go at all. I started hanging out with one of Andria's friends who is bisexual her name is Lelia Moehead. I have to say she is very attractive. Lelia and I are good friends.

Beth meets Lelia and right away Beth starts accusing me of having sex with Lelia. I stood up, and I said enough is enough.

"I'm done with all this shit Beth. I cannot take your jealousy anymore. and I am not going to Michigan with you either. I stormed out of her house and I never looked back. A week later Lelia invites me to her house. I said cool. I went over to her house. Lelia lives in a co-op. Just so you know, a co-op is a place where both sexes live in one house. They all share everything equally in the co-op. Everyone has their own bedroom, but they share the common space. Such as bathrooms, kitchen, utilities.

We went up to her bedroom and I let her seduce me. We had a lot of sex. We played for a while. Damn she was fricking erotic, sensuous and extremely freakish. I just wanted to keep going, I was in heaven. As we were deep into our passion, the phone rang. It's a guy calling for Lelia. She stopped having sex with me to answer the phone. The person on the phone was a guy. She actually left the room, and so did I. I got dressed, walked down to the front door and out. I never looked back.

Andria and I decided to go to this gay bar in Illinois. We went to the "Lucky Haven Club." We were dancing together. This slow song comes on. By the time I realized it, the song was over. We did not care. We just kept on dancing, talking, laughing, and telling all kinds of jokes. I just thought if I kept on dancing with Andria, she would realize how much I liked her. At least I hope so. Andria and I are getting closer and closer. We decided to get a job together at Eons Pizzeria. We both got hired. About the third week into our jobs, I was constantly looking and watching Andria. I felt after eight months of doing nothing with her, I wanted to do everything with Andria. I couldn't take it anymore. I pulled a pizza out of the oven. I handed the pizza to Andria I said,

Andria I want to sleep with you tonight!

My girl just stood there with her mouth hanging wide open. The pizza in her hands and all of a sudden, you hear this loud crash (splat silly nilly) Andria dropped the pizza on the floor. I turned around. Andria still standing there with pizza all over her shoes, legs and her mouth still is hanging open. I just started laughing. She is looking at me as if a Mack truck just hit her. I reassured her I was being very sincere. We both start smiling at each other. I did not think this day would ever end.

Finally, it is 3:00 in the afternoon. Time, for us to go. Thank Goddess. We hop in her ride and we drove to my house. We went to my room and I basically teared her clothes off. She was surprised by my behavior. In the car I told her what I wanted to do to her. Her face turned beet red. My clothes came off a little at a time. All of Andria clothes were all over the floor. I start kissing her and I am lying on top of her. I'm holding her head in my hands. I kissed her. I felt her tongue. Andria's tongue felt so good and wet inside my mouth. She started tickling my tongue with her own and my body is experiencing extreme passion. I took off my pants. My pussy is dripping with wetness from Andria's tantalizing touching, and erotic kissing. I wanted Andria. Her body is sexy. Her size beautiful. She is such a beautiful amazon womon. Her nipples are as pink as roses, her skin is dark ivory, and so soft to the touch. Her stomach so round, pudgy kinda. Andria felt she weighs too much and she is afraid of lying on top of me.

I told her I don't care what she weighed. She laid her pretty, sexy, hot body on top of mine. My body shivers from excitement. She took my mouth like it was her own. She stated kissing me and I sucked her tongue like there was no tomorrow. I drank the wetness from her mouth.

Her tongue is long and soft. My tongue searching, for her BOSS deep within her. My tongue rolled over her lips. My body yearns, for her touch, aches to release itself. Without a word, Andria was reading my thoughts and my desires. She entered me with her finger. Then she used two. My body climaxes like crazy. My body is a faucet that won't turn off. I enter Andria while she is still inside me. There's no end to our deepness. Just a deep curiosity to explore and touch each other. To seek out the treasures awaits each of us. Her pussy is wet, and her hair so long. I wanted to get tangled up in it. Andria is lying on her back. I am finally home. Safe, and sound between Andria legs. I licked her very gently I waited for her response to my tongue. Her hips moved in rhythm. I heard her hips call my name. I went to them.

I took my tongue as far I could inside of her. I wish my tongue were longer. Andria moaned to the touch of my tongue. In a soft rhythm, I oh so loved to hear. My mouth followed the beat of her body. We were in synch, harmoniously together. Our bodies rode the waves of desires, and we hungered together. I hear Andria telling me to stop. I said between breaths, I can't stop. I want to drink all of you. I move my tongue against her clit. Her clit and hips moved, trying to reach my tongue. I teased her in slow motion. I stopped moving and now her clit searched for my tongue again. She found my tongue on her own. I heard moaning. Was it her or me? I don't know. I can't tell if Andria already released what I had been waiting, longing, desiring, craving for. I wanted to drown in her river of wetness. Her BOSS so full of hair, and her pussy so wet. My tongue wanted more. I crawled on top of her. I laid my body my body down on hers. Andria liked my face. We kissed passionately. She rolled over, and I laid on my stomach. Andria massaged my body. From head to toe. I felt little kisses all over my body. The heat in my body started to rise and my pussy yearned for her touch. This time I found the rhythm. You know that ole sayin, "And the beat goes on" I heard my heart beating or is it my clit again? I cannot tell the difference. She rolled me over on my back. She massages my clit. My body moved with her hands

"Stay still Jaynie."

I can't my body won't let me. My hips reach for her fingers,

Andria doesn't want me to climax yet. However, my body said yes. My body reached for Andria's fingers again. Her tongue found my BOSS instead. Lying and waiting for her thirst to be quenched. She is thirsty no longer. Andria is drinking from the never-ending BOSS. She enjoyed the BOSS very much. After many hours of pure enjoyment and intensity we laid in arms and legs entwined together.

"Jaynie I have not felt like this, before," as she whispered in my ear. Neither have I Andria. I like the feeling very much.

Andria and I became lovers soon after many days of festivities. Andria was living with a womon named Kathy Schulte in a one-bedroom apartment on the west side. I was living on the east-side and to see Andria was sometimes difficult. I didn't have a car but she did. I didn't want to depend on Andria always picking me up. Andria's roommate Kathy moved out with some guy. Andria had this big apartment all by herself. Andria suggested I move in with her, which made a lot of sense to me so I did. Why pay rent at two different houses? Andria helped me move my things to her apartment. We made five trips back and forth. Thank Goddess I didn't have any furniture. Andria and I are having a beautiful time together. We made dinner together, go dancing, to the movies, and to visit our friends. We both work full time. We missed each other so much we couldn't wait to see each other until we got home. **Still 26 years-old**. When we did see each other we would hug for a long time. We kissed each other, for the longest time. We made dinner early go to bed, play around and be tired the next morning. There was a lesbian couple living across the hall from us. I told Andria I think they are lovers. She didn't believe me.

One day I went over to say hi to them. Madalye & Kelsia invited me in. I introduced myself. I checked out their apartment and it was filled with womyn's literature, posters, and they even had cd's of womyn's music. Oh yeah they're lesbians. They have two cats. You know you're a lesbian when they have cats, ha ha ha. They are nice womyn. Do you remember the movie Color Purple? We all decided to see the movie together one weekend. I swear to God; the theater was packed with womyn. A man scattered here and there. It was just nice to see that womyn were the majority, and the men were the minority.

I even saw my seventh grade German teacher Ms Hackett. I always had a crush on her. Now I know she is a dyke; to cool. The movie was excellent and the crowd cheered when Jaunt kissed Shug. I loved that movie. I am going to buy that movie when it comes out on VHS. We get back home after a night out on the town and we go to town. I love making love to Andria. Through the next several months Andria and I were talking about a three some down the road. Wouldn't you now that Madalyne and Kelsia wanted to have a foursome with Andria and I. Wow a foursome, four womyn. Kissing, touching, fingers, pussy, wetness, tits and nipples. Oh hell yes. I am game. How fricking cool is this? I never had a foursome before. Oh man here we go again. Maybe this one might work out. We decided why not. One day Andria and I invited our neighbors over for chat and drinks. All of us started kissing on the couch. I can tell Andria is uncomfortable with the situation. I tried to get her to relaxed. I really liked Kelsia. Of course I want this foursome to happen. We all went into our bedroom. I see Andria became becomes extremely nervous. I asked them to leave. They could see Andria wasn't feeling comfortable. We remained good neighbors. The subject was never mentioned again. We both decided to quit the pizza joint. The was a boy and he was a dick. He did not care about his employees. He just wanted to make money. We quit right in the middle of summer. Unfortunately, we both knew we had to find jobs very soon. Andria and I tried working at the "Suga's Hamburgers Juke Joint." We started to gain lots of weight big time. We both quit job.

There was an ad in the paper for cleaning people wanted. We answered the ad and we both were hired. The company we worked for was called "We Clean 4 U." The owner's name is Marva Redburn. Nice woman. After about three weeks. Marva made supervisor, Andria was on my team. Andria didn't like the fact I was her boss. She booked up her speed. I never seen Andria move so fast. She did so she could get the other supervisor position, and she did. Thank Goddess because when we worked together we fought like cats, and dogs. When we went home we continued to ignore each more because of our fighting all day. (I knew not to work with my lovers in the future; if I wanted to be happy).

There was this old man I had hooked up with in the past. It included cash. He had a trashy trailer. I cannot believe I had sex with this man for only $275. 00 It should have been $500. 00 for as messy as his place was. Grin and bear it, is my motto. Well any way, he had this pregnant cat. This cat was beautiful, and so sweet. I just love animals. She was gray tiger

WITHIN THE CHILD'S CORE

stripe. I talked him into letting me keep her until she had her kittens, and he agreed. I took Ms. Kitty home, and she stayed with us for the several months. I'm thinking everything is cool right? I had my cleaning team and Andria had hers. I was told to clean the houses like they were my own. Not once did my team make any mistakes or have any complaints. After six months on the job. Marva the owner calls me into her office.

"Jaynie, your team members have been complaining about you. … They said you were too picky about the houses; you're are too bossy. … and if you don't go they will!"

I literally sit there like a rock just hit me. Marva, what do you want from me? …. You fired the last person. She was getting calls left and right about the mistakes she was making. … Now you are going to fire me because I am too meticulous. What kind of shit is?

"Jaynie I have no choice. It's easier to replace one person then to replace five! … I am sorry Jaynie. I think you are one of my best supervisors I ever had.

That made me feel good to hear. I am angry and sad at the same time. Damn now what? I get my shit from my locker, and as I head for the door I turned around and said see ya Marva. For some reason, Andria I started falling apart. All the fighting and arguing has taken a big toll on our relationship. It doesn't seem to get any better.

Andria was still out cleaning so I waited around for her. I was thinking about the fact we had been arguing. Finally, Andria arrived and I told her what happened.

Hi hon, how was your day? I sat on the on the curb as she is unloading her car.

"Real busy Jaynie. And yours."

Well Marva fired me about an hour ago. My team members told her I was too fucking picky and to damn bossy!

"Don't take this the wrong way Jaynie, but you are."

Like I really need to hear this right now especially from you Andria. Thanks a lot. Andria continues unloading the work car, and I went and sat in our car. She got into the car. The hostility is so thick you could cut it with a knife.

The ride was very quiet. We are starting to pull apart and it is scared me. What is wrong with me, why am I attacking Andria? God, help me, please! The dreams about the shiny penis are getting bigger and stronger. and I can't stop the dreams from coming. I am even having dreams of killing my father. I really don't know why. Wait yes I do. I hate my father for what he had done to me, and how he raised us. I just can't seem to forgive him. I don't know if I want to forgive him. Most importantly I don't even know about forgiveness and I must admit I don't how to forgive him. I would wake up in a cold sweat from dreaming about my father. (killing him.) The dreams were so real. I felt the gun in my hand. I saw him sleeping in bed, passed out from drinking, and I let myself in the back door. I made sure he was asleep. I walked into his bedroom, took a pillow, and covered his head with it. Put the gun up to his head. I pulled the trigger. Then I would stage a robbery. I left and went back home to Crows Town and act as if nothing ever happened. I felt so guilty for having such a heinous, socio-path re-occurring dreams.

I felt maybe he knew I had these dreams about my father. I thought I had better call him, before he called me. I told him I loved him. I started crying whilst talking to him and he told me he loved me too. I knew that was a lie. He doesn't know what about love. I didn't love him. I truly hated my father with a passion. Winter is here, and the holidays are around the corner. I am trying not to attack Andria with words, but now I am thinking stupid. Maybe she is seeing someone else because Andria started doing things without me. That's why I start resenting her. I have abandonment issues big time. I want to do things with her, but I notice my depression is getting stronger. Holidays are the hardest time for me. Because I had not spent any holidays with my family since I moved out in 1981. The only real person I had in this world really loved me was my grandmother, and my aunt Amegic, my lover Andria. Andria was my heart. My world became Andria. But I wasn't her world. Andria world was her friends, her family, and me. And I had to share her with everybody. I had no one outside of Andria. I had a real problem with my jealousy of Andria. She claims she's not seeing any one, but I don't believe her. I felt can't trust her. Why am I accusing her of something she is not doing or would not think about doing?

Thanksgiving is here and my mother has invited me down for dinner. I was really shocked. They never invited me down in the past. I will go, only if I can bring my lover with me. At first, my mother said no. I told my mother if Andria cannot come then I won't come.

I do not. My mother gave in and Andria came with me. When we arrived my two brothers and they're girlfriends were there. Maye was living out of town so she could not make it. Everyone was very polite to Andria. I really appreciated it. They asked Andria questions about her family, which by the way both families, mine and Andria's lived on the same side of town. My mother wanted a picture of us kids so we posed. I had Andria in the picture with me and that was the only time my mother was accepting of my lesbianism. I shouldn't had said accepting.

CHAPTER 9

I SHOULD HAVE said tolerant. The drive back to Crow's town was nice. We talked about things wouldn't set either of us off. I really dreaded Christmas because I knew Andria was going home to her parent's house, for the holidays. I knew I wasn't going with her. Christmas Eve is here, and I felt very depressed. I watched Andria get ready for her trip and I try to help her. I cried so much. I couldn't stop crying. She is finally ready to go and I give her a kiss and I tell her I loved her very much. I'm also sorry for my actions, all the fighting and accusations. I didn't mean any of it. She hugged me and she left. I watched her load the car. and she looked up as she is getting into the car. Andria waved good-bye to me. As she pulled away, I'm crying uncontrollably. I called out her name, but she can't hear me. I watched the car pull away. I sat around the apartment. I cried I tried to clean, and I cried. I tried to watch TV, and I just felt worse, and cried even more. Boy depression is a bitch. It's like a drug you don't want.

I just felt worse. I decided to go out. I though back to how much we were arguing, which was a lot. Over the stupidest things. However, I have to say Andria was the longest relationship I ever had since coming out in 1980. We hooked up in the summer of 1985. I really truly felt like I was losing Andria. I was extremely jealous of Andria she could go home to her parents' house any time she wanted to. I couldn't. She had a bond with her family that I so longed to have with mine. I wanted a family like hers. I remembered all the holidays

Andria went home and I cried for days at a time hiding in our apartment. I missed my family so much, it was killing me inside. The pain that hurt the most was with my father. I wished I could explain to Andria how hurt I was by what my father said in the parking lot at "Al's Hangout." He called me a faggot because I cut off all my hair. Also what he said to me when I was moving out of my parent's house. The two situations kept replaying so loudly in my mind over and over again. I can't get it out of my mind or my heart. Even If I told her, she wouldn't understand my pain or sadness.

After I moved on my own in 1981, at the age of 19 years-old. I spoke to both my parents a six times in four years. That's pretty sad. As a matter of fact, I had seen them less than I spoke to them. To take my mind off Andria I went walking. I still don't have a car. I started to hitch a ride. An older white man pulled over and asked me if I needed a ride? I let him pick me up and he asked me where I was going? and I told him. I guess his age was sixty-five. He was looking at me in a way I had seen before.

Why are you looking at me like?

"Well you do look pretty young to be hitching don't you think? …. By the way how old are you honey?

Why does it matter? I am an adult!

"What's your name?"

Jaynie. …. Yours?

"Bennet. …. I am just staying over in Crowns Town, for the weekend. …. Want to have some fun Jaynie?"

Sound good to me. …I don't think you can afford me!

I should have been reluctant. I figured I'm younger and faster than he is. If he tried anything, I would kick him in the balls and run. We got to Bennet's motel room. This is strange because his motel is located all the way out by the airport. He was 'on the west side of town just driving around. Hum, seems to me he was searching for something or someone. All of a sudden this man is all up in my face.

Hang on there, Bennet, now wait a second! … What is it exactly you want from me?

"I want sex."

Okay.

"How much do you want?"

Whatever you feel is fair.

"$50. 00 okay?

I looked at him and started walking toward the door.

What about $300. 00 ok?

I nodded my head yes and walked back to where he was standing. He gave me the money and he starts to undress himself and then me.

While he was undressing me I was thinking about Andria and if she missed me as much as I missed her.

I actually left my body and I didn't even feel anything. I made the right sounds and said the right words. Such as "oh feels good and don't stop." I really wanted him to stop and I wanted to get the hell out of there. Everything was over in about ten minutes and he gave me a ride back to my neighborhood. I felt like shit in the end. I felt so ashamed of myself I just wanted to die. I wanted to tell someone, to talk to someone about what's happening to me mentally and emotionally, but who could I tell?

Who could I call. where can I go, and talk to someone. I Nowhere and no one. People and friends will judge me. They wouldn't understand what I am telling them and why I'm telling them. I knew for sure I could not tell Andria I knew she would definitely leave me for sure and I could not risk it. I felt like I am in this tunnel, and the light is getting dimmer and dimmer. What is happening to me? I felt like I am alone all the time even when Andria was here in the same room with me.

I was playing a role with Andria, and I was playing too well. My dreams are turning into nightmares. The thoughts killing my father getting stronger, and Stan's penis is chasing me. I'm getting sexually excited just thinking about Stan what he used to do to me. In my dreams he doesn't stop touching me. Stan keep's penetrating me all the time. Using his penis and his fingers, and too much Vaseline. I felt guilty of dreaming about my father and about Stan, but I can't help it. Andria has awakened me up several times in my sleep because I would be crying, or yelling in my sleep. The same dream walking into the house, and pulling the trigger. I woke up in a heavy sweat. Crying uncontrollably every time I had dream I always called my father. My guilt was stronger than my emotions. Andria and I argued practically every day.

I felt abandoned even though she wasn't leaving me. Well Ms. Kitty is getting the closet ready for delivery. She has been sleeping in there for the last several months and boy let me tell you she is pregnant. Ms. Kitty came out into the living room and was talking to us, as if to tell us to follow her. Andria and I were just watching T.V Andria Ms Kitty is going to have her babies. Andria didn't believe me so we waited.

Ms Kitty did it again she would take a couple of step, and look back at us, so we followed her. She went into the closet that she made a home since she came here. Actually Ms. Kitty seemed quite content sleeping and living in the closet. Andria told me earlier that is where Ms. Kitty will have her kittens. We laid in front of the closet and Ms. Kitty started giving birth to her kittens. To cool, I was very amazed. I have never seen a cat give birth before it was really beautiful. Ms. Kitty was cleaning her baby and just when she's was about done, out comes another one. Then she was done for a while. She delivered the rest of the kittens sometime in the night. When we got up, we noticed she had three kittens. They were absolutely beautiful. As I promised, I took Ms. Kitty back to the old guy when the kittens were able to be on their own. Unfortunately, we lost one of the kittens.

Andria had her bike up against the rocking chair a where the kittens were playing. I had told her to move her bike, but she did not listen to me. The kitten I really liked who looked just like the momma kitty. Fell on the bike, and broke his neck. Eventually, Andria and I broke up because of all the fighting. Also because of my depression. Andria moved back home to Lexington Ia. I had just turned 26 years-old. Andria and I were together 1 1/2 years. She told me she wanted to see other people. Andria was the first womon I fell madly in love with. I really cared and loved Andria very much, with all my heart. I have to say I never felt like this about anyone before her. I was pushed her away from me and I didn't know it.

That was when I decided to seek therapy. I felt like I was losing control of myself and I didn't have anyone to turn to. I was deteriorating rapidly. I was her very first relationship. I knew she wasn't happy with me and I appreciated how she left me instead of giving me guilt. That's why we broke up, and I had no other choice but to let her go. I couldn't seem to let her go; my problem was on an emotional level. I didn't know Andria's leaving me was the same feelings I had when my parents would shun me. I had the feeling of abandonment again. I was going through those same feelings all over again. It hurts so much; the pain is very deep. After Andria moved back in with her parents, I called her to see how she's doing. After the first week of Andria being home, she became cold, and distant to me. When I would call her she asked me things like, why am I calling her all the time? Why can't I just leave her alone? She wanted me to leave her alone, and I didn't get the hint even though she was trying to be kind. When you really love and care about someone, its hard letting go. The pain can be very damaging. It's almost intoxicating. I became a stocker. I would call our friends, trying to find out what bars Andria would be. In my mind I felt I needed to be at the bar where Andria might be. Do anything to try to make her notice me. Things like trying to make her jealous by dancing and talking with other womyn.

I knew I was making a complete ass of myself. I just didn't give a damn. I just wanted to be around her, no matter if she would talk to me or not. Let me tell, you the more Andria seen me the more I felt like she hated the sight of me. After Andria moved out. I had to find a more affordable place to live. I found a house for rent and I would be sharing it with a womon named Lois. My room was in the basement and the basement smelled like mildew. The kittens really enjoyed it. They could climb around stuff and run up and down the stairs. After a while, the kittens started getting on my nerves. Andria didn't not have to worry about them. All she had to do was give me money for litter, and food. I was trying to find a job and take care of the kittens.

Andria and I would try to be civilized to each other; it was hard for both of us. After about five months of basement living I told Lois I was moving. I also told Andria I didn't want to deal with the kittens anymore and she would have to take the kittens to the humane society. We fought about the kittens for a while she finally came picked up the kittens. I asked her if she had a carrier case and she said she didn't need it. I looked at her and said hum. Later on night she told me she would never transport kittens without a carrier. She said the kittens started hyperventilating and they scratched her all over her legs and ankles. Oh well, I tried to tell her. I found a nice room to rent right down the street from where I was living. I finally got a job working at Larry's Discount Store in Crowns Town out on the high way. This black guy would come into the store every day and tried to talk to me. I didn't want to hear anything he had to say. I walked away. Whilst I on the floor working the same black guy comes back again. What the frick does he want from me? He told me his name was Ramien Wakamie from Africa. I said good now, will you please leave me the hell alone, please! What the hell is wrong with me? What do I feel like I am in this black whole? And why is this guy trying to come on to me.

I'm becoming confrontational and defensive at work. I am not getting along with my co-workers, I need this job. I can't afford to lose it. Something is happening to me. I missed and needed Andria. I couldn't function, or think, I haven't not eaten in several days. I can't eat. I don't want to eat. I just wanted Andria back in my life. By this time, I have really started losing my mind. I was at the bar in Crowns Town, I was depressed. (When you are in a good mood people acknowledge you and say hi to you. When you are really down in the dumps, I swear you are invisible). I was walking towards the door to leave because I was depressed. I kept thinking about Andria too much. I should have stayed at home to be honest. For some reason someone tapped me on the shoulder. I turned around, and it was Jill. I had a crush on Jill but she drank too much for my taste.

I honestly didn't know what she was saying to me. All I heard was Jill yelling at me. I was already mentally ill. I walked away from her and sat at the bar for a long time. over two hours, and not one person said anything to me. I just started to cry. I no longer had Andria or my family. I just don't know how you can miss something you never really had. Meaning my family. Jill kept fucking with me. I kept trying to tell Jill to leave me alone. She had grabbed my arm, and I told her to let go of me. She starts to push me and I told her to knock it off. Jill wouldn't listen. So I slapped her and then I grabbed her throat. I squeezed her throat as hard as I could with my left hand, and my nails were long. I looked at Jill I was actually thinking, I could kill her and no one would have noticed. They would put me in jail and wouldn't even give a damn. My problems would be over. I have nothing else to live for.

I lost my lover who genuinely cared for me and I never had my parents to be proud of me so what's the use of living? I saw Jill's right hand coming up to clock me on the right side of my face. Let me tell you I was ready to blocked it with my right I was ready deck her with my right, but some guy grabbed my hand and told me to chill. I snapped out of it. Everybody was staring at us. I was standing there, like what the fuck just happened? I felt very bad for what I did to Jill. I really liked Jill, however I warned her. I need to talk to my therapist. I should call her tomorrow.

I had found a therapist a few months ago. I was attending some free event for mental and physical wellbeing. I met a therapist there and we clicked instantly. Later on that night, Jill walked up to me and splashed a drink in my face. I just smiled, casually walked up to the bar ordered a pitcher of beer. I walked up to Jill with same smile on my face. I poured the pitcher of beer all over her head. "Now you fuck off and die, and stay the fuck away from me. I'm not going to repeat myself again." I walked away and went to the back of the bar. Damn I just wasted $5.00 on that pitcher of beer and I didn't even have a drink. I noticed Andria playing pool. I was so happy, my spirits picked up. When you're depressed and the person you were missing shows up, and just to see them picks up your spirits. You change from bad to good in a flash. There is definitely something wrong. I walked up to Andria to say hi and she asked me to leave her alone. I walked away depressed. Trying to make Andria jealous again by dancing with other womyn and didn't work. She just ignored me.

Eventually the group Andria came with, was about to leave. I followed the group outside and I started yelling at Andria.

"Andria why don't you love me anymore. … Why can't we be together and have our relationship back?"

I knew the reason why we are not together. I knew Andria still loved me. I'm the one who fucked up the relationship; not her.

"Don't you understand Andria I love you?"

Don't you get it Jaynie I don't love you and I don't want to be with you any longer. …. I want you to leave me the hell alone!

I snapped again the same night. I pushed her towards her car. As she turned around to get into the car, I kicked her hard in her ass. Andria looked at me as if she was going to hit me.

"Hit me Andria, just hit me please. She would not. She left and I stood in the parking lot and cried. I was thinking of walking out in front of a car. Or jump off a bridge. I really just wanted to die, or I just thought I did. I've been crying out for help, for so long, and I didn't even know who I was any more. I am having a nervous breakdown. Finally, someone heard me (myself) thank Goddess. I finally listened to my little voice inside my head.

Eventually, I started to walk. I was looking for a pay phone. I realized I was thinking of killing myself. I knew I needed help. The thought was getting stronger, and stronger. I couldn't handle I lost Andria for good. I couldn't understand why I kept having those same dreams of my father, and Stan. I called Sophie at 1:00 a.m. (that was the name of my therapist.) I told her I needed to go to the hospital now or you won't see me the next day. I met her at her office, and we drove up to Lexington Iowa together. That particular hospital is the only Mental Health Hospital in Iowa. All this stuff happened when **I was 27 years-old**. I was quiet on the drive up. Sophie asked me how I was feeling. "I said I just wanted to sleep and never wake up."

We arrived at the hospital and Sophie checked me in. I was taken to the psychiatric ward; on the third floor. The next three months I was at the "St. Jude's Lutheran Mental Hospital The third floor was for mentally depressed. The 2nd floor was, for the severely mental depressed. The second floor was under lock down every night. The floor I stayed on, you're was able to leave for the weekend if you got a pass. The pass had to be okayed by a doctor or nurse. All I wanted, was to stay in my room. I didn't want to live, breath, walk, talk, or go away where. I just cried all the time, and I really truly hated myself. Mostly, I hated my parents, for having me. I wished I had never been born. The nurses made patients go to support classes which met three days a week. Also there was occupational therapy that met two times a week.

Three days a week we had an hour session with the psychiatrist whose name was Dr. Wendall Ausenagart. He was on duty for week. He was very tall, and extremely nice. I had to discuss my personal problems, my depression, and my family issues with this doctor I don't know. I didn't have a choice. After the hour session with Dr. Ausenagart I would go back to my room. I would cry because I felt good talking about my problems. I thought there were no solutions. I'm back at the point of wanting to kill myself. It was hard talking about family issues, when you are always told to keep your mouth shout all the time. In 1986 I even bought the book "Why Womyn want too much when it comes to love." I was hoping it would give me some insight on what was going on inside my head. The only thing helped me about the book, it made me look at myself as I read the stories. It was something to read, and occupy my time. Actually book described me to a tee. I guess I was not ready to listen. I wanted to tell the doctor about my activities, hitchhiking, prostitution with old men. Discuss what I was doing in hotels rooms with men. I was ashamed and afraid Dr. ASugenagart would tell my parents. (That is strange that I am afraid he would tell me parents. What could my parents do if they knew what I was doing. Beat my ass?) I had no contact with my parents. I am of age. I just couldn't tell him. I tried and I started to cry I left the session. I just kept my mouth shut. I had been in the hospital for two months. One-day Dr. Ausenagart asked if I want to confront my parents on what had happened in our household. I said yes of course. Finally telling my parents how I felt would be great, and a relief off my mind. I knew I would never be able to confront my parents by myself not with Sylvet temper. I got the nerve to call both my parents. They had been divorced for over a year. I told them I really needed to talk to them.

I felt reservations from both parents, but they agreed to come to the hospital. On top of all my depression, for the longest time. I thought I was the cause of their divorce. Sylvet showed up first, and Othea followed behind him. Dr. Ausenagart introduced himself and told them why they were both here. My parents nodded their heads. Dr Ausenagart looks at me and said, okay Jaynie it is up to you. I stared at my hands and I began talking. Everything came out in full force. I told Sylvet what Othea did to me, and he never even knew. I said vice versa to Othea about Sylvet. After two hours, I accomplished nothing, but more hatred toward my parents. All Sylvet did was switch from one leg to another and I could tell he was very angry. He never even spoke one word. He just looked at me as if I was a child. The look on his face was wait until we get home. I'm going to beat your ass good! All Othea did was cry, and she didn't say anything. Sylvet did say one thing he said in front of Dr. Ausenagart these are private family issues, which should be discussed at home behind closed doors. See Dr Ausenagart that is what I'm talking about. Everything happens behind closed doors. Keep the world out and the secrets in. Keep the doors closed to hide the physical abuse, beating, molestation, the shame, the pain and the hurt.

I told both my parents there is no way I'm going to try and talk with you guys at home. Sylvet my father, with you having a gun, I don't trust you. You have too much rage and anger inside of you. At any point and time, Sylvet has shown us he is capable of killing us, and not even think twice about his actions. If I would have said those things to my parents alone, my father would had beat the holy shit out of me. Probably my mother would not have tried to pull him off of me. Both my parents left the hospital and I went back to my room crying. All I wanted from them were answers to why they raised me (us) the way they did. Hateful words, beatings and abandoning me. Why they never showed any emotion toward me? Why Othea my mother blackmailed me into giving up Jennifer my baby. Why Othea felt I was a shame to the Corevine's pride? Why Sylvet made me wash his back, why he made me sit down stairs as he played with himself and pretend to watch TV? Why, why, why why why why? Why should I have to ask all the time? There will never be any answers to my questions ever. I know that now. What hurt the most, my parents couldn't look at me.

Dr. Ausenagart kept trying to medicate me, but it wasn't pills I needed. I needed, and wanted so desperately, to have my parents hold me, and tell me no matter what they will always love me. My time in the hospital is almost up. I started asserting myself in my support group meetings and in occupational therapy. My wooden plaque was almost done. I made two things, one is a leather wallet that had stars, the moon, the sun, roses in the corner and my initials A & J on the back.

Which were Andria and mine initials. On the wooden plaque read,

Womyn lovin Womyn
Is an extraordinary
Experience all in itself
By JC

I loved my plaque. When I got home, I hanged the plague on my wall. I made two things that I can take with me. With my own two hands. Wow to cool. I was very proud of myself. It was finally time to leave the hospital. I felt I was ready to face that big ugly world on my own again. Mentally, I knew I wasn't. But physically I was.

I went back to work for Larry's Discount. My boss was very happy to see me. I was happy he didn't fire me because of my sporadic, uncontrollable, unacceptable behavior.

I packed my things and looked for a new place to live. I found one, and moved out the next week. The house I moved into was a co-op. The house was white with and two stories and has two bathrooms and five bedrooms. I have the bedroom on second floor. I should have asked the property owner if the house had roaches? Oh well too late now. I had been living in this big house alone now for three months. And I am really bored. Ramien is still bothering when he comes into the store at Larry's and he always finds a way to talk to me.

I had to say for a man is only 5'7 he is very consistent and persistent in pursuing me. The bars were not doing a damn thing for me. I knew Andria would be out so I stayed away to avoid confrontation. I am in the kitchen and I hear this party going on in the back of my house. I decided to crash it. I met this guy by the name of Paul Ryewild. He was attending Crowns University; he was 6'0, 23 years-old, and extremely good looking. We are drinking beer together and talking and smoking some weed. I really needed some fresh air. I said Paul I'm going to walk for a while, and Paul asks if he could walk with me. I said suit yourself. We had walked around the block, and we ended up at my house. I asked if he wanted to come in. We talked in the living room and the next thing I knew I was kissing him. I had anyone touch me for over three months. I was lonely and very depressed and I just didn't care what happened to me. We are undressing each other we fooled around for a while, and we go up to my room. We started having sex. Paul uses his mouth very nicely. I really like how he used his tongue. I enjoy sex with Paul, enough that we decided to hook up the next day. I really liked Paul. I guess he was convenience to fill a lonely void from Andria. After about a month of seeing Paul I noticed my period was late. I thought oh no not again. So I told Paul, and he said he is too young to have a child. Eventually my period came, thank Goddess, and that was the end of Paul, and me.

I wanted to talk to my therapist Sophie. I thought she was really nice to me when she took me to the hospital. She was telling me my behavior was wild and uncontrollable. I told Sophie her about my relationship with Paul. I still wanted to be with Andria and a stranger from Africa named Ramien guy at Larry's Discount, was still trying to talk and chase me.

"Jaynie you just got out of the hospital. Please take your time and make healthy cognitive choices."

Yeah Sophie you're right. I know. …. I was there for three months trust me I remember. I think I am capable of taking care of my mental state of mind on my own. Please don't give up on me. I know I am bound to make some mistakes until I feel I am on solid ground. I am not this weak womon that I can't function on my own. Since I have moved out of my parent's house I would constantly call my parents and ask them to come over sometime or call me on the phone. My father came over once and so did my mother. I said to them so many times, I love you with all my heart. My parents never said it back to me. My parents would call and visit my other brothers and sister. Why not my place? Othea told me one time,

"I don't have time to see your place Jaynie and I don't want to make the time. Besides you don't have any kids" I am thinking in my head. Are you kidding me mother? You mean to tell me you won't come visit me because I don't have any grandchildren, for you to play with! Then I tore into her. Oh that's really rich. Othea you don't seem to remember five years ago, when I had a child your grandchild. You blackmailed me into giving her up. You had said I was a disgrace to my family My child the grandchild you were ashamed of. Now you are punishing me for it. Othea you know what? I won't ever ask you to call or visit me again and I didn't. I started to talk with Ramien. I told Ramien how I felt about womyn over and over.

Ramien said he wasn't interested in me that way and after months he finally told me what he wanted from me.

Ramien would pay me $5000. 00 to marry him for four months so he could get his visa. He showed me all his paper work. He had such a sad look on his face, and I was feeling and I was fucked up in the head. I thought Sophie would be proud of this choice I made to help someone out. I still 27 years-old when all this shit took place. My sister and I had been talking for a while. Maye informed me grandmother Odemesse had passed. I will always miss my grandmother. I wished I could have had another child. If it would had been a girl I would had named her after my grandmother. I knew that will never happen. I thought I was thinking clearly, so I told Ramien yes I would marry him. I never thought to check up on what Ramien told me. I assumed he was telling me the truth. If I could have made this decision all over again, I would have said no to him. When will I learn to stop being a rescuer? The next week Ramien Wakamie took care of all the plans for the justice of the peace. I had my witness and he had his. He got the ring at a pawn shop. We stood in front of the justice of the peace. Said our I do's, and we were married. Ramien moved into the house I was living in. He had the far bedroom down the hall away from mine. He started working two jobs because he said he would pay me the $5000.00 he promised me. I had already collected $1,000. 00.

After about five months, the landlord wanted to raise our rent. We moved and found a house to share with this really cool womon named Suzy Treutts, and a tall gypsy womon Her name was Wendy Macanlent. They both were gay. Which was fine by me. Suzy had a strange physical attraction to Ramien. In addition, I had an attraction to Wendy. Suzy only had one bedroom, but it was big enough for two beds. Ramien had his single bed, and his own phone line, and I had mine. Behind closed doors we were roommates, but in public we were married, which I couldn't stand. Also I didn't want the gay community to think this man was my boyfriend or my man. However, I did like Wendy.

We would go dancing and we would go for walks. I had noticed Ramien did not like Wendy. However, I did, and I did not let him scare away Wendy. Since I met Wendy, we talked constantly. We started dating each other after months of getting to know each other. Sometime into our relationship, she told me she was moving to Toledo WI. I was sad she was moving. Of course, I did not want her to go. I finally found someone I felt I clicked with. I am smiling and thinking about Wendy and guess who called me unexpectedly. My sister Maye can't believe it. I asked her why she called? Maye told me she would like it if I could walk with Othea my mother.

I told Maye that ship sailed a long time ago. Besides, Othea can't stand me, and I sure don't care or want to be around her. Maye and I will talk through the years, but not much. After months of dating and hanging with Wendy she did eventually move. We promised to stay in touch. Wendy, and me are writing to each other at least once a week. Wendy had this uncanny ability to write backwards. I mean this womon had perfect penmanship backwards. She would write me three to four letters at a time. I would have to sit in front of the mirror and read them. Of course I would practice writing backward, but never as well as Wendy. I had emotionally grown to think I didn't care what the community though of me, and who I hang out with. As long as I was happy with myself. After a while, Ramien started trying to treating me as if I was a real wife. Wanting me to cook him dinner and do his laundry. Please really, being a wife to a man! Be a wife to a man! was to funny. He would put it like this.

"Jaynie you are my wife and you should cook dinner for me."

Are your fingers broken?

"No."

Then you know where the kitchen is. .… . I am not doing any cooking for him or anyone else if I don't want to.

Ramien felt since he was working two jobs, I should pitch in and help him. "! Good luck on that one." He just didn't want to do his own shit. The contract we agreed on was. I do my own laundry, cook my own meals, and vice versa. He started to take advantage of the nice things I was doing for him. That's when I started to think what the fuck did I get myself into again? When I went to the hospital, I for depression over my bad behavior, family issues, and, Andria. When I got out, I was feeling good about myself to a degree. How could I do something so fucking stupid. Married a man who begged me too marry him. I should have said no. When I married Ramien I felt my depression get stronger. I have been out for three months. Now Ramien had to go to the hospital for knee surgery. When he left, I started doing some checking and I called the Naturalization Immigration Services. I talked to his attorney, and he told me Ramien had lied to me. This process was going to take four years not four fucking months. I was telling Wendy everything was happened with Ramien. She suggests I go to a womyn's abuse shelter. At first, I thought no, I wouldn't need to stay there. Ramien would never hurt me. At least I don't think he would. Damn lying bastard! I fixed his little red wagon. I moved out of the house we shared and went into an abuse shelter for women. I would be better off inside the shelter and I don't have to worry about living in fear of my life.

I would be living there for the next six months. This went on in the summer. In the meantime, I had the use of his car. I was driving around this cop pulled me over. I had filled the fricking car up with gas. The cop asked me if I knew this car was reported stolen. You could have knocked me over with a feather. It couldn't be stolen, it's my husband's car. He knows I have it. They took me to the police station, no had cuffs. Just a lift. I told them my side of the story about Ramien then they let me go, but they kept the car. Ramien was charged with filing a false police report. When Ramien got home I told him I found out the truth about him being able to receive his green card.

Also that I moved out, and I'm filling for an annulment. We never consummated our marriage. He hit the roof, and he also threaten to kill me. Remember what Wendy suggest. I had already gone into hiding. This man was really crazy. My friends told me he came into the bars looking for me. When he saw me he tried to run me over with his car. After living in fear for the last six months, and trying disparately trying to complete my education, I couldn't because of Ramien. While I was staying at the shelter I sill continued to see my therapist Sophie. I was just starting to understand I had been physically abused my both my parents.

Sophie why do parents do this shit to their children?

"That was all parents knew growing up in their own household. Abuse was their only way of life."

When I left her office I was crying, so badly I could not think straight. When I finally got back to the shelter, and I went to my room and cried uncontrollably. One day in my counselor office at the shelter, we were talking about Stan my pedophile and out of nowhere, I finally felt my pain, agony, and all my suffering. I had held all that shit in my soul toward my parents and Stan. I hated my parents and Stan with a passion. I started thinking back on all the times Sylvet would beat me and how much Othea would let him beat on me. Thinking about all those times Sylvet would put his foot on my head or my back and beat me until my skin came off. My ass had no skin left on it. I would be sore for weeks. I just kept crying. The flash backs were, so strong and my ass would have no skin and it would be sore for weeks. I would cry all over again the flash backs were, so strong, and so real. I started wearing big clothes to hide my body fearing people could see my scars. I never showed my body in the light. I was so ashamed of my body.

I started hitching even more. I just didn't care about myself anymore. I let my teeth get cavities, and I started gaining weight big time. I took Wendy's advice, and moved out of town.

I put everything I owned in a truck. I moved Toledo WI. I guess you can say I ran to Toledo, and I ran fast. And all that shit came with me. I had let Wendy know when I was coming, and we were both excited about me moving there. I had arrived in Toledo at **28 years-old** in the dead of winter and I mean winter. When I arrived at her apartment we just hugged each other, and she helped me with my things. Once settled Wendy made hot cocoa, and talked. Wendy told me she was seeing someone. Get this it was a guy. Was Wendy bi-sexual? I was crushed. That's was why she being distant. Damn and we never had sex. We were naked before, but no sex just a lot, of cuddling, kissing and holding each other. That's why I stayed as long as I did. I wanted her BOSS so badly. Wendy said I could stay at her place until I found a job, and a place to live. This living situation is not a good thing. I'm here now, so I have to adjust to it. Why didn't she tell me in her letters she wrote me? Wendy was nice enough to tell me there was a job position opening up at where she works at called "Barton University Book Store."

I went in to apply and I got the job too cool! Wow second time at being hired on the spot. Wendy worked down in the shipping department and I worked on the third floor in the computer room. I share a cubbyhole with another other wom-on who was a bitch. Boy talking about your coffee drinker. This womon drinks more coffee then a dog licking his balls. On top of that she is a smoker and loved her cigarettes, which makes her breath smell like shit. I mean damn she could eat a hundred mints and nothing could penetrate foul breath. The room was actually big enough, for just two people. My job was boring. My label was a computer programmer, and all we did all day was entering serial number of books, titles, and authors, into the computer. Then arranging books on the shelves I'm still living with Wendy, she doesn't offer me a lot of food.

I don't want to eat all her food. The sad thing was for the next three weeks I would eat peanut butter and honey sandwiches. Once in a while honey and cheese sandwiches. I became extremely constipated because that was the only food I would eat for lunch, and dinner. The second sad thing was I had no money to ride the bus, which meant I had to walk to work every day. Hell, I did not even have money for anything. I was trying to stay strong I guess. I didn't want to start hitching at all. I am fighting like hell to stay strong. I felt the less money I had in my pocket the more I was tempted to prostitute myself. My strength did not last long. I needed money and my depression was still there and I went backward instead of forward. I relied on my survivor in me. I only did it a few times. I still am a good person, and I'm proud of me. But sometimes a person's actions are stronger than their mental state of mind. Let me tell you I lost my strength here and there because sometimes it would rain and I would have to walk to work and home. I would be wet all day and I hated being wet. The people I work seen me walking, and do you think they would have offered me fricking ride? Hell no.

I saw them at work and said "Thanks for offering me a ride when it was raining yesterday." I knew co-workers aren't obligated to give rides if they don't want to. I feel badly giving them guilt. However, I was extremely resentful of my co-workers. They had cars, bikes, busses, for transportation and I did not have any transportation. It was no one's fault but mine own. I had been walking around with a very negative attitude against the employees I worked with. I felt the employees were extremely racist, homophobic, stuck up cliquish people that I ever met in my life. I couldn't be myself. I was carrying around this big secret on my shoulders and every day it was wearing me down. So much I started hitching to avoid my depression which by the way only hurt me even more. Going to work every day and hated every minute. I don't know how Wendy lasted as long as she had because she couldn't stand the people either at work.

Wendy let me stay with her until I was able to save enough money for a deposit and first month rent. I should also say Wendy's place was just small efficiency. She had her own bedroom, and bathroom. I was sleeping out in the living room floor. I hated it. We are living in a breadbox. We started to get on each other's nerves. Wendy would complain about the stupidest things. For instance, I was using too much bread or too much of her cheese. Or I left the light on too long.

It felt so fricking good when I finally got my first paycheck. We were able to cash our paychecks at work. I cashed mine and they counted out $375. 00. I walked out of the bookstore in tears in my eyes. I was on top of the world. It felt so good having hard-earned money in my pocket the healthy way. If I want anything at all, I could just buy it. I didn't have to feel guilty. I can eat anywhere I want to. When I didn't have money I wanted to eat everything in sight. Now that I have healthy money. I just want to hold on to and not spend a penny. While living in Toledo, I felt very alone, I did not know where or how to get find the lesbian community or the gay bars, and last, but not least I could not come out at work. The people I work with is so straight lace. I hate it. Well on to the good news after months of sleeping on the floor, I finally found a place.

My new roommate is Rachel, I will be renting out a room from her, and she leaves in a two-bedroom flat right across the street from this little lake. Rachel is nice and she is a womon of size, which is cool with me. And she gay. Wooh. My first gay womon I met since I have been here. On top of, she even hooked me up with a lesbian softball team. I love softball. Now I have finally found the Gay Community I have been desperately searching for. Rachel asked when did I wanted to move in, and I said as soon as possible. Rachel also took me to a lesbian bar called "3 Strikes You're Out." Nice bar and they have two pool tables. Oh yeah. In the past I played a lot of pool. I still had the touch. I started playing pool at "3 strikes Bar". After the third week of coming down to the bar, I noticed this black womon. We played some pool and talked and drank. Her name was Wentra.

I swear to God, she looked like Janet Jackson. I had to admit she was an awesome pool player. She told me she was bisexual and she has never slept with a womon yet. I was not ready to bring anyone out of the closet just yet. We just hung out together the next several months and became very close friends. There was a woman by the name Jacquelyn. She was about 5′5 and long curly black hair. I really liked her, but I just could not get over her shortness. Nothing ever became of Jacquelyn. To bad, she was a very beautiful womon. I just like taller womyn. One night I had been playing pool, and it was a very hot summer night. There was a womon standing against the rail by herself. Stupid me walked up to her to say hi.

What's your name? … Why aren't you on the dance floor?

"There wasn't anyone to dance with. … My name is Gertrude Bale. What's yours.

My name is Jaynie.

The signals were slapping me in my face, at a fast rate. I did not see them coming).

Would you care to dance?

We danced together all night and I thought she was nice, and sort of cute in her own little cute way. She was a kinda grow on your type of person. We hung out together all night long. We talked about this and that, where I'm from, where she is from, who my and her last lovers were, and why we broke up with them. She had broken up with somebody three months ago. She was looking for another lover. I was truly just seeking a friendship. That same night I should have noticed how I was constantly reassuring her she was a beautiful womon inside and out. I didn't see it coming.

Gertrude don't you need some time to get over your last relationship.

"I DON'T NEED time to get over anyone. I just keep looking until I find someone."

Eventually the night came to an end and we exchanged phone numbers

Just so you know Gertrude I am dating other womyn right now.

"Then I don't want to go out with you. Sorry Jaynie I don't date womyn that are seeing other womyn. I just date one womon at a time."

"Gertrude replied, I've been alone for a long time." and "I've mourned enough and I can't stand being by myself", and I really hate sleeping alone. .... If I can have someone then I rather stay single."

I thought to myself dam why didn't I see those damn signal. She gave me a way out. And I didn't see it.

Her being a lesbian got the better of me, and I decided to invite her over to my apartment, for ice tea and talk. She was still standoffish especially when I tried to help her with her confidence and suggest she and I should meet other lesbians in the community. After inviting her over to my house, we talked, and she is not interested in getting to know the Lesbian Community. That's just the way she was. She left later on that night, and there was no sex; not even a kiss. I told her I would call her tomorrow. I went to bed and slept on it. I should have taken off running, but silly me called her the next day.

Hi Gertrude, Jaynie here. I would like to go out with you

one on one. … What could it hurt?

See there I go again with feeling sorry and being a res-cuer. I stopped dating all the womyn I was interested in so I could have a clear head with Gertrude. We decided to make it work. Being with Gertrude was one of the biggest mistakes of my life. The next year would be a year I wish I could forget. The first time Gertrude and I went out for dinner and dancing it was okay.

I was hanging with Gertrude only after one week of meet-ing. I knew it was the biggest mistake I made! After moving to Wisconsin six months ago. Gertrude and I became lovers, which was way too fast. After the 2nd week of dating the words fucking cunt, bitch, slut, and whore came out of her mouth. I just stood there and took it because I wanted to show her I cared about her. I had to let her know someone out there be-side her ex's cares about her. I was on a rescue mission, and she was the mission. Little did I know I was walking into a thunderstorm? She was outgoing, and willing to do many dif-ferent things together. We went out to dinner together, mov-ies and dancing together and took road trips together. As we spent more time together, however I noticed she was becom-ing very possessive of our time and me. We never went out with other couples, or any of her friends. We were always, always by ourselves.

I started falling apart quickly and did not even notice it. A month into our relationship, she started treating me warm and then cold. Guilt tripping me, and saying I did not care about her or us. When I would ask her to meet a friend of mine, she would make excuses to get out of it. At first I thought she was just really nervous about meeting new womyn friends. I noticed when she met my friends she would be very distant, standoffish, as if like she was too good to meet my friends and it was a waste of her time. After a while, she did not want me to depend on any friends for anything. If I need anything, I should not ask my fucking friends. "I'm your lover not those bitches." I am sorry Gertrude, next time I have a problem or need a favor, I will come to you. By this time now she is getting angry whenever I saw or called my friends. Especially when I called them from her house just to say hi.

She'd became irate and yelled that my friends were whores, bitches, and fucking cunt-sucking sluts. Eventually, I stopped calling them altogether.

I was so embarrassed and felt ashamed of making apologies to my friends. I tried to tell her how and what I was feeling. I was always apprehensive because she was always angry about something, and then the names would start spurting out of her mouth. I hated walking on egg shells. I grew up with egg shells all my fricking life, and now these damn egg shells were back again. I just don't know what to do anymore. I started feeling isolated, and very much alone all the time. I had no real friends anymore because she had scared them all away. Gertrude was now the only person in my life and the more isolated I became the happier she got. I tried to change her anger into something positive.

Gertrude, let's go dancing, hold each other and stop all this yelling and fighting.

"Why so you can ignore me for hours, while I sit there, and watch you fucking hug, and kiss on those fucking whore and bitches there? No way!

And then the yelling and arguing would start all over again. During an argument, which lasted over two hours, I told her I had had it and was going to leave. She blocked the door.

"This is my fucking house and you are not leaving." By now I was crying and just wanted to go home. She was called me names and told me to relax. I shouldn't try to leave; she was doing what was best for me. How could this woman decide what is best for me? I felt I am going crazy. Suddenly like a light switch, she became this forgiving, understanding lover. I'm sorry, I didn't mean it. If you didn't say and do things to make me angry, I wouldn't be like this.

I'm saying this in my head. If you could would just be good little girl and not say or do anything; everything would be all right.

"Jaynie I do love you and wished we could stop all this nonsense.

Yeah right same old song and dance. I thought instant replay of yesterday. I think I have a Dr Jekyll and Ms. Hyde. I allowed Gertrude talked me into staying. All I wanted to do was sleep. She wanted to kiss and make love to me. I didn't want to. I rejected her. She got angry, and stormed out of the bedroom. calling me a bitch. I started laughing, hysterically, and asked if she could just take me home.

"If you want to go home so fucking bad; fucking walk home."

I just sat there in the dark and wondered what the fuck I was doing here. I finally was free to go home, because I had to work.

The next day I'm sorry phone calls started.

"I am sorry, please forgive me, please." "I didn't mean to push, or hurt, or yell at you."

If we went out to dinner she wanted my sole attention. If I saw someone I knew, she made it so difficult for my, friends, I just stopped introducing her. That's what she wanted from the start. We have dinner and just look at our plates. Conversation is very touchy. I do not know what to say or what to talk about. I let Gertrude do all the talking. It had been seven months since we started dating and we are still in fighting zone.

My eyes are still closed. (My eyes are closed to my

friends but they are not closed to Gertrude and abusive tendencies) Even though they are closed, I am not delusional. I asked Gertrude to see a therapist and she agreed. I was rather shocked, but happy she said yes. I found a therapist within the Gay Community. I was starting to learn about boundaries, and getting back into the community again. I met a nice couple and they invited us over for dinner. I was really happy and excited I was meeting people again. I was excited but Gertrude was not.

"Who are they?"

I am sure you would approve. I talked to you about them before? Lori and Sandra, remember?

"No, I don't and I don't want to go."

Gertrude started yelling again cussing at me. Then I get the guilt just for wanting to be with new friends. I gave in. All all the while thinking, why did I ever get involved with this fricking crazy psycho bitch from hell? A year after we met, there still fights. NO love loss, no making love at all. I have isolated myself from myself and from her. I had allowed Gertrude (my batterer) to control my emotions, and actions to the point I had to ask her to do this or that. If it was something I wanted to do and she didn't like it we'd fight until I just didn't ask anymore. I guess I stayed as long as I did, Gertrude told me no one would love me, want me, or touch me, the way she did. I am ugly bitch; who would want me?

"Jaynie everybody always leaves me."

I really wanted to be supportive, but not abused by her. I have been secretly seeing a therapist If Gertrude would have found out she would have hit the roof. I felt I needed one because every time I would go out without Gertrude, I would be thinking about my depression.

I also found a lesbian support groups. My therapist was a great source of support for me. I didn't told Gertrude about the group, out of fear of her rage. When I finally did, she first said

"Good. Maybe this group will do you some good."

Gertrude then turned around and accused me of sleeping with the womyn in my group. I just didn't know how to stand up to her, to tell her what I was feeling.

When I tried, she laughed, and mimicked me, made fun of me. Physically I am strong, Emotionally, I didn't have a leg to stand on. I did have three things that gave me strength, my therapist, and grandmother in my heart, and the lesbian support group and my will to survive, and to get healthy and the ability to break away from Gertrude. I started to hitch hike and prostituted myself because of all the depression.

The one thing I was trying to stop, but I couldn't because it is so embedded in my system, thoughts, and actions. So instead, I tried to get drunk and did not work either.

I was so exhausted from constantly arguing with Gertrude. Her goal was to break me down, and it worked. When we would go out for dinner, I had to ignore any one I might know so she wouldn't off on them in the restaurant or at me later. If everything went well with dinner and if I behaved the way, she wanted me to behave, then on a good night we might, go to the bar for a while and dance as long as I danced with her. I missed dancing so much was one thing besides pool I really enjoyed in my lesbian lifestyle. After I met her she made us stay away from the bars sometimes weeks at a time. If we did make it to the bars I had to sit with her I could not talk to anyone, unless she knew them and they were not a threat to her or our relationship. If someone just looked at me on the dance floor, she would just walk right up to him or her and take my hand and we would leave just like. I could not even say good-bye to my friends. Then we would argue all the way home to her house. I would say something like,

"Just take me home Gertrude, I want to sleep in my own bed tonight!"

"Yeah right your slut, you just want to go back to the bar so those fucking bitches can lick your fucking asshole.

"No you are going home with me."

After we arrived at her house, I started going toward the bedroom because I did not want to fight any more, and she said I could not sleep in her bed I had to sleep on the floor where all the other whores slept. So I said fine and I was walking away she pushed me over the coffee table and then she picked me up and dragged me to her bedroom tore off my clothes, I am really trying to get her off me and she fricking rapes me throughout the night. When she was done with me then she said now get the fuck out of my bed. During all the shit was going on with Gertrude, I was seeing my therapist Leannie and she was such a cool womon and therapist.

She kept asking me why did I stay and I tell her I am afraid to leave because she threaten to kill me so many times I honestly believe she might succeed one day. Leannie told me of a support group was going on in Toledo and the group was called Lavender Lesbians, which was womyn who was against lesbian violence and battering. I went one night and I really liked it.

I thought this group has a lot to offer if I want to get out of my abusive relationship with Gertrude. Our being together was getting so bad she told me on many different occasions if I die, I would be taking you with me. When we are in her truck, I just keep my mouth shut because I could just see her hitting a utility pole at 80 miles an hour. After a while, Gertrude would ask where I was going and I told her I was going to a support group about incest. If she knew, I was going to a support group about lesbian domestic violence she would yell, and scream until I quit going, but I have no intention of quitting. Finally, after 81/2 months of going to Lavender Lesbians support group, and over a year of seeing Leannie, I finally gained the strength and confidence I needed to leave Gertrude on our one-year anniversary. It was very hard at first because I could not and I know I would not last if I made myself live the rest of my life in taking mental, emotional, psychological abuse and rape. I also knew if I did not leave either she would die or I would. Also during the last months of our sick relationship, I was walking on eggshells all the time, every day. They were everywhere. One day

Gertrude said, "I to me I love you so much Jaynie, but you keep pissing me off. 's why I treat you the way I do."

How could a womon who uses the hand she used to touch me, and make me feel so good. Then turn around and use those same hands to push me over a coffee table. If you would just be a good little girl, I would not hurt you all the time. I swear to God, she honestly said to me. I knew I was going to leave her and I had a month to decide how I was going to get my stuff out of her house. I first had to take my bird patches back home. More than once, she said if I left her she would kill my bird. After the cage back home, I started taking my stuff back to my apartment little by little. I used the excuse saying it was dirty, and this or, and she never had a clue.

I also knew if I didn't get my stuff out of her house before I decided to leave her she would hold my stuff for ransom until I came back to her. I didn't allow her to have any leverage over m when it was time for me to leave. She had nothing of mine except for the stuff I gave her as a gift. I was being nice to her. After the last week at the being of spring, I took the last load of my stuff into my house and I told her I would be right back. I took my stuff in the house; I came back out to her truck. I walked around to her side, I look down at her, and

I said, "Gertrude I want a three-month separation.

Gertrude said, "Yeah right! Who are you having an affair with? …. What bitch is licking your pussy tonight?"

"How can I have an affair, I am always with you, we are always together. …. I can't go anywhere without you. … Yeah right an affair! … I told her I was serious, and I didn't want her to call me, see me or anything."

I walked into the house and locked the door, and kept the phone by me just in case she would try to break in. She starts yelling and honking her horn, and I just stayed in the house eventual she left after sitting in my driveway for several hours. Then the phone calls started coming. At first I would fight with her on the phone, would go on for a few hours, and again I would be tired.

The next time I say my therapist, I would tell her about our conversation and my therapist said for me to stop combating with her. When she would call me again I just started hanging up on her and it felt wonderful. Guess what it worked. She soon got the hint I was very serious.

I originally asked for three months, but it turned into five in order to gain, my power and assertiveness back. After my five months of separation, I started feeling really good about myself. I really liked the fact the eggshells were gone also; I like not having to worry about Gertrude at all. I liked not having to have her touch me, and me not touching her. I really like the fact those horrible name-calling has stopped. To be honest sometimes, I felt bad for Gertrude because I knew she was hurting. I would call her once in a big while, and ask how she is doing and she would hassle me for calling her. I finally called her on the phone and told her I was not coming back, and for her to move on with her life.

There were fun times Gertrude and I had, but the bad times outweighed the good times by far, and I just couldn't see me settling, less. I settled for less for 365 days' way too long. I started getting on with my life without my batterer. I was not sure I could survive without Gertrude, not sure if I could stop wanting her, stop wanting to make love to her, kiss her, drink her, but I knew I had to. I deserve better. Even though she was abusive to me, I still miss being with her. I have to keep reminding myself not to want her too much. In addition, keep thinking about what happened in our relationship. Remembering all the shit, pain, and agony, I had suffered at the hands, and words of my batterer. When Gertrude and I did talk, she would tell me she has changed, but she would still call me names, and accuse of sleeping with every womon I meet. I would call her and

I asked, "Why we get along, can't we just try to be friends instead of yelling at each other, and hanging up all the time."

I know she hasn't changed.

Gertrude asked not to talk about our past relationship with other people. It's over so I should keep my fucking mouth shut.

However, I can't keep quiet. I have to do what best, and healthy for me. I feel ashamed enough as it is, and if I kept quiet, I would feel 100 times worse. In addition, I would be saying it was ok for you, to abuse me. It is not ok. Abuse is never ok. I do not want to be embarrassed or ashamed, for wanting to get healthy, and confident again, and self-assured of my choices, and decisions.

I definitely don't ever want to be co-dependent on you or anyone ever again. I want to feel good about my lesbian-little girl womon-self. I have a long hill to climb. I know I would rather think with my head instead of my body. I am attending Al-non for lesbians who are lesbian domestic abusive survivors, and co-dependents. I continue to see my therapist. I figure give myself two to three years, and I should come up fighting, kicking, and wanting to live. I will never again let another womon kick and hold me down low again. My self-worth, self-esteem, and self-confidence are far too important to me. If there are womyn out there who have been through what I have been through, do not worry, you are not alone. Let us get together and stop lesbian violence. We need to stick together, not fight and kill each other. And I know I want I was single for the next two years and I was losing weight hitching rides with old men, seeing my therapist going to the YMCA. **I am 29 years' old**. I was working out in the water and meeting these old men there. I felt like I had the control over these weak crunched up men. I felt if they called, it was up to me to see them. But I was so wrong, it was up to them, I didn't have a lot of money all the time and I was so thankful they did call I couldn't wait to see them, and after I seen them I felt like shit.

I was really fucked up in my head because of Gertrude and my own pain I thought I was doing better, but I wasn't.

If you are driving 60 miles an hour in a 35 mile zone and you want to be arrested, and put in jail then you know something is definitely wrong. She treated me like I was her property. I was even hitching rides with men when I was with her, and I did not want to, but the thought of seeing her just sickened me. So I took my mind off my troubles on a cool night I was really bumming and I decided to go to a straight bar called the Turn Table was down by my house. I was dressed and started walking. When I got there, the music was flowing and people were bumping into each other on the dance floor, and the place was packed. I had noticed this guy sitting by himself on the dance floor. Right away, my radar went up and I was searching his face to see if he was a undercover cop. I casually walked up to him and said

I said, "Hi, would you care to dance?"

He said, "No, but I want something else if you are interested?"

I am thinking my God, look like easy type, or something. Here comes my dark side just creeping up. I don't know how my dark side knows when to jump in, but she does.

Any normal healthy person would have told this man to go and screw himself, but I just stood there and let him offer me whatever he could afford. We took off to his house in his car; it was about 11:00 at night when we go his place. His house was an ugly yellow from the rain and the dirt hitting against the house. I do not even think it has been painted in years

He let me in first and Wickert followed and turned on the light so we could see. He lived in a one room, on bathroom efficiency small house. As you walk in you saw his rocking chair on your left and next to it you saw his bed. His TV was to your immediate right. I should say Wickert meant well, but just went all about this whole scene all wrong. I found out later with talking with Wickert he was an extremely lonely man. was how I first met Wickert. HIs dog was his only companion. I was still careful to make sure I did not allow Wickert into my private life.

As the night went on, I was still apprehensive about Wickert so I asked Wickert to leave the cash on top of the TV, and he did. Wickert did not even argue with me because if he would have would have been out of there in a heartbeat. He turned off the light and we both got undressed, and had sex. I finally left around 2:30 in the morning with $300. 00 in my pocket, and feeling like shit because of what I did. However, the next day I would go out and buy all kinds of stuff for the hell of it.

I never bought food or the stuff I really needed or should have bought. I just bought material items. I would see Wickert almost every week and each time he would pay me $300 to have sex with me. However, as the months came, and gone

I would feel so guilty for taking this poor man's money, even though I did like the sex I softened I lowered the price to $200. 00 instead and he agreed. Actually, he felt he should not have to pay for it anymore because I liked it as much as he did. I told him to go, and find some other womon who will have sex with him. He shut right up. Sex with Wickert would last about a year, or so. I would still hang out in the gay bars, but I just could not bring myself to go there after the shit happened with Bertha. (the womon that hit me in my mouth). I am 30 years old. I decided to go down to 3 Strikes Bar because there was a pool tournament going on and I was feeling ok about myself at the time. I had lost about 40 pounds and I had quit drinking.

All I would drink is water. I met this womon named Mallory Shevia and I thought she was cool, or so I thought. She was attending truck-driving school, she was about 32 years old and I had been dating for about two months, and I thought it was ridiculous she was staying, and living in hotel while we were going out together. I asked if she wanted to live with me, and save money on hotel costs, and she said she would appreciate

She thanked me, and she moved in. I felt I had made a wise decision by letting her move in, but again, I felt sorry for someone, our relationship only lasted six months. Even before she had moved in with me I had been on. General Assistance for three years all ready (in case you don't know what means something like welfare except I don't have any kids and I get food stamps to be able to purchase food). I was still seeing my therapist, and I was still very much stuck inside my damaged world. When I first met Mallory, she said she was a virgin and I thought too cool. After Mallory had finally moved in. Everything was calming down, and even for a while I felt happy with her. She would write me letters telling how could I make her feel and what she wanted me to do to her later when she would get home. I wanted to please her the best I could. I did what she wanted, but after about three months of living with her, she started getting phone calls from her ex-lover Monna and with our relationship started going downhill very fast,

I said, "Mallory who is calling you almost every night?

Mallory replied "With a look on her face, like must you know everything, and everyone I talk to. …. It's my ex-girl-friend Mona she needs someone to talk to."

Why you? … How did she get our phone number?

"I do not know!"

Yeah right.

After a while, I was getting jealous. Mallory felt she need-ed to go see her ex up in Michigan some place, I thought and felt I could trust her to be with her ex so I felt cool about her leaving and seeing her. She even told me she would miss me. I said I would miss her too, and all I said was just be good to us. She leaves and two 1/2 days later she comes home and she had hickes all over her neck. What the fuck, I was so pissed I wanted to kick her ass. Then she had the nerve to tell me she did not know how they got there. She claims she was passed out on the couch and her ex gave them to her when she was sleeping. Yeah right. I have some swampland to sell you in Florida do I look fricking stupid to her? I guess so! I looked at her at Mallory with such anger. I started shaking bad. I had to go into the kitchen to calm down and I know I scared Mallory. I thought two can play games o I went to an all weekend softball tournament up in WI and I had as many womyn could give me hickes and let me tell you they did. I am not going to lie I liked it. Womyn just sucking on my neck. I met this nice looking womon, and we hung all day and into the evening and I invited her back to my tent and we started fooling around.

The next morning, we said this would never happen again and it didn't. The tournament was over and I went back home, thinking to myself, now Mallory will have a taste of her own medicine. As soon as I walked into the house Mallory had made dinner for me, and also bought me two dozen red roses. I opened the door and there she was with roses in her, hand and. Dinner was good. She was so sweet and I now I felt like shit. Later into the evening when I took my shirt Mallory hit the roof. She saw my neck and we argued she was calling me names and I just sat there until she was finished and when she was done I asked her how did she feel? She left the house, and I didn't see her for three days. But I didn't'' tell her about womon in WI until two weeks later. I eventually told her and was the starting end to our relationship.

After I told her what I did she asked me to leave and I did. I guess she thought I was going to hit her or something, which of course I would not. As I was leaving the house, I heard Mallory yell she had enough. I didn't even stop to listen I just kept walking. After about five hours of staying away, I decided to come home. When I got home Mallory wasn't home. I was not to see her for four days. When she finally came home I was so happy to see her we ended up in bed. I had not touched Mallory since the weekend she got back from Virgina.

She came back with more hickes on her neck. This time she was with some bitch I can't stand. Yet I was still blind and stupid. I can't believe I still stayed with her even after what she did. But the following week were lying in bed and.

Mallory says, "Jaynie is your cycle here yet?"

I look at Mallory with such a shock,

Not yet. …. Why?

In my head it clicked, but I didn't want to accept it.

Mallory said, "Do you remember guy who would always

give me a ride to work and take me home?"

I replied, "Yes. You mean Clint?"

"Yes."

I can see her eyes in the dark and she is looking at the ceiling.

What about him?

"Well the other night we hung out after work and we had a couple of beers and ended up having sex.

I just laid there and I collected my thoughts, and I sat up and looked at her and said,

"You make me sick; you only had sex with this guy to get back at me." But you know what Mallory. You only degraded yourself not me. I still wanted to make love to her, to wash guy touch away from her body, but I couldn't. I didn't care anymore. I just stopped caring about our relationship after. Another time there was a party and Mallory's ex-girlfriend was there and Mallory was all over her and I was getting jealous and so I was ready to leave and of course Mallory wasn't. But she left with me any way. We got home and Mallory starts yelling at the top of her lungs about stupid shit, starts throwing shit all over the apartment and then she starts throwing my plants, I couldn't calm her down so I started to dial 911 and I even told her I was calling the cops and still didn't stop her. I told them what happen and they asked Mallory to be quiet, all they were going do is give her a warning.

She was calling my name from the police car as the car was pulling off with her inside it and I wanted to go out and help her, but, the womon cop told me to stay inside, and it was not my fault, it was hers. Regardless, I felt like shit. Mallory called me from jail and told me to get my ass down to the police station and get her out and I told her I couldn't and also because I didn't have kind of money to get her out. So she hung up on me. I just had to wait until she came home.

When Mallory finally did get home from jail two days later, she told me, she was getting her stuff out today and I was not to talk to her period. I did not. Mallory proceeds to get drunk following weekend at a party and she started attacking me about being on food stamps, and she knew before she even moved in with me. The funny thing is she had no problem going grocery shopping and me buying anything and everything she wanted. At this party, she had a big problem with it. Hell when Mallory first moved in with me. She didn't even have to pay any rent for the first two months. Shit I did her a huge ass fricking favor and this is the thanks I get.

After months of being with Mallory and all her shit including her alcohol problem, she finally moves out of my apartment. After all the shit she did to me I finally broke up for good with Mallory. I think she did what she did because she didn't want to make the first move to break up.

Well, I did make the move and we did break up. After Mallory moved out the phone, bill arrived and she left me with a $60. 00 phone bill, which really pissed me off. I noticed all the calls were to her Monna, her ex in Virginia and adding to my anger her stuff was still in my attic. After months and months of me calling her and bothering her, she finally came over and got her stuff and paid me for my phone bill.

I had liked this womon so much, when was in her drunken stage, she would, ask me if I would marry her and like a stupid fool I said yes. Thank Goddess I did not. Marrying Mallory would have been another big mistake. Our relationship only lasted six months, and after, I hardly saw Mallory again. Finally, finally, I got my place back and I am miserable again. I noticed with Mallory, she was showing me the same behavior and saying the same words, Gertrude called me over two years ago. Why do I continually seek out unhealthy people in my life? Because, I have learned to break the fucking fricking abusive cycle yet, but I am working on it. After Mallory moved out I went and I go even deeper into my damage. It was easier for me to stay in my damage than to totally deal with the present. I was seeing my friends less and hitching more.

One afternoon I was walking down the street and I see this guy walking out of his house. He asks me if I would like to come in and talk with him, and this guy was at least 58 years old, and I didn't see any harm in it so I said sure. We sat talking with each other and just shooting the shit, and he looks at me and said, he wanted to have sex with me I just felt like shit and I thought fuck it I am going to take advantage of him and I didn't care so I did. Then I had second thoughts and told this old man he could not afford it. He asked me how much and I told him and boom, he leaves the room and comes back with $275. 00 in his hand, smiling big time. I said okay your money. After it was over I was starting to leave and he asked if he could see me again and I told him to call me and me did. He was calling me every other week, which was good because I needed the cash and the sex. Sometime he had the cash sometimes he did not so I just called it even. All my friends were asking what was wrong, and Jaynie what can we do to help you? I would just look at them and start to cry. I mean really cry. I never had kind of of real friendship ever. I know I needed to talk to someone about my problems so I thought I could confide in my closet friend Wynter.

I was very hesitant about telling anyone except my therapist, but I thought I would try it. Wynter was dating this white womon by the name of Bertha Bombsdead. Wynter's girlfriend drank all the time so bad she would pass out and would not remember a thing, or she would beat the hell out of Wynter and then deny she even hit Wynter. This womon could just look at you and all you could see is the black in her eyes and you would be scared, but I was not. When I told Wynter what was bothering me I begged her not to say anything to anyone and she said she would not I felt I got along with Bert ok. I tolerated her because of Wynter. I just wanted Wynter to be happy. About a month later, we all are at softball practice and it is extremely hot outside, I think it is the month of July and all of us are just sweating buckets. After we had been out at the softball diamond practicing for over two hours, we decided to go down to the Rainbow, for a few beers. We get down there and somehow I end up sitting next to Bert. We are just talking and laughing at nothing in particular and all of a sudden, Bert turns to look at me and then socked me, right under my chin. I just stood there and stared at her. For a fraction of a second, I thought to hit her, but the pain was much more than I could take.

When I left Crowns Town I had left with the mental impression I am ugly so I didn't give a shit about myself and included my teeth, body, face, and any other parts. After my arrival in WI within the first month, I started having tooth problems and being on G. A. paid for all my hospital and medical care so I had all my teeth fixed and I started taking good care of myself. However, as far as trying to keep a job forget about it. I would find one and then I would do something, or say something to mess it up, and be fired. When would happen, I would go back on GA. I truly wanted to work and not be on GA. When Bert hit me, the first thing I thought about was, oh my God, my teeth. They took me into the bathroom and put a cold pack to my mouth.

Then Wynter showed up and she told me to get into the truck and the next thing I know Bert is yelling for Wynter to get out of the truck, and Wynter rolls up the window and we pull out before Bert reached the car. She took me to the E. R. and took care of me and I had to file a police report against

Bert. I really did not want to, but the doctor said I might need to have braces and one possibly two-root canals and I knew I couldn't afford on my own. I finally go home about four hours later and my mouth hurt so bad I just cried all night. I had to file a police report because it was an assault. I found out later the police were looking for Bert; I also found out later Wynter was trying to hide Bert, which really hurt me. Why would she even think to protect abusive bitch just hit her best friend? In addition, let alone herself. Eventually Bert was found and she taken to jail. She was charges with assault and battery. Later that day I started receiving threatening and prank phone calls. I still didn't back down. I was in the process of getting my teeth fixed also going to court. There was a trail with a jury and everything. In the end I won and she had to pay for my entire medical, and bills, and the E. R. room. I have not talked to her since. I had to wear braces for seven months.

What she did was when she hit me in the mouth, she knocked my front tooth inward. There was trauma to the second tooth. I eventually had to had a root canal to both front teeth. Then after was all completed I had braces put on. I really did not like them too much, but I survived. Always remember when you get braces the first time just know in about two hours your mouth will hurt like a son of a bitch. I stayed out of the bar for the longest time until I felt things were back to normal, which was eight months. Boy was I wrong! I thought after amount of time I felt I could be able to walk into any of the gay bars and hang out with me even knowing Bert would be there.

When I finally did see her she again had made my life a living hell. One night my friend Adele, Lauren, and me decided to go to the Rain Bow to shoot some pool. We had been in the bar for only 30 seconds and Bert came around the bar and she started talking her shit, and out of nowhere, she went into my secret world I only had shared with Wynter. I just stared at her and she started telling everyone who was around area everything I had shared with Wynter. I mean Bertha told all of it. I looked around and I could see their reaction. Now I just wanted to die. Actually, all she wanted was for me to hit her so she could beat the shit out of me. I never raised my hands. I just stood there looking at her wondering why she hates me so much and then out of nowhere she spits in my face because I would not react to her shit.

I just turned around, and left, I just started walking and I could not stop crying. Lauren and Dena were in the car following me asking me to get into the car, and they were trying to console me, but it was a waste of their time because I felt lower than snake shit. I just yelled at them to leave me the hell alone. I just kept walking until I quit crying and I finally got into the car and the silence was so intense you could hear a pin drop. I finally got home and I went directly to the shower, and I washed, and scrubbed for over an hour trying to wash her spit off me. I just felt so dirty and ashamed, and I had done nothing wrong to make her expose my private life like the way she did. I guess Bert felt it was her territory, I was stepping into it, and she was just defending it. I came to realize she was extremely jealous, of me. I have not given her a reason to be jealous, but she was. Oh hell I do not know, but I just drifted further into my hitching and prostitution, and I stayed away even longer this time. I just went to bed, and cried myself to sleep. The next few weeks I just kept seeing my therapist. In my mind, Bert gave me the okay to hate myself even more because she hated herself just as much I guess she wanted anybody and everybody to join the band wagon. My therapist felt like I was progressing forward one day and then other times I would be taking four steps backward. Occasionally I saw progress then it would go away.

I felt like I was splitting into two different personalities. I honestly felt there was me and then there was my alter ego. I would not let people into my dark side of me, every time friends would ask me how I was doing, I would just break down and start crying and I would literally run out of their house. However, you know what is so funny. Even though Bert said those terrible things to me not one time did any of the people were there said anything bad to me. Actually, it was the opposite. This guy approached me and said to me later don't worry about her, she does not know her head from her ass. After several months of being a hermit, I felt it was time for me to be around my friends. With the help of my therapist and the wanting to be mentally and emotionally strong, I finally started taking back my power from Bert.

No longer do I want to be in the darkness held me down so low I could not breathe. Only the future is the bright light guides me, and pulls me forward no longer wishing to be alone to fit in to live, you just do it. When I went back to the bar, I spoke with the owner and he said if Bert fucks with me he would kick Bert out. When she saw me she looked at me and I just turned around and gave her a look like yeah bitch I am back and this time I am here to stay, so if I were you Bert I would not fuck with me. One time she confronted me and I said when you feel like you want to have a piece of my ass make sure I see it coming this time. She just looked at me, said fuck you, and walked away. Which was fine by me because as I said Bert is a very crazy womon and when she was in my face my whole body just shook and I was trying not to show how actually scared I really was. I no longer hang out with Wynter because I could not be her friend if she continues to be lover with Bert who abuses womyn. It has been over a year and a half I left Mallory and I see her here and there, but no biggie. I would see Mallory at the bar and she would be getting drunk as usual. I felt sorry for her and I felt obligated to drive her.

Will I ever stop feeling sorry for drunks? One night I am at the bar. I see this beautiful small womon and find out her name was Zoey, and I felt she was so damn beautiful. We hung out together, went to movies, and dinner and I felt this womon was getting to attracted to me in such a short time. I am 31. Zoey was coming over to my house almost every day, and I could not understand why, but I knew every time she came over she kept talking about sex. I was not ready for step yet.

So one night we decided to meet at the bar on a Saturday night and we both decided to wear dresses. We were dancing and having an okay time. Zoey decides to wander around the bar and I am at the bar getting another drink and I remember it was warm day in May. I happened to be standing next to this tall womon, she was leaning up against the bar, and her back was to me. (Little did I know this womon would become my lover for the next three years). She had on a long sleeve khaki shirt and a pair of green shorts. I am standing on her right, she is facing the window to the street, I said, "The next time you see me again; you are going to buy me a drink!"

As she turns around to fact me she say's

Stranger, "Oh I am, am I?"

I replied, "Yes you are, I retorted?

I heard a cool song come on so I asked if she would like to dance with me! She stood there looking at me and she is actually thinking about my question. After a few seconds of me waiting for her answer.

Stranger replied, "Yes."

Thank Goddess because I really wanted her to dance with me. I really liked her.

Stranger say, "Yes whatever your name is I will dance with you. …. I wa just to leave. …. But I guess I could stay for one dance, I guess."

CHAPTER **11**

I TALKED HER into staying. As we are talking another song is playing I like. I find out her name is Agnes Smagma, and she is from Kurtisville WI. I was under the impression she lived two to three hours away from me the way she described it, but actually it was only 45 minutes away. I am thinking this womon is fine. We are dancing and I see Zoey watching us dance, but I already forgot about her. I am totally into Agnes. I was so surprised she dances the way I do so I thought was somewhat cool. Agnes had auburn hair brown big beautiful eyes a real nice smile.

She has a gap in the middle of her front teeth and with I thought was one of her better qualities. Nice size set of lips on her. Little did I know when I met her she was already drunk so she definitely fooled me! I noticed she was stumbling over herself, but I never thought anything about it. We get to my place, and it is late and I offered Agnes a pair of shorts, and a tank top to sleep in. We are both tired. We lay in bed for a while, then we cuddled next to each other, and we started kissing. We both fell asleep in each other's arms, just cuddling each other and I have to say, I thought it was wonderful. Let me tell you, the thought of making love to Agnes was extremely strong, but I knew in time we would share intimacy when the time is right. Just lying next to Agnes was good enough for me. It will not be boring I know for sure.

During Agnes and my conversation Agnes told me she wasn't a heavy drinker and I am thinking is exactly what I have been wanting and waiting for in a lover someone who does not drink a lot. She also said she does not drink on weekdays only weekends. I felt oh this is so cool I could accept. I fell for crock of shit, hook line and sinker; I was very naive and blind. The storm is brewing. Little by little, I was falling for Agnes, and I just could not stop it. She was the black widow spider waiting in her lair for me her prey. What I didn't notice is Agnes drinking habits were a lot worse than what she claimed. Morning finally arrives, and Agnes and I are eating toast for breakfast. As we are getting dressed I still wanted to get to know her more so I asked if I could hang with her for a while, and maybe go to her neck of the woods.

Agnes had such a surprise look on her face (like or shit what do I do now look). She did not answer me at first, I think I had waited at least two minute for her reply. The reason for her procrastination was because she was afraid of what her cousin, and friends would think of me. She finally says yes. Agnes told me she was from a small, very white community; and the community is racist. I thought, oh great! I can just see the good old boys riding in their trucks and calling people names, with empty bottles of beer being thrown alongside the road. She mentioned to me I would probably get some stares because my race, which in my opinion should not make any difference; but then again it might matter to others. I am so used to getting stares from people it really would not bother me at all. Understand, I have never been out of Toledo except when some of my friends and I would travel to Wanten Iowa, which is an hour and twenty minutes away. The drive down was nice, and the scenery was breath taking. The drive also gave us more time to talk and get to know each other a little better. We finally arrive in Kurtisville, and the town is not booming with people as I pictured in my mind. It was extremely hot outside so I was happy the Agnes borrowed her cousin's truck with air conditioning. I looked all around me and I never saw any black, Asian, or Mexican people. Agnes mentioned that Arnie, who is also gay, was a racist. It didn't bother me. I kept statement in my head. We finally pulled in front of her house she shared with Arnie. The house the house was a beautiful sea ocean bluish green, with black shutters. Arnie came out to greet us, and you know what, he was very cordial and very polite to me and I was cool with. He did make a comment to Agnes.

Arnie said, "I see you made it back alive with my truck, all in one piece

Agnes replied, "Yeah."

I didn't understand it at first, but I understood it later. Arnie felt by letting Agnes use his truck, he was afraid his truck would not come back in one piece because she would drink to get drunk. Agnes showed me around her house and she also introduced me to her miniature German Shepherd who name is Lazy. I have to say he was a beautiful dog, until you wanted to get close to Agnes and then he became Mr. Terror on four feet. He didn't like any one getting cuddly with Agnes. I kept trying to tell Agnes there was something wrong with her dog! Agnes just said the dog was over possessive. I just thought whatever. While I was there visiting, she took me over to meet her mother, only three blocks away. Her mother was very nice, and her name was Jorlynn.

After meeting everyone, Agnes and I made dinner together; I think I stayed the next three days with her. Sex was awesome, and I needed and wanted it really badly. She had my head in the clouds for at least a week or two. I would be traveling back and forth every weekend after. She brought me back home on Monday morning because she had to work Monday night. Now it has been over a year and six months since Mallory and I broke up. I am 32 years old, and is when

Agnes came into my life. In the month of Sept, I tried to stop hitchhiking for a while any way. As far as finding a job, they come and go. Agnes knew I was on GA. It did not bother her as it did Mallory. As I said earlier, I spent most of my time in Kurtisville with Agnes and hanging out with Arnie, just having a good time. There were times when I would hardly have any money. I remember buying clothes or shoes I really needed for myself. If I did not have any money I would return them to the store, and get the money back so I could go to Kurtisville to visit Agnes. I always took a bus to go and see her and took the bus back home because Sunday she would have a hangover, and she did not feel like driving me back home. There were times I thought about going back into my damage, needing money so badly. However, I stayed strong because I did not want to have to lie. Just in case Agnes was to ask where all this money was coming from, with no job?

You and I both know, when you lie once, you know you have to lie again to cover up the first lie. Sometimes I would do yard work, babysitting to make cash. Sometimes I would even borrow money from friends, but I didn't like doing because I would have to pay them back with money, I didn't have to borrow with from the first place. Borrowing money was always my last resort. After hanging in Kurtisville, I was getting to know Agnes's friends. One of her so-called close friend in particular was a womon by the name of Buela Herbesitis. When I met her she seemed nice at first, and then later through the months she became terribly rude, stubborn and extremely opinionated. In my own opinion, I found Buela to be very curt with me and I felt like she had a fricking big chip on her shoulder and she was just a fricking back stabbing bitch. I could not understand why I felt was very jealous of me because of my friendship with Agnes. We would invite Buela out to hang with us and right away, she always wanted to sit next to Agnes, never next to me. I also noticed Agnes always was in the middle. Buela made it seemed when I was around she was willing to tolerate me. Our friendship if is what you called it was a short tolerated social friendship. Buela was Agnes's friend not mine, which was fine with me. I even tried to strike up a conversation with Buela, and she would always correct me on this or.

I was really growing tired of Miss fucking know-it-all, never can be wrong attitude. I even told this info to Agnes also too started to ignore Buela when we went out. After about the second week, Agnes pipes up she does not like being in the middle of Buela and my battles. So I said, "Take yourself out of it, and let Buela and I handle it. Agnes did not like idea at all, but oh well. So in the end she still stayed in the middle. The third week I am at Agnes home waiting for to get off work, which would be around 10:30 in the evening, and bored out of my mind.

Buela comes over around 8:30 same evening, and she said she was bored and asked if I might want to go to the Cliff Hanger 51, I said sure.

My first night at the Cliff Hanger 51 was cool. I guess because of the Airport being right next to the bar, and the bar lights on the dance floor lit up just like the airport runway lights did. After Buela asked me I thought to myself we don't know each other well, and maybe this would be a good thing, and plus I had nothing to do at the house, but watch TV and eat. I have to say Buela was a welcome sight. I told Buela I needed to be back by 10:15 in the evening to be there when Agnes got off work, and she said no problem. We left and when we arrived, the bar was dead so we played some pool, and Buela was talking to some gaud ugly womon.

and I just sat there and drank my beer and left the two of them alone. I was having a real boring time. I do not know, which was worst. I'm having a boring time at Agnes's house, or having a boring time at the bar. I kept looking at the clock, it was getting close to 10:30, and I was starting to worry because I didn't want Agnes getting mad at me, for not being home when she got home.

I went to look, for Buela and her new womon and they were kissing, and making out in a corner by the dance floor. I felt bad, but I had to interrupt their love affair, to tell Buela we should be leaving soon. We left and when we got home, Agnes was already waiting for me. I had told her what had happened, and you should have seen the look she gave Buela. If looks could kill, Buela, have been dead four times over. After night I decided not to go anywhere with Buela unless Agnes was with me. I never want to be on Agnes bad side. Now I have been going back and forth to Kurtisville, and Toledo almost every weekend, and still between jobs. I would get a job and then lose it for whatever reason. I know it is because I have a real big problem with authority figures. If I did not get a handle on it soon, it would become a major problem in my future. Sometimes I would lie to my property owner saying my check has not come in, or I just started a job or there is a two hold on the payroll checks

I never told Agnes my actions because I thought she would be ashamed of me even though I was ashamed of myself, for lying to my property owner. He had been very good to me, but in my mind, (I am thinking hey love costs but damn this bitch is expensive.) I started to realize I was always spending mostly if not all my money on Agnes. I always bought the bus tickets there and back, and she never even offered to help. I felt I wanted to impress her. I wanted to make sure she was having a good time. Make sure she always had a beer to drink. I did not care if I had something to drink, or not. I did not care if I had food to eat in my apartment, or private things for myself. I gave up myself for Agnes and she knew it, and she was just reeling me in. The more I pleased Agnes the worse I felt emotionally. Isn't that funny? When you meet someone is so controlling it's very hard, for the victim to see straight. Do you agree?

I only saw Agnes on the weekends so I am not sure on how much she drank, or if she drank on the weekdays. I'd find out soon enough. In the beginning when I was going back and forth, Agnes would pick me up on a Friday, and then she would drive me home on Sunday. And after a while she told me she didn't want to keep taking me home on Sunday because she wanted to sleep in on Sundays. I thought great, this really sucks. Stupid me like an idiot I said, "Oh I understand honey, don't worry about it." I do not mind taking the bus home. I fell right into the trap, and didn't even see it coming. Boy I tell ya', when you like someone you allow yourself to look the other way, and to avoid any shortcomings. What I did recognize was Agnes would drink so much on the weekends she would not be sober enough to make the drive, which by the way was only a fricking 45-minute drive, there, and back. By bus it took an hour and 30-minute drive there and back. I also noticed I started to become very insecure when I was away from Agnes.

However, when I was with her I felt secure. I know is strange, but my intuition was telling me something and I didn't want to hear it. I felt like I was becoming very possessive of my time with Agnes. We have become lovers by now, and it's been already three months. Maybe because of my insecurities in my old relationships, I do not know. Seeing how Buela was always hovering over Agnes didn't make the situation any better either. When I could not get down to see Agnes I would become extremely depressed. My head would be running with all kinds of strange thoughts. Like, maybe she's having an affair, and not telling me about it. You would think if I can't get down to see Agnes she would come up and visit me for the weekend. She did, but was very rare. When I could come down to see Agnes, I did practically anything and everything she wanted to do, believe it, or not, with a few exceptions. I mean, I would have had sex in front of Agnes with some else if was what she wanted, and such stuff as. We decided to go to the bar in the third month into our relationship. We had, had a good time considering the fact Agnes was extremely argumentative when she got drunk. Sometimes I don't know what I said, or did, to piss her off, but I guess whatever it was it must have been really bad. Agnes would be talking to me one minute and then all of a sudden she would just ignore me. When I would try to talk to her and I would ask her what I did to make her so mad? Or what she's so mad at me about? In addition, she would not tell me why. We are in the bar and she wants to leave so we get ready to leave, we are on our way home and not a sound out of Agnes, just silence.

What I didn't see was Agnes had been trying to dump me and I didn't even see it. She gave me every indication, but I was blind from trying to save her. As we pull into the driveway Agnes turns to look at me, and she tells me she wants me to pack my shit and go home. I looked at her with such an expression on my face like (are you on drugs, or what?)

I said, "What, Agnes are you kidding, you can't be serious, it 2:30 in the morning. There are no buses running at this hour, with tears rolling down my face!"

Agnes replied, "she was serious as a heart attack, I don't give a fuck what time it is. …. I want you out of my house and out of my sight, out of my life tonight and right now."

At first I really thought Agnes was just joking. But then I went over to hold her and look into her eyes, and she pushed me away, and she was not joking at all. Right then I knew she was completely serious. Her face was as cold as ice and her eyes were as dark as coal.

By now I am crying hysterically and I am asking her Agnes what I did, just tell me what I did was wrong, and there still was no answer. She let met me into her house like I was a stranger to get my belongings. I went upstairs to pack and I realized how much stuff I had brought over to her house. Little by little of course, but it does add up. (The next time I stay at a girlfriend's house I will only bring what I need to wear and not any of this extra crap). I had so many bags packed to go you would have thought I was a bag lady. Well, anyway, I packed what I could take with me. I will pick up the rest of my things later. I started down the stairs almost falling because I couldn't see through all my tears. The last thing I wanted was for Agnes sneering at me.

I held my head up as I walked out the door. I even packed the gifts I had given her. If she is kicking me out then I will be damned to let her keep all the stuff I had given her, no way in hell. Not after the way she was treating me. Screw her and the drunken horse she road in on. Now my mind is racing, who can I call to come and pick me up, not one person came to mind. I had met several people at the bar, but didn't know them well enough to exchange phone numbers. And even if I did know someone to pick me up Agnes would not let me use the phone to call them anyhow.

I thought to call a cab, but I didn't know any of the names of the cabs in Kurtisville. I am thinking to sleep outside on the porch until the morning and call my friend Delphine in Toledo. I am standing in the front of the door and I look at Agnes;

Agnes says "Don't look at me like Jaynie because your crying isn't going to help you.

I replied, "Where do you propose I go? ... I am sure as

hell; don't know my way around Kurtisville, yet.

I am practically on my hands and knees begging for Agnes to let me stay

"Please at least let me sleep on your couch and I promise by morning. .... I will be gone from your life for good."

Hell no Jaynie, I don't want your ass on my couch. .... Hell I don't even want you in my house.

"Why, just tell me why .... Since when did you stop trusting me?" I will even sleep on the floor next to your bed if you felt it would make you more comfortable."

Agnes changed her mind and I was grateful because it was now 4 a. m. in the morning, and I was dog as tired. She goes up stairs, and I lay out on the couch and I cry myself to sleep still wondering what the fuck I did wrong, and now wondering what the fuck am I going do." .... Who am I getting involved with? .... What am I getting involved with? .... Why am I getting involved with this sick fricking flip flop womon?"

To think I honestly wanted to love and be with this womon for the rest of my life. What the hell was I thinking. (What kind of drugs was I on?) Morning was just around the corner and I still didn't have anyone I could call to pick me up lives in Kurtisville boy I am fucked. Finally, the sun peeks out, and I wake up and I am hesitant about going up stairs to ask Agnes for a ride to the bus station. But I know I couldn't carry all this stuff to the station by myself.

The city buses don't run on SundayThe only action that happens in this town is if there is a fight, robbery, murder, parade, or the county fair's in town. I quietly walk upstairs to her door, I knock softly, and I let myself in.

"Are you a wake Agnes?"

Yes.

I said, "Agnes would you mind taking me to the bus station?"

You know what, she had the every lasting no good ass gall to say no, and I just looked at her, and I really had to hold back and not want to scratch her got damn eyes out of their eye sockets, or not want to beat the holy shit out of her. was how mad and angry I was at this stupid drunk ass bitch. Then she comes back with.

Why do you want to go to the bus station Jaynie? …. You don't normally leave until six p. m. or so."

"Well, early this morning you told me you didn't want to see me anymore. …. Also, you wanted me out of your house and your life forever so I am leaving."

Jaynie, I never said. … Why would you say such a terrible thing like, you should know me by now?

"Agnes you did say those horrible things to me, do you think I am making this up?"

I honestly don't know! Are you?

"No I am not making up this story, you even told me to pack all my stuff.

Jaynie I swear I never told you to do any such thing. …. Just to show you I want to give you a kiss. Well, after was I was just imagining all of this. What the fuck just happened. Why would this womon, kissing me passionately? Then out of know where Agnes starts touching me, and one thing lead to another, she takes all my clothes off, and we had sex as if nothing ever happened.

I was very dumbfounded and I was totally at lost for words. I am thinking maybe she is trying to get rid of me and I'm not getting the hind. I didn't not know what to say to Agnes, or what even to think to say to Agnes. However, I was happy she was not mad at me and she was kissing me. This would be the very first episode I would experience with Agnes when she would drink over her limit. Little did I know there would be worse times to come, down the road! After fucked up crazy night, I was extremely cautious around Agnes when there was alcohol around in the picture. I didn't want to upset her, or get her angry at anything I say, or did. Whatever she wanted to do we did, whatever she wanted to watch on TV we watched and when she wanted sex she got it. I had no say in it all.

The next two months were pleasant with Agnes. Our relationship had been going on four months now and I have to say she treated me really well. In her small, minded way I think she was feeling guilty about what/how she treated me, and she was apologizing for it. I felt we were getting along so well I thought I could tell Agnes about my past before some-one else did. Agnes remembers what happened to me at the bar with Bertha a couple of years ago, and she busted me out in front of those gay guys. I felt very humiliated. Well, I don't to ever feel way again, or have to go through kind of humilia-tion again. Also I wanted to tell you about my past so there are no lies, or secrets between us. Including the fact, I want to be straight up with you, and on top of all I don't honestly think I could take the embarrassment again.

When I first met Agnes she was going to school for draft-ing, and architecture, I thought was cool. I was proud of Agnes. I have never been with anyone had/or wanted to have a college degree. Anyway, back to me telling Agnes about my past. I was at home in Crowns town thinking on how I was going to tell her, I had thought about it for a long time. I had been talking to my therapist about my telling Agnes about my past. My therapist mentioned I have a choice. I could tell Agnes and have her possibly walk away from me, and never speak to me again, or I could not say anything and act as if nothing ever happened to me, I was just playing with her.

Then she would be mad at me for not telling her, and think had been lying to her all this time, and I have been keeping secrets from her from the start. I was between a rock and a hard spot, but my therapist told me, it is up to me to make the decision, not matter what the consequences. I cannot predict the future. For some unknown reason I wanted to tell my mother about what had happened to me with Stan when I was three years old. Do not ask me why!

I feel now she was not there for me when I needed her the most. Now I am telling her because the damage no longer affects my life. (So I thought). When I finally did tell my mother, she had the audacity the absolute gall to ask me,

"Why did you let it happen?

How, in the world does a little girl at the age of three tell his/her parents, a man is touching him/her in private areas, where he should not be touching? When the man show's them him/her more love then their own parents.

How dare my mother ask me? What Stan did to me wasn't my fault. How dare she try to blame me for his actions?

"Why weren't you there for me when I needed you when I was growing up?

"Why didn't you have a clue something was going on with me, when, I got caught having sex in the second grade?

"Why didn't you ask me what was happening to me then. I would have been very scared to tell, afraid of being beaten by you, then by Sylvet. I would have told you. At least I would have tried to tell you.

So do not sit there Othea and try to put the blame on me, I think you should put the blame where it belongs. would be on you and Sylvet.

But let's face it, if parents ask you a question and you are too scared to answer them, well, then what is the next step to take? Let me tell you! The parents are already mad you will not tell them what they want to know because you know as soon as you tell them you get a whipping and one way, or another they will find the answers to their questions. Therefore,

I guess I probably would not have told her.

"Othea why did you allow Sylvet to beat my hands, so bad they turned beet red?"

"Why didn't you tell me what I did wrong?

By the time I finished asking her all these questions, I was crying so bad I just hung up the phone on her. I never even called her back and she never called me back either. After I just wiped my eyes and I felt so good and so high like I could actually float across the room. After my phone call with Othea was when I decided to call Agnes and tell her the news of my past, including the conversation with my mother.

I called Agnes up, on a bright sunny Tuesday afternoon,

"Hi Agnes, how are you doing today?"

I'm fine, getting ready for work. How are you?

"I am honestly feeling really good! In addition, it's so damn good to hear your sweet voice today."

Well thank you, and it's good to hear yours as well.

"Agnes I need to tell you something about my past. …. I've been wanting to for a long time. …. I couldn't because I didn't feel the time was right, and now I think it is."

I am listening.

I took a deep breath, I started talking, and telling her little by little and after two hours on the phone with Agnes she finally knew about my past and my damage I have carried for over 31 years.

I have to say I felt so good after telling her. My therapist made me do a lot of mind searching and had me think about the pros and cons.

It was just if I told Agnes about my damage, I was afraid she would leave me, and I was afraid of taking chance, but I knew it was something I had to do.

The good thing is Agnes did walk/run away from me, and most of all she did not judge me. Agnes said I love you for telling me, and being honest with me yeah baby.

You want to know something else, I felt so high, and so good, if Agnes had standing in front of me, I probably would have attacked sexually and smother her with kisses. Her mother would have been so worried about Agnes her mother would have put a search party out for her. We chatted a few more minutes about the weekend. Nothing changed in our relationship, and I felt we grew closer than we were before. After my very lengthy conversation with Agnes, I was finally able to let the past stay the past and move forward with Agnes into our future as lovers so I thought. Sat morning and Arnie, Jonas, Agnes and Buela and me are getting ready to throw a June child's party. For all you readers out there a June child's party is where all your friends whose birthday is in June, just has one big gigantic party instead of individual's ones. The party thank God, is for over 25, and older. Jonas took care of the festivities for the evening. The party was a success. Agnes birthday was also in June; she is turning 39 years old.

For being 39 years old, I thought Agnes was looking damn good for her age, and I did say (at time). Not to mention the dark bags under her eyes also not mention her crow's feet. Everybody in the house is preparing something. I was making the potato salad.

Agnes was making the barbecue sauce. I tried some of it and it tasted like crap, but of course, I told Agnes it was very good. I feel if you want to make a good barbecue sauce you have to use Open Pit, it is the best. The party finally got under way. Agnes invited some of her womyn friends, and among them was this interracial couple of names Leah and Maxlene. I really like Leah because she was a very beautiful black womon and I wanted to get to know her, and Max, but especially Leah. Max was nice. I thought she had a beautiful head of hair; it was down to her waistline and all sandy brown. Max is white and I had no problem with that at all. I was watching Leah and Max on an off throughout the party. In addition, I thought there is no way Leah is even remotely attracted to Agnes. I even spoke with Leah and she told me they have been together, for over six years. I was praying Agnes and I could make it long, or even longer. Eventually all good things must end. It was 11:00 in the evening. I met more of Agnes friends and I was sad to see Leah and Max go, because they had their own party to go to. Agnes was getting drunker by the second and of course, I was embarrassed. Eventually Agnes said she was drunk and she was going to bed, and of course I went with her. Why because I knew what would happen if I did not go with her, plus to avoid any arguments. last scene was still fresh in my memory. All night long, I have been very fortunate not, to step on any eggshells. The following morning, we all got up and Agnes and Arnie, Jonas, and Buela had their several cups of coffee.

She was at the party and she was a total bitch to me, and so the more I tried to be nice to her the more of a bitch she became. I truly did not mind Buela being at the party, but why does she have to be so evil. Everybody knew her called her the walking talking dictionary. Just because she had a few years in college, it does not make her Ms. Einstein. I still feel deep inside my soul, Buela and Agnes had something together. I cannot put it into perspective yet, but I will. Clean up was quick and we just rested, for the rest of the Sunday afternoon. Everything is still going smooth with Agnes and I am growing happier. August finally rolls around and the air is getting cooler. We decided to go to Mumboley's Bar & Grill for a drink, and to celebrate our six-month anniversary. You can tell by the cool breeze winter is just around the corner. (yippie). Finally, after months of fighting with Agnes I honestly can say we are going to make it. I can say puts a happy smile on my face, and I guess you can say I am falling in love with Agnes. Agnes called me early at work. She told me to get ready, and we were going out tonight! OH my Goddess she remembered our anniversary, how sweet. Thank goodness for the weekend. Therefore, I go home, I get ready, and I knew the drive would be long so I just took my time getting ready. Agnes arrives, she honks the horn, and I fly for the door because I know how she hates having to wait for me. When I get into the car, she tells me of her week and I tell her about mine. Every Friday and Saturday, we go out and so this time she took me to a different bar, a straight bar. I thought it is a nice place.

The music was old, but it was cool. I really like the fact she does not mind gong to straight bars occasionally. We finally get to Mumboley's and she wonders over to a table full of womyn, and of course, I follow her, as a good dog should, oops, I mean lover. She introduces me as her friend, and I thought (friend, what the fuck), what is going on here? However, I just keep my cool, and kept thought to myself, but be sure I would ask her later, now was definitely not the time. All the womyn I met were Buela's coworkers. They all have worked there together for a while. The last one I made an acquaintance with is a womon by the name of Sandy Headcheese. I chuckled to myself because of her last name, but I did not let her see me laughing and I just said hi to everyone. As were sitting down with our drinks, I asked Agnes if Sandy was a dyke and she said no, she is a breeder with three kids and a hubby.

Again, I feel safe with Agnes and without fear of losing her. Sometimes when I meet her friends, I feel threatened because they see her every day and I just see her on weekends. I miss that about Agnes. I would love to see her every day, but she lives in Kurtisville, and me in Crowns town, and I do not have a car now. When I meet someone knows her I am a little standoffish. After meeting Sandy, I noticed a very, extremely, attractive men sitting next to her.

Actually, he was just looking to damn good if you know what I mean. I wondered to myself if he is with Sandy and to my sadden surprise he is her hubby. His name is Trumont, sad to say they make an ok couple. Sandy is 5'5 with brunette hair and nice brown eyes. Trumont has just the same color hair, and same eye color. Trumont is full Italian. I have to say Sandy has good taste in men. The night went on and Trumont and I dance almost all night together, and all Agnes and Sandy did is talk and dance a couple of times together. I got a few dances with Agnes, is not thoughtful of her. Sandy asked me sometime evening if Agnes and I were lovers, then I in returned to Sandy what was Agnes answer when you asked her the same question. She replied Agnes said we were just friends. After hearing I just hit the roof, but I kept my composure and I told her the truth, about our relationship. Sandy looked at as if I were lying about Agnes and I being lovers. I could not understand why she would think I would like about my own lover. After night, I never imagined what would come next, but little by little, the picture started falling into place. Through the next two months Trumont, Sandy, Agnes and I are hanging together almost every weekend. As times goes on I am still living in Crowns Town. I'm traveling back, and forth to be with Agnes by bus. My addiction to Agnes is growing stronger, and feeling I get when I think of her makes my heart shine. I just wanted Agnes to know I would not walk away from her no matter what; we could make it through anything.

As I stated before I was still stuck in my damage and I have been trying hard not to do it with the help of my therapist. November is here and almost gone and all four we are still going to straight bars, and so I suggested to our little group we check out Cliff Hanger 51. Whenever Agnes and I would go there, we would always have a good time. I have, to tell ya the more we hung out with Trumont, and Sandy the more I wished I could have hooked up with Trumont once. Little did I know I would get my chance? This man is drop ass kick ass gorgeous and I mean with everything I say. When I first met him he did not have a mustache, or beard and now he does, and I have to do everything humanly possible not to want to touch it. I would have sex with him 24/7/ 365 if he wanted to, oh well, wish-full thinking.

We all agreed to go the Cliff for the evening. This would be Trumont and Sandy first time in a gay bar to my knowledge. On our way to the bar Trumont asked me, "What he should do if a man hits on him and I told him of it happens tell the guy you are not interested and you are happily married and walk away with a smile." We got there and Sandy and Agnes talked practically the whole night as Trumont and I again danced together by ourselves, which to be honest was fine by me. As weeks and months went on Sandy would want to come out and Trumont would not. After a while it came down to Agnes asking me to talk Trumont into going out I would feel horrible because he really did not like coming to gay bars. I felt I was begging him. Why would I care if they did not go out on some weekends? I did what I was told, and he would give in and come out, and Sandy and Agnes. They were happy as they can be. Actually I was too because I got to know Trumont on a more personal level. Why were they so fricking happy? Why did I have to convince Trumont into going out with us? If Trumont had stuck to his word, and he wanted Sandy to stay home, she did. She didn't like staying at home, and neither did Agnes as far as goes. I felt if Sandy didn't go then Agnes didn't want to go out either. Something is happening, but I just could not see it, or can I?

One time I said to her you were excited about going out

all this week and now Sandy can't go, now you want to stay home. Well what about your lover, there is one other person in this relationship? Agnes said if I want to get out damn fricking bad, then go, but without her, and if you do go out, don't come back here. I won't let you in. At moment, the lights started to come on, flashing like crazy. One weekend there was a drag show I had wanted, to go to with Agnes for months. Our plans were to get down, to the Cliff early, and get a good table for the evening. We got down there and we saw Buela was drinking as usual and trying to hit on every womon she sees. Buela would be very curt and cordial to me when she was sober, but when she was drinking to where she got drunk she was unbearable. I don't know who treated me worse Agnes, or Buela They were both nasty, vicious, disgusting drunks. I could complain to Agnes about Buela and all she would do is stay in it, but and out of it at the same time. (Do you know what I mean?)

They both went from one extreme to the other, and both of their facial expressions changed. Anyway were sitting at our table waiting, for the show to start, and guess who shows up without Trumont. I have been feeling uncomfortable about Sandy in the last month and a half. She has been spending a lot of time with Agnes after work, and I am trying to trust Agnes, but so far, she is batting strikes). Sandy walks over to our table and she was about to sit down. Would you like to know what happen, this should have been my cue to say fuck you Buela I am out of here. Instead, I did this. Agnes looks at me and she told me to get up so Sandy could sit next to her, I was so shocked, I just looked at her with a surprise look on my face and my mouth just hung open, like huh, are you kidding. (I am thinking what in the hell did Agnes just tell me to do?)

Like a big stupid idiot, I got up. would be the very last

time I would move for bitch (Agnes). I looked at Sandy and she totally avoided my eyes lucky for her. Now Sandy is sitting right next to my lover while I am sitting across from Agnes. I honestly felt like I was the third person; I should leave the two of them alone so they can be together. is exactly what I did. I left, went to get a drink, and did not return to the table. Now I am fricking furious, and I did not even notice the show had started, and finished because I started putting the puzzle together. really pissed me off. I honestly thought Sandy was a cool, and the fact I trusted her, and Agnes. So now, I am the one who is looking very stupid. I cannot even tell you how the evening went. However, this I can tell you, the bitch, and I went home together, and Sandy when home to her husband where she should be. The days to follow I was very scared. I knew I would not see Agnes until this weekend. Because; of not paying my phone bill so I can have money for Agnes to party with my phone got shout off during the last part of November. I had to call Agnes collect, and I was afraid she would not accept the charges, but she did. I made a promise to myself to call her once a day in the evening, and only talk for 20 minutes.

In addition, I told her I would pay, for the collect calls. Geez am I stupid, or just brain dead. weekend Agnes was to graduate after going to school for two years. I took her to dinner, for her graduation present. After dinner I took, her to Mumboley's where a few of her co-works, Buela and Sandy for a surprise graduation party. Trumont and Sandy gave her this beautiful black tweed jacket, and I thought, damn I wish I had friends like. Not to mention I thought the jacket was a bit extravagant for only being friends with each other, for only four months. The bar was quite boring after little scene. I couldn't wait for Agnes, and I to leave. After evening, I was really starting to resent Sandy. She practically hung to Agnes all night long; we didn't even dance together at all the whole night. Shit we hardly even talked. Agnes gave Sandy all her attention, and yes, I am very jealous. I was givi9ng all my attention to Sany's husband Trumont. The more time I spent with Trumont the more I wanted to have sex with him.

The whole time I have been with Agnes we both had been contemplating me moving to Kurtisville, but we had not found a place for me to live in yet. The months are going by so quickly, and stupid me is looking forward to Christmas. Maybe it will make us happier. At least I am spending it with Agnes, her mother, and brother. We did not have a lot of money to buy Christmas gifts so we just bought what we could afford and was a book, and a calendar. We all made dinner together, and were nice. If I had to compare, which dinner tasted best, I would have to say thanksgiving.

Agnes, and I only celebrated thanksgiving dinner with her mother; her brother was out of town. New Year's Eve is next weekend, and I was asked to baby-sit, for a friend of mine, and I told her I would. Agnes was going out with Sandy, Trumont, and Buela to a party, and I would meet them at our favorite breakfast spot. I told Agnes I would meet them at 1:30, and she said she would be there. I was sad I could not party with them, but at least I can eat with them. For the weekend I was in Kurtisville, and had to drive to Crowns town to baby-sit, and then back to Kurtisville. I drove like crazy to get there, and flew back home to spend time with Agnes. In addition, maybe because I did not feel good Sandy and Agnes were spending so much time together because I wanted to spend at least part of the New Year, with Agnes. Everyone was at the restaurant, and again Sandy Buela was sitting next to Agnes. When I walked in, I noticed the nearest chair was three away from Agnes, and this time I gave the bitch (Agnes) a taste of her own medicine. I walked up to Agnes, put my hand on her shoulder, looked over at Sandy, and asked her to move so I can sit next to my girlfriend.

Agnes, and Sandy was about to say something and I put pressure on Agnes shoulder to tell her to shut the fuck up. I looked into Sandy eye's, and she saw the look in my eyes, (Which said, now bitch start something I dare you). She got up quietly, and moved. She did not even get to sit next to her Trumont, oh darn. Goddess felt so good. You see readers (good things come to those who wait). I have, yet to have my day in court so to speak. They showed me pictures of the party at the bar, and I have to say Agnes looked okay and so did Sandy. Trumont looked very hot, in his three-piece suit. Buela had it going on. Looking at the pictures you would have thought Sandy, and Agnes were lovers instead of her and I. After a while, Agnes would be going out with Sandy practically every night. If not to the bars, then over to each other's house. I would be in Crowns town, just wishing I could be there with her.

I am just crying all the time because I know she is going to leave me, but hoping for the best. I could honestly feel there is something wrong. My intuition told me they are having an affair, but you know silly me, I didn't/would not let myself believe it. I would be saying the (I love you's), and Agnes would be saying them back to me. I asked her what she thought of Sandy, and she honestly said she thought Sandy was ugly, and a loud mouth, and not her type, and she was very cocky. I thought cool maybe they are not fooling around after all. I would grasp at anything to just to believe they were not messing around. Everybody said they we looked damn good together. Then there were those same people who were constantly telling Agnes I was no good for her. She could do so much better than me. On a cold sunny day in Jan I called her.

I said, hi Agnes how are you?"

"Fine", I am just sitting her debating about going to work.

"Are you tired? Don't you feel well?

Yes, I do. I just hate going to this dead end job.

"Oh honey I am sorry you feel way about your job. You know you can go out, and find any job you want!"

Yes, I know.

"Agnes, you're really quiet, what's up."

(LIKE I DON'T know what's going on, the bitch is having an affair. …. How to you tell your lover you are having an affair.

Nothing!

"I am still coming down this weekend to be with you right?

Yeah why wouldn't you?

"I don't know. I have been feeling funny all week. … I felt you were going to change plans or something like! Is funny?"

Yes, I guess so!

"I have been cleaning house all day, and I thought I would call to say hi….. And to say I am looking forward to making love to you as soon as I walk in the door."

Oh you do, do you?

"Oh hell yes, at least I hope so. …. Agnes what's up? …. Do you want to tell me something?

Yes, I do.

"Well what is it? Come on, you know you can tell me anything."

I knew the answer; I just wanted her to say it aloud. So I can finally believe it.

I am seeing someone.

My heart just dropped to my feet. I felt numb all over

"Excuse me!

Just what I said.

"While you and I were together?

Yes.

Goddess I want to beat the fuck out of her. Damn her.

That's just fucking great. Why would you do this to us? (Now I start to blame myself)

"What have I done to make you want to fuck someone else?

I don't know Jaynie it just happened.

"That's bull shit Agnes; you just don't sleep with someone out of the fricking blue! … Do you think I am stupid, or something? …. Was I born fucking yesterday?

Jaynie, you have not done anything. It was me, it's not your fault. I'm really sorry.

(I want to say this but don. t You make me sick you fricking bitch. I trusted you, I confided in you, I let you call me all those names, and I still stayed with your drunk, stupid ass. Goddess what a fucking fool I have been. I am sorry is all I can say.)

"Your sorry well honey won't help me now will it?"

Right now, I am so full of rage I could have killed her if she had told me in person.

My heart is so heavy I can hardly breathe. I am shaking right now; thank God, Agnes is in Kurtisville as we spoke.

"Agnes I want to know who it is! … Is it Sandy?

Who I see is my business. … I have to get ready for work good bye.

The phone went dead in my hand. I looked at the phone, and just cried.

Then I thought if it is not Sandy then she just might tell me who it is. She claims to be both of our friends.

Therefore, I called Sandy on the phone.

Sandy picked up the phone on the second ring.

"Hello."

Hi Sandy, this is Jaynie can we talk?

"Sure what's up?"

I just got off the phone with Agnes. She told me she was

seeing someone. …. Do you know who it might be?

"I can't do to Agnes. … I don't want to betray her!"

What about me and my betrayal? …I trusted that bitch with my life. …I opened my heart to her.

If I guess who it is will you tell me? (I have to fucking play this damn game with this bitch. Really!

Sandy replied, No, but I will do this for you. …. . If you ask me names I will tell you if you are getting close or not."

I replied, "is fair as I was sniffling."

In addition, right away I started asking questions about Sandy, and her family. Such as is the person short, or does she have kids, is she married. By the time I was done, I could have ripped her conniving little throat, for pretending to be my friend, and all along, she was having an affair with my lover. After my long hour, chat with Sandy. Agnes called within in a few minutes of me hanging up with Sandy. She said she was pissed at me, for talking to Sandy. I asked her if she was disappointed in me, and she said yes.

In addition, she did not want to talk to me anymore. I just hung up on her, and cried because of our conversation on the phone, it took a lot of thinking, but I finally got the courage to call Trumont. It took a few weeks, and even Trumont did not even know what was happening. We started putting our heads together, and then we both got angry. Now this is how sick (mentally) I became. I felt I still wanted Agnes back even though what she did to me was so fricking bad. I know if I called her she would just think I was harassing her. Therefore, the only way I could see her was at the bars, and is just where I went. I did not have a place to stay so I made friends fast. I met this nice lesbian couple. They would let me crash on their couch, and I would go home the next day. I felt I was becoming obsessive over Agnes. I would dance every time she was out on the dance floor. Sandy would start talking shit, and I would just ignore her because I know if I would go after her they would kick me out.

Agnes taught me a very valuable lesson. is there is always a time, and a place to talk about anything. I was just biding my time. Months followed Sandy moved out, and left Trumont. Trumont and I just had sex once. We did some heavy kissing. I thought it would be mine exploding, but it was not. He was dating other womyn. Agnes and Sandy started having problems. Sandy needed a car to get around town, and to take her kids to school. Some kind sweet, helpful Agnes gave her car to Sandy to use. Isn't that just sweet of her?

Shit, I needed one for months, and she never even once offered to let me use her car. Then Sandy needed this and, and Agnes played right in to it. How does it feel to wear the other shoe Agnes? When I heard about this I just had to laugh because Agnes was now being played like she played me, and the funny thing is she does not even know it. I had left some things at Agnes' house, and I knew I did not want to go there alone, and Agnes said she did not trust me in the house with her alone. Yeah right as if I want to destroy Arnie stuff, or hurt, or maim Agnes. Hmmmm. At least she would not do this to anyone else. Ha, but she should be afraid. I could easily hurt her. Nevertheless, would not be a good thing would it. Leah picked me up at the bus station, and on our way over there, let me tell you I was nervous, and I do not understand why. When I got there, Sandy was there, she had this ha ha smirk on her face, and I just wanted to choke her. Well anyway, Agnes had everything packed for me. There were a few items that Agnes had forgotten. She went to go get them

I had brought my favorite comforter over at her house to snuggle with; t told her I wanted it. She went to retrieve it and it was damp because she just washed it. I guess she and Sandy fucked on it, well it was the least thing she can do. Little did

I know Agnes had told Sandy everything I had shared with Agnes in confidence? I would soon see how much her giving me her word was worth. I was at the bar with Leah and we were shooting pool. I was looking fricking damn good too. In addition, Sandy starts calling me a fricking whore, a prostitute, and I sell myself for money, and all of a sudden, the bar got quiet. Sandy kept screaming at the top of her lungs about my past. Everyone almost at the same time turns their head to look at me, as I stare at Agnes, with such anger in my eyes. I am thinking you fricking bitch how could you to this to me. I could have gone ballistic up in bar, but I did not and then all of a sudden, people started talking again. Everyone started ignoring Sandy with her loud mouths antics. People were behaving as if the comments were no big deal.

I just turned around to Leah, and said we should go, before shit hits the fan. As we were walking out the door Sandy starts up again, and we just ignored, and kept walking to Leah's car. As I am walking, I heard someone running up behind me and I told Leah to look to see whom it is, and Leah said it was Agnes. Just when Agnes was behind me I turned around, I grabbed her neck with my right hand, and I said I do not care if you live, or die, Agnes, you decide here, and now, it is up to you. You make the choice, and you make it now. Then I out of the corner of my eye, I see Sandy running toward us. I released Agnes, Sandy got there at the same time, and she was in my face. I took my right fist, and clocked her in her face. I told her I been waiting to hit you, for a long time. Now stupid bitch Agnes is trying to hold Sandy back from me; I look at Agnes.

I said, "Hey please by all means release Sandy."

Well Agnes did let go of Sandy, and Sandy never moved from where she was standing. Leah and I are about to get into the car, and Agnes is yelling something, but I can't/couldn't understand her. My hands were shaking bad, I felt like shit, for what I did

Months following, friends told me Agnes could not talk, for a couple of weeks. I bet was a relief to people who think she is full of shit anyway. Sandy had a black eye for a few weeks. At some point down the road, Agnes and I started talking again. She informed me she and Sandy had finally broken up. I said oh Agnes should I feel sorry for you and let you cry on my shoulders? Agnes replied no. I said (to myself of course) it's kind of funny how you guys only had only a three-month relationship, and ruined a six month so called healthy relationship, for a little romp in the hay. You put me through pure detrimental hell. My addiction to Agnes brought me to talk to her, and eventually back in to her bed. I was truly happy to have her back as a lover. I know I should have left her alone, and moved on with my life, after all this shit came down, but I wanted to show her just how stupid I mean how much I loved her.

When we decided to tell people we got back together, and trust me I got a lot of flak from my, and Agnes friends about going back to her, but you see I thought I loved her. Understand when Sandy and Agnes were together, I did whatever I could do to make sure Agnes saw me dancing, and looking good, and I wanted to make Sandy jealous. Also for Agnes and Sandy to see how it feels to wear the other shoe. I have to admit I pissed Sandy off bad, my just being in the same room make her face turn deep red and I loved every minute of it. The love I had for Agnes was gone, but there is something about Agnes, I just cannot seem to let go. I think it was the sex. I did not want to be without sex. Not she was better than I am, but how we had sex I liked so much. I decided to give her another chance with my heart. After two years, and several months of talking about me moving to Kurtisville,

I finally gave in.

My property owner lived down stairs, and I lived upstairs, he was divorced, and I have to say quite attractive. His name was Duvane with two daughters. I had seen the ad in the paper, I liked his voice, and I truly wanted the place. When I finally saw the house, and instantly fell in love with it, and calling Duvane every night to let him know how much I wanted the apartment, really was a big help. Was it because when I met Duvane I found him attractive, or was it the thought of fricking him on a lonely evening. Hum, not sure. The apartment was eight blocks down the street from Agnes. The house has a real nice big back yard. I had Agnes, and my friend, Leah, help me pack, and move. Packing took a week, on the way to Kurtisville, I drove Agnes car, and she drove the U-haul-it truck. With me moving to Kurtisville did not bring us closer, it just made me weaker against Agnes, and she had more powerful over me. Her drinking became worse. In addition, the attacks against me mentally and emotionally were becoming more, and more frequent. I did not know when they would hit, but I knew when they were starting, I can feel eggshells everywhere.

Moved in finally and Agnes was coming to visit more often, which I was happy for a minute. The last year with Agnes was the worst. Her drinking had taken a wrong turn. I was slipping back into my damage, seeking out older white men, which looked sad. However, my damage was coming out in sexual ways for instance, the thought of fricking my property owner. However, the prostitution happened after a month of my moving to Kurtisville. It was not even intentional. I just was not happy anymore, and I was feeling like I wasn't worthy to be with Agnes. I kept trying to play as if I was. All this time I am just loving my new apartment, but wishing I had stayed in Crowns town. At least I would not have to see Agnes all the time. How does saying go, loneliness heals an aching heart?

I really do not know why I took her back, I guess out of loneliness, and wanting the relationship to work, and not wanting her to be with Sandy. I really truly wish I could leave her, and every time I decide I am going do it, I think of all the other womyn who had hurt Agnes, and left her, and didn't even bother to try to work it out, I just didn't want to be like all her other ex's, to bad huh! Maybe I should have left her as they did, I do not know. I should have left in the beginning, or after the shit happened with Sandy, or all those times she called me a whore, cunt, bitch, slut, nigger, and any other degrading names she came out of her mouth. I could have, should have, a lot of should 'a's, could a's, but did not have the strength to walk away. At one point Agnes was living with her mother for the last two years since her stay with her cousin Arnie didn't work out. Jorlynn would ask Agnes to do things around the house, and Agnes did not want to do them.

Maybe out of laziness! Jorlynn was becoming real tired of constantly asking Agnes to help around the house. I even tried to offer a helping hand, but it was not enough. Eventually Jorlynn finally kicked Agnes out. Of course, I felt sorry for Agnes because she did not have anywhere she could go. So being the kind person I was, I let her move in with me, which by the way was a big mistake! Trust me when I tell you this, I have made mistakes in my day, but this one beats all of them. As I said I had a one-bed room apartment, and I wanted the company. However, her drinking was getting out of hand. I told her one condition was if she lives with me she cannot be drinking at all. In addition, if she did, I will leave this time, and I will never be coming back. You know what Agnes took me at my word. I was serious. I truly wanted her, and not her abuse. (Seems somewhat funny, I am realizing for the first time I am taking my power back with Agnes, and it feels damn good. I guess Agnes did not want to lose me so she quit drink-ing. I had only a handful of friends because of Agnes. She did not like them for whatever reason. One in particular was my 17-year-old friend Trabelica Catchstead. This girl had long red hair down to her ass. I really enjoy red head womyn.

In my opinion, I found Tribella to be a knockout. Agnes knows how much I like red head womyn so of course she could not stand Tribella. This gorgeous womon stood 5'10 her eyes were a beautiful green blue, or sometimes hazel depend-ing on the weather. Tribella eyes, hair, height, and her cocki-ness were traits I admired about her. The story behind Tribella runs like this. I met her in the summer of I was **35 years old**, she was 18. Now if you notice there is a 17- year age gap between Tribella, and I. The weather was so hot you could fry an egg on the sidewalk. Sandy was living on her own with her three girls, not too far from my apartment.

She was hosting a party, and somehow I came to this par-ty. I did not like Sandy, but I knew the same womyn she knew. I was sitting on the couch just chatting with some womyn, in the living room. As I am talking I turned to see who came in the house, and I see Tribella. I'm thinking to myself I must have found a four-leaf clover. In addition, I am thinking I hope she is single. I was just awe struck. I could not take my eyes away. I asked someone who she was, and they told me she had a lover, dammit to hell. To be honest I was not single either. However, you readers know me. I engaged in a con-versation with her, and we were laughing. About a half hour later, I am smiling like crazy, talking with Tribella her girl-friend was also a womon of size, and she was bi racial chick. She walks up to Tribella, calls her honey, and kisses her. My heart sank. Therefore, we continued to talk but now her girl-friend is sitting next to her. Tribella introduces me to her, and her name is Winda. So eventually, I said I had to get home to my girlfriend. If you had not noticed, I am growing rather tired of Agnes. Then I do not see Tribella for months. The funny thing is we only lived five blocks away from each other.

When Agnes moved in with me, she brought two air conditioners. She would run both air conditioners at the same time. My electric bill was outrageous. She would sit in her chair when she would get of work, watch TV, and fall asleep for at least two to three hours. Before she would fall asleep she told me she wanted me home when she woke up because she wanted someone to talk to, and didn't want to wake up to an empty house. By now, this womon has been living with me for five months. I looked at her one day, and I said you must be mad or fricking insane if you think I am going to sit here in this cold house, and wait for you to wake up. So I left but before I left I called my friend Leah who has a swimming pool, and asked if I could come over and hang out, and she said sure. Little by little, I am slowly sparking up conversations with Tribella, here, and there. Kurtisfield is not big of a town. In addition, I should tell you Winda does not like me either. I told Agnes I would see here later that evening. I left the house with my bathing suit in hand. I called Tribella, and asked if she would like to go swimming, and she said sure. I was so pissed at Agnes day is why I was evening paying attention to Tribella to be honest.

I was so pissed at Agnes day is why I was evening paying attention to Tribella to be honest. When I picked her up, she had on her bathing suit, and a pair of cutoff jeans. Therefore, we get to Leah's house, and get into the water. She still has her shorts on.

I said, "Tribella how come you don't take off your shorts?

She replied, "I knew you wanted to see my body, and she wasn't ready, for me to see it yet."

I replied, "is the reason huh? "Okay you can think."

Now I am thinking oh cool take our time make me crazy with desire, as I watch her swim. I told Tribella what Agnes wanted me to do, and she too could not understand why I should be able to have fun while Agnes sleeps.

I like being outside, and riding my bike, going for a walk, or doing something active. Not sit at home and grow old. Agnes would rather stay home unless she is going out drinking, and partying. However, Tribella likes the same things I like.

I really want our friendship to grow and I have come to the decision I am not going to let Agnes run my life anymore. The next three years I spent with Tribella, and I trying not to let our attraction for each other grow. In the beginning of our friendship Tribella, and I were just platonic friends, and her girlfriend Winda did not like the fact Tribella, and I were hanging out. Winda did not like it when I would come, and visit Tribella, or even if I gave her a call. It is somewhat funny both of our girlfriends were jealous. Of us and there was no reason to be. The more Agnes did not like Tribella, the more Winda did not like me, it made Tribella, and I hang out together even more. When I am around Tribella, I don't see age. I just see a womon, of beauty. Just hanging out with Tribella makes me smile. Back to swimming.

We had three hours, of pure fun. When Tribella, and I got back home, from Leah's house we were sitting at the table talking quietly, and Agnes was waking up from her nap. She starts yelling at Tribella and me leaves while Agnes was yelling at the top her lungs. Before she

Tribella leaves and she says, "Will you be alright?"

I replied "Yes and thanks, for asking. .... . Then I said her bark is worst then her bite."

I just stood there allowing Agnes to yell, and after she was done.

I went to the kitchen to make something, for myself to eat. What are you making for dinner?

"Fish."

You know I hate fish!

"Well you better make something to eat for yourself because as of today I am not cooking, for us anymore. .... I am cooking for me."

Months down the road, we co-exist in my apartment together. I was very proud Agnes had remained sober for five months and I was truly happy about it. Every year is the Foaming off the Mouth Street Festival, which is held in Crowns town every year.

Agnes asked, "Would you like to go to the Foaming Festival this weekend?"

"Sure, it could be a lot of fun."

Let's stop at the bar.

"Why, I asked?"

I already knew the answer.

Come on baby I just want to have one drink.

"Okay, just one drink."

Then were off to the festival and I will buy you anything you like.

"Agnes you don't have to buy me. .... In addition, I don't want you to drink either. .... You know how I feel about you drinking. .... . And remember what I said if you start drinking again?"

Agnes thought I wasn't serious. It seems she did not believe me so we are heading to Crowns town, and we stop at the Watering Hole. The bar is almost empty, and for being a men's bar I am surprised. We get there, we are sitting at the bar, and she orders a Tom Collins in a glass big enough for two people. In addition, I just ordered a wine cooler.

I was kind of hoping she would not drink it, and then

again, I knew if she did, our relationship was over. It seems strange, but also elating. I just sat there watching her drink this enormous glass of alcohol. After she was done, I asked if she was ready to, and she said yes. Just so, you readers know, I had quit drinking with her to show my support for her. The drive to the festival was strange; I did not talk to her the whole time. Agnes was drinking at the festival, but didn't. Someone had to get us back to Kurtisville.

The drive home was very strange, and very quiet, so quiet you could hear a pin drop. I feel deep inside she knew if she starts drinking you knew I was not backing out of my decision. I think she wanted out, but she did not want to be the one to leave. Therefore, she drank to leave. I also believe she did not like the conditions, and she really missed drinking. Agnes would rather drink, and be drunk all the time, rather than be with someone who really tried to care for her and not judge her. was her choice, not mine. As I am driving us home I look over at her, and I tell her very calmly

I said, "Agnes when we get back home I want you to pack your stuff, and get the hell out of my house, and my life." I do not want you in it any more. .... I want nothing more to do with you."

I heard those words before!

Do you remember, she said those to me over three years ago at 2:30 a. m. in the fricking morning? Well now, I am reliving this same scenario, and this time the shoe is on the other foot. In addition, to be funny now I am kicking her out.

Agnes replied fine, "If is how you want it."

"I replied, No Agnes is not how I wanted it. .... it's how you made it happen."

We finally arrived home, and I just sat down on the couch, and watched her pack everything, and she asked if I was going to help her, and I replied oh hell no.

You did not help me three years ago in your supposed black out drunken state. After the third load to Agnes car, I did not see her any more. I forgot she left with my key. I called Tribella, and asked her if she could take me to Agnes house to retrieve my keys back. She said no problem. Went to Agnes's mom's house and I got my keys back, and found out Agnes did not even tell her mother what happened. However, I made sure Jorlynn knew the whole truth. Now I finally got my life back, and Agnes is no longer in it. When I left Agnes house for the last time I knew I was not going back. How I knew this is because she had called me those names I mentioned earlier, and she betrayed me, and she

had promised she would never do to me and for the fact she was going to kick me out of the house at 2:30 am, and not knowing where I can go at time of night.

She accused me of having sex with my friend Corry, which was not true. Corry had dropped me of from the bar at 2:00 am in the morning, and Agnes and Buela had gone to Crowns Town to party. I waited outside for a long time. Agnes claims she was home at 2:00 and I was not there. I knew I was there, and so did she.

She just placed her quilt on me, and trying to make me out to be the liar, when in fact it was she was lying. I even drove to Buela's house several times night, and I did not see her car there. I went back and forth trying to see if I could catch her coming home. I was up through the night tired as hell. I just cannot believe I let her treat me like. I allowed her to. I did not see Agnes until 9:00 the next morning. We are sitting on the couch, and I am dead tired. I was doing everything to prove to this fricking bitch I was home waiting for her drunk ass. I even called Corry at 9:00 am in the morning to verify what time she dropped me off and still Agnes did not believe me. I think Agnes, and Buela spent the night together, or somewhere, and they both promised each other never to tell. Many times Agnes said to me if you let people know we are back together, again she 'd deny it. I am sure Agnes secrets are very safe with Buela. Looking back on all the incidents have happened in my life, I always want to believe I have grown stronger even before I met Agnes in 1991. When I broke it off with Agnes in 1994, I realized my self-worth, self-esteem and confidence was a lot more important than taking care of Agnes' needs. I will never let her, or anyone else control, me again. At least I will try not to.

Back to the story of Tribella. I am growing and liking Tribella more, and more every day. Well let me tell ya. It has been over a year since I kicked Agnes to the curb, and it has been 10 months since Tribella, and Winda went their separate ways. Our friendship has been growing every day since the day I met her in 1994.

I wanted to see how Tribella and I lived on our own and I did. We have decided to hook up because we had so many things in common. When we first met, I felt she was excessively young for me. Now finally she is 21 years' legal age, and I really do like the fact she is of age. After dating her for over ten months, we decided to make a commitment to each other. We both have decided we want to make a lifetime commitment together. My grandmother would be very proud to know just like my grandmother I found my soul mate, after 33 years of searching. I still have my bird patches, and now I have a baby kitten named 2Ring. In addition, Tribella cat Smooch, who is the Othea cat of Mascara. There is talk about children, but not for five years at least. Therefore, I still have enough time to spoil Tribella. We live in the Midwest. Where the summers are warm, and the winters are long and freezing. I would like to think I have mentally come along away. Tribella and I have traveled far in the last several years.

In 1994, I started writing this book. I had my apartment back, and Tribella and I are just dating. I felt the need to write down my emotions, is how I started; my therapist gave me the idea. After a while, I had so many pages and my hand was growing tired of writing. I purchased a used computer, and found out about AOL. I allowed the computer to come into our lives, which caused many problems, and a lot of lying on my part, and distrust on Tribella's part. I was unemployed and just staying at home working on my book, and playing on the computer. I was having cybersex with men trying to find a master. I was into the bondage, submissive, life style.

It excited me to let someone dominate me. was why I was playing on AOL. If they could not dominate me, then I would dominate them for money. Tribella was at work, and I just got bored. Then I started giving these strange men my phone number, and I would have phone sex. I know now it was stupid thing to do, but back then, I was only thinking of myself. What I wanted, and what I could get away with. I met this guy. His name was Jim Dudaken. It was 1996. I was 37 years old. We had been talking for several weeks. He said he was seeking a submissive to own, and I was seeking a master. He told me he was married, and I did not care. I just kept thinking I finally found a master, and then on the flip I am thinking I am trying to change my life, and become stronger. However, my hunger abusive side wanted the affair to happen. As we talked further, he told me he was a business owner (which actually was a lie. He was a manager for a business) who was looking for a receptionist and I was actually looking for a job. I am thinking a job, a new place, a master, I can have sex with this man, and he can play with me, and tie me up. He was head of a company called Mighty Air Duct Corporation. They were a traveling air duct company. Therefore, he invited me to Maytop WI.

I was telling Tribella I wanted to get the hell out of Kurtisville Ia. There was no was no true reason for me (us) to stay here. I was leading two lives, and being dishonest to Tribella, and I was thinking if we left Kurtisville our lives might just get a little better. I know now you cannot run from your past, you can only stay, and face your past so you will be able to move forward in your life. In addition, she agreed. Tribella was hoping the move would be a good start for us. Therefore, I drove to the site where my future boss (master) would be.

They were in the middle of building a big baseball stadium called Hitters Stadium.

In addition, I really wanted this job. I would be making $12. 00 an hour. When we met face to face I found him gross looking. He was tall, 255-pds long hair thick mustache, and Caucasian and his stomach was so big, he could not even see his feet.

He was 47 had three kids and those were his words. I had some time to think after telling Tribella about the job, and trying to make a better life for ourselves. I told my potential boss, how I truly felt. I told my boss I did not want to pursue the affair, or the dominant and submissive life style. The real reason why was because he really truly looks disgusting. He did not even look good. He was disheveled, he smelled nasty, he drank coffee like it was going out of style, and I just could not see me letting this nasty looking man dominant me! Oh hell no. I think because he had talked so much on the phone, and his voice really did turn me on. So much I would get wet just hearing him breathe. That is how and what happens when you have phone sex. You get excited talking to a man, and talking about sex, and then you become conditioned on the phone. Therefore, I was hoping if he can sound good on the phone he must look fricking good in person. Boy was I wrong. Therefore, I did tell him I would be a very good receptionist if he gave me the job. When I left the work site, I had the job. I could not wait to drive back to Kurtisville to tell Tribella the good news. We celebrated, and all we could talk about was Maytop WI. I was supposed to be starting my new job in two months. Hitters Stadium was starting at ground zero. I was preparing for the move, and while up there, I would find a place for Tribella and I. She would stay behind and take care of our apartment. I had called Maytop WI Casta Marta homeless shelter for womyn, and children way ahead of time, and explained my situation.

I didn't have enough money; I was able to stay there for only 30 days. By then I would have accumulated enough money for rent, and a deposit. is one big load off my mind. I did not want to leave Tribella behind, but I did not want to stay in Kurtisville. Finally, it is time for me to be heading to Maytop WI. I just could not let her go. I cried so hard I could not even breathe. I loved her so much, but I was lying to her. I felt like I was literallybeing pulled in two different directions. After an hour of crying and holding each other and telling each other how much we would miss each other, and to make sure I call her when I make it in. I made myself get into my car. As I pulled out, I held my hand, and was waved to her as I was pulling away, and kept saying through my tears I love you, be good. I have had seven long-term relationships in my 27 years of pretending to be a lesbian. Tribella was the seventh relationship. However, she was the only one I truly fell deeply in love with, and I really truly cared for her. Actually, I cried for a very long time. I finally, rolled into Maytop W. **I was 36 years-old**. It took over two hours to get there. Finding the house where I would be staying was very scary for me.

Knowing where I came from, and how my life was so sheltered I was even afraid of saying hi to anyone. The house was three stories tall, looked rather gloomy on the outside. Almost like the houses you see were boarded up, or the houses you see they use for Halloween. The season was fall, rainy and rather chilly. Winter was just around the corner. The day I arrived it has been raining, and was dark all day. It was around five p. m. on a Friday evening when I pulled in front of the house. The leaves were turning, the grass somewhat green. Garbage was along the streets, and on the side of the grass. When I first walked up to the house I met a nice womon from Africa, her name was Nubamba. She was the housemother. She did the entire intake for people coming in, and cooked there three days a week. She also was going to school to get her Masters in Nursing. Some of her kids came with her to the United States from Africa,

However, the rest of them, including her husband she had to leave behind. I liked her instantly. I grew very close to her. She lived down the street. When she was taking my information, I had asked her the room I would be sharing with another womon, had a lock on the door, and she told me no, and there would be no locks on any doors. Now I am confused and slightly mad. I asked Nubamba what I to do with my computer, my personal belongings. I could not afford to buy another computer, and I did not have much stuff to steal, but it was all I had.

Moreover, she told me there was nothing she could do about it. There is no way I could keep all my stuff in the car, I am not going to sleep in my car, and there is no way I am driving back to Kurtisville. I do not belong in a place like this. I am not saying I am better than this place or am I? My mind is reeling, and as she is walking me through the house, I came across a womon in the kitchen who also worked for the shelter. Billeann was a mother of two with one on the way, and a husband. They lived in a separate house right next door to the shelter. I being to tell her about my dilemma and she told me she had a bedroom I could use and not have to worry about my computer, or my stuff stolen. I was going to humble myself, and stay in the shelter. However, Billeann offered me the chance to be able to be safe I could not pass it up so I jumped at opportunity. She also gave me a key. Billiann reminded me not to give it to anyone. I would eat my meals at the main shelter. If I wanted something from the store, I would have to buy it. I thought no problem. I had enough gas money, for the next two weeks. I knew I had to be careful on how I spent it. I called Tribella, and told her I made it. I also told her I missed her very much. In addition, I started crying because now I am on my own, and I was fricking scared to death. We talked a few more mins, and hug up. The womyn at the shelter were from all different walks of life. Some were from abusive relationships, and some were use homeless, no job no family no money. In addition, some were prostitutes. Me, I had a job, but no place to live. Isn't that funny?

Some of the womyn I could not trust if my life depended on it. In addition, some I truly felt very sorry for. I walked around the neighborhood to familiarize myself. I truly did not fit in this shelter, but I had to swallow my pride and tough it out, for the next 30 days. Even though I wanted to turn back around, and go home. Friday evening dinner was good. I did see a cockroach on the wall, and I thought oh fricking great. I told Nubamba, and she called the exterminator the next day. There were rules we all had to follow at the main house. You have to be out of the house by 9 am. Return the house at five for dinner. If you were later, you did not eat. You could not leave the house after 10pm. If you did, you needed an excuse as to why you are late coming back in after 10 p. m.

In addition, sometimes if you did not have one, they would not let you back in until the next morning. Saturday, and Sunday you can stay at the shelter all day. evening all the womyn in the shelter sat on the porch, and talked as the kids played in the back yard. I was smoking at the time. Therefore, I let a few womyn ask me, for a cigarette, but I stopped gesture right away. It was getting close to bed, and it was very hot. I went to Billeanns' house, took a shower, and headed to my room. I was happy I had my own room, and bed to sleep in. I woke up Sat early for breakfast. I showered, and did my daily rituals. Saturday was my first day to actually see how the house really looked inside. The sun was shining so bright, and made the house look bleak. There were not any colors at all. There were no TV's, just a radio. There was a playroom for kids to play in. I spent all day walking around the neighborhood. Did not drive anywhere. Had dinner took a shower, and prepared for bed. Tomorrow I start my new job. Monday came rather early. My first day on my new job. I drove there, and was ready and excited all at once. Jim was a nice guy and a cool boss. I had been searching for a place while working, and staying in the shelter.

I finally found one not too far from my job. Right off the highway. I informed my landlord that my girlfriend, and would be moving in at the end of the month, and she is fine. After 30 days, I moved Tribella, to Maytop WI. She got a job filling vending machine at an all-womyn's college campus. She was ecstatic about job. However, I was not, and just a little bit jealous. A college full of lesbian professors. She told me she was selling drugs to have pocket money while she was by herself. I was angry as fuck. What if you would have been busted? She said she just sold it to some druggies lived down the street.

I loved Tribella very much, and missed her terribly. I just let it go. She is not selling it anymore, not at least while we are together. The only two drugs of choice we were doing were pot and coke. She had never done coke, before so she claims. I had done it in the past, and stupidly I felt I was the one turned her on it. Maybe I did maybe I did not. I will never know. However, my intuition tells me I did. I will always feel bad about. It first started out somehow; we met a guy who we would see when we would wash our laundry. We started talking, and joking around, and the word weed came up. Our friendship took off. He was nice. His name was Lorenzo. He was actually hot. I am thinking, boy would I love to fuck you.

I said, "Hey Lorenzo do you know where I could get some coke?

Lorrenzo replied, "Shit yeah, how much do you need?

I said, "Just enough for the night."

He said, "I could get you an eight ball."

We both said yes, was how we got started on an eight ball of coke. We both agreed to do cock only on the weekend, and to use it by ourselves alone. Tribella was always befriending womyn, and she me this one neighbor, and told her she should come hang with us. I thought at first ok. However, Tri offered her some of our coke, and the womon would not stop coming to our place. I told Tribella was enough. I am not supporting her fricking coke habit. Hell, we can barely support our own. I told Tribella her cokehead friend was no longer welcome. She was mad at first, but Tribella got over it. We would do an eight ball occasionally, which was fine by me, but then I noticed she wanted more. I told her was too much, but she said she could handle it. Soon it grew to two. I had to stop coke all together because Tribella was doing it all the time. In addition, it was too much for me. She would do coke all night, and sleep all day. She eventually loses her job, for not showing up. Moreover, one month to the year I would have become a full time traveling receptionist.

However, on the job site a big yellow crane fell and killed three workers were working on the crane. They had to lay off several workers and I was one of them.

I realize trying to break dysfunctional behavior is a hard and trying process. Denial is a strong emotion keeps survivors stuck in their damage. However, fear is the strongest of them all. I have been in therapy since 1979. It is a constant healing in the works concept.

I also have met new friends along the way. Such as Morgan Gentry who is a real cool womon. When I first met Morgan, she was quiet and she was in a relationship where she was not happy. A year later, she is going out dancing, playing Softball, and meeting plenty of womyn. By hanging out with Morgan I have managed to lose a lot of weight from dancing, and skating, and just breathing fresh air, and loving Tribella. Making friends with Morgan and Lilly has helped me realize you have to have friends. I am still in therapy but now I am in it to change my old patterns, and erase those old tapes to make sure I do not go backwards. I just want to keep going forward. In addition, I am trying to learn from my past, and to stay in the present. It cognitive choices, I have to look at every day. I have not hitched hiked since 1998.

I do admit it does get easier. I have to admit I have been feeling good about myself in the past two years. I am starting to see things about myself, and my personality I never knew before. It is scary, but good. All I can say is once you are ready to break the dysfunctional cycle. Lift your hand high with a hammer a slam it hard. Just take a big step, and put one forward. I would like to add do not be afraid. If you need help, and please do not be embarrassed to ask, for it and do not turn it away it comes knocking at your door. The road to recovery starts within your heart, and deep inside your soul, and mind, and especially your CORE. You will know when you had enough. When you start to see the light trust me it will be the most beautiful light you have ever seen or imagined.

CHAPTER **13**

THE ONLY LIGHT you will only want to see. It was another year after I had been laid off. I had been supporting the two of us on my unemployment. Only receiving $400 a week. Tri would not go out, and work I was doing everything. Unfortunately, I had to tell Tri she had to move out. That was the hardest thing I ever had to say to her. I did not want to, but I did not know what else to do. We were fighting all the time, and always-about money. All she did is lay around the house, and eat and do coke. She never did any work around my apartment, no cooking and not even a little help with laundry. She just kept telling me she wanted more coke. I told her no. I really didn't have the money. She loaded up her El Camino and packed up the animals, and I cried and hugged her good bye. And she moved went to stay with family in another city in WI. She told me we were still together. But I knew better. We just broke up. **I am 41years old**. I stayed behind, and started a cleaning business. I did wonderful. I made enough money to support myself and live comfortable. I had remained single, for a long time not dating womyn or men. Just surviving and living in Maytop WI. and I found a job working at Webart Department store.

I had met this guy in my line, and I really felt sorry for him. Again the feeling sorry for people when will I fricking learn? He got courage to ask me out and I could not say no. Now you see my weakness as if I had in elementary. His name was Mitch Burrows. He kept pursuing me, and wanting to hang out. Therefore, I did go out with him. He totally was not my type and I even told him, but he could not take no for an answer. My therapist has told me, before I have to learn how to say no and I just have not gotten use to word. After only three to four months of I was thinking to myself when I first met Mitch I thought to myself there is no way I could start or even/have a relationship.

He was short, and did not keep himself up at all. Mitch was calling me every day, wanting to see me. I kept trying to see if there was something remotely, I could find attractive about Mitch, and sad to say there was not anything. We kept going out and after several months of dating him, he asked, for my hand in marriage. I am thinking to myself why he is rushing this. Why is he so persistent? For whatever reason I told Mitch if you bought me an engagement ring I would marry him. Two days later he bought me, a ring I was 43 years old I accepted with high hopes. I was thinking of how to tell him about his oral hygiene. When he came home from work, I sat Mitch down, and we talked for a good hour. I told him he needs to go to the dentist, and he did. If he would not have, I would not have gone through with marriage. Mitch told me of his past relations. How these women used him financially, the sad thing is they never paid him back. I will be asking myself this question over, and over. Why did I stay? My intuition tells me he has hardly any self-esteem. I felt sorry for Mitch. I actually pitied him! For months, Mitch was always coming to my place all the time so I asked him why we could not go to his place. Mitch gave me all kinds of excuses not to invite me out to the house, however I pushed it. Same weekend we went to his house. It was a four-bedroom two-story house. The outside needed some work, but it was ok. Once you walk in, I cannot believe my eyes. I was looking at total squalor.

I turned around, and said "Mitch how can you live like

this") Mitch replied, I don't really live like this"Man you could not even see your floor. The whole house on both floors, were in disarray.

I said "Mitch where is your room?"

Mitch said, "Awe Jaynie I think you seen enough let's go back to your place."

I said, "We will, but for now show me your bedroom."

I open the door and it is the worst room in the whole house. The smell is unbearable.

Cat feces everywhere, empty food containers scattered everywhere and clothes were everywhere. You couldn't tell the clean clothes from the dirty ones."

I asked, "Mitch without even looking at him how he could sleep reeks of shit, and such a foul odor? He didn't answer me he closed the door, and headed me toward the stairs. He was trying to steer me toward door, and I told him I was thirsty. As I walked through the house all I saw moldy dishes, and open food containers on the couch, the chairs, and the floor and cat feces everywhere. As I walked into see the kitchen, and I fricking could not believe it dirty, filthy dishes everywhere. I mean you could not place anything in the sink, on the stove, on the table, in the stove! (How does one live like this? I mean really!) You turn me to look at you and again you tell me you don't normally live like this. You just did not have the time to clean up. Bullshit. Then you break the news you would like it if we lived out here

I said, "Mitch! OH HELL NO! Not in this, old foul oder, smelly, rotten, decrepit house. I would not live out here if you truly paid me a million dollars. …. Uh thanks but no thanks."

I am thinking you are a fricking filthy man. After I just seen how Mitch lived and he promised he would not live like this in our new apartment. We found a two-bedroom apartment on the east side of Maytop WI. We started moving his stuff in. and mine and oh my gosh! All of his stuff had a foul smell. (You know when you stand next to someone and they have an order. In addition, you can smell it when they move. I am talking about foul smell.)It stank so bad I had to hold my nose. While Mitch was at work, I had to wash all of his clothes, bedding, and coats. Anything I had to hang it had to be washed first. They smelled so fricking bad. What I could not wash went into the garbage. The smell was so bad I had to place all of his stuff outside of the laundry mate. I washed several loads little by little. The funny thing I saw the signs and the bells were ringing, but I felt pity and I stayed.

He saw how I lived, how I took care of myself, how I cleaned our apartment. However, he was not happy. I can see it was hard for him to contain his behavior. Not picking up after himself not brushing his teeth. Our sex life was so sad. I clean the house, and straighten it up for Mitch and he did not even notice. I started nagging Mitch all the time, complained about his messy behavior/habits. I was telling Mitch more we should not marry. I allow him talk me out of it. He is trying to control his messy behavior After three months, we decided to get married. We should have never walked down road. We try to be happy. I like the label Mrs. We get married and try to get pregnant and no luck. We even went through in-vitro-fertilization and sill no pregnancy. I am so sad and crying all the time. Mitch is blaming me, and I start to feel like I am less of a womon. Finally, after months, and a year of plead-ing Mitch finally decides to go the doctor office to check his sperm count. My conceiving is not my fault; it is you. It's not your sperm count is low, dammit to hell; you don't any. In ad-dition, you tell me it is all me! RIGHT!

Mitch started belittling me in our first year of marriage. I just ignored him. Then he starts blaming me for everything goes wrong. He started calling me names, and his favorite is

"I am stupid." and I was a fricking idiot.

He has called me a bitch, whore, I knew more wanted to come out, but I know he dare not say them, to my face. I grew weaker every day, and I noticed Mitch became stronger, isn't funny. However, we both knew he was the weaker one. I allow all stuff to happen. Maybe for the fact I was just too weak to do, or say anything. You had been telling me for some time you wanted a divorce. I tried to tell you it is a good marriage! we can make it work. We just have to try harder. You tell me you don't want to try any longer I am devastated. I am so against divorce. Believing, feeling as if I have failed in every way. I wonder what I did wrong and how can I fix it.

Agreeing to whatever it is you want me to do, lowering myself to your level in order to make you happy, and make myself more miserable. I thought if I stay with Mitch he could realize he found someone who genuinely cared for him and not how much money he had. I over looked so many of Mitch's bad, nasty, filthy, disgusting and perverted habits and still I stayed.

Even through all of his entire idiosyncrasies because I really felt sorry for him. And I genuinely cared for him. So now, Mitch is wanting a divorce, it has been three long sad, depressing years. So I can only say is for the last three sad years is you have blackened and hardened my soul. You have pecked at my heart until it was deflated. My eyes were puff, and red from constant tears. You constantly tell me I am full of shit and don't know what I am talking about. Now I realize Mitch you do not get it. You have destroyed whatever caring I had for you. You have deliberately sabotaged our marriage, and our relationship. And with I will forgive you, but I will never forget. You can have your divorce. I should say from the start I have forgiven my ex-husband. He is the product of his environment. We are not friends but acquaintances. Now I am slowly mending my heart with bandages, I am giving my mind the strength to heal from the mental and verbal abuse Mitch had put me through. I am giving my eyes a rest to know, they are not just used to shed tears. One thing most of all I am giving myself is a reason to live, and to move on. I will not allow myself to live way with you for the rest of my life. I know I have a long road ahead of me. I do not know what the future will have in store for me. But I do know one thing is you won't be in my ride. I still wondered why I stayed.

You see readers, even when you try to be strong, and seek healthy relationships, one still gets by you, and all of a sudden, you back to square one. Watch for those signals, like their living patterns, or their behavior patterns. If the man or woman that you are seeing they take care of themselves in hygiene. If the person you are liking pick up after themselves. If you notice how men live, and you do not want way of living. You just want your life to be nice, calm, and tranquil. Good luck to anyone who is going through what I have been through.

I got the nerve and I reached out to my old social worker Leo Hiker to find out his point of view dealing with the adoption of Jennifer. I wanted you to read a social worker perspective, and see how they feel knowing they are separating a child from the mother even if it is for the greater good. So I sat with Leo on Sat May 4th 2013 I was 52 years' old

1. "How did you sense there was sexual abuse in my life?

Leo – "Mostly with seeing how much pain, secretiveness I was hiding. It is as if you were not forth coming. I could see you didn't trust men, period."

(I wanted to tell you something about what was going on in my house, but the words were lost because of the adoption and the pain it was causing me.)

2. "How did you feel knowing I was 18, and young going out into the world with a child on my own?"

Leo – "More than anything I was scared for you. I was not sure if you were equipped to take a care of a child on your own. However, I didn't want to deny you."

3. "Did my mother confront you about letting me have Jennifer?"

Leo – "She was very convincing in me not letting you keep the baby. I was starting out in social work.

I was ignorant. However, I was trying to learn about black culture. I was pretty naïve. She may have convinced me it was wrong idea to let you keep her."

4. "Why did you really change your mind about letting me have my child?

Leo – "After talking with your mother, I saw it would

be a rough go, and not having adequate tools at your disposal. You had no support from home, or family. It was like you were all alone."

5. "Did you give her information on how to contact the adoptive parents? If not how was my mother able to talk with them and get pictures?"

Leo – That would be a no no with social services. Not sure how she got the information."

6. "What were your feelings about my mother?"

Leo - Perturbed at her for not being supportive of you any away. Your mother treated you, as if you were not her child, just some girl in the street.

7. "Were you sad? And how did you feel when I had sign the papers?"

Leo - Yes was very sad, feeling of helplessness for you. There was no glee having this child available for adoption. My heart really ached for you."

8. "How did you feel about when Alex came into the office to sign the papers? Did he talk to you, about the adoption?"

Leo – "No memory."

10. "What was your feeling when we spoke after my mother's passing?

Leo - Happy to hear from you, and I know you are finally happy, and you are finally moving on in life, and away from the past. I am sad you lost your mom. But I am happy you are going out, and getting what you want, and desire in life. Again, I was feeling helpless; I was not able to do anything for you. Want to see you again and tell you how proud I am of you for you and give you a hug."

Now you have it for the first time I had the opportunity to ask a social worker his point of views about dealing with adoptions. He is what you call the intermediary, and trying in vain to make some sense out of it all. However, you see when the controlling parent plays the part at home and in public, it is not easy to fight.

To break abusive, dysfunctional cycle, YOU CANNOT KEEP ANY MORE SECRTETS. is how the abuse started in the first place.

My road to recovery started back in 2010 when I started realizes I was not getting any better. I still had anger issues, and hatred. Every time I tried to bring up the past with my dad, he said he did not want to hear it. My brother Towan was not taking my calls at all. I finally made the decision to call my father on December 31 2012. My uphill battle with my father began. I wanted him to tell me why he treated us the way he did. In addition, what he did to me when were alone. I told him I wanted a sincere apology. My father is hard of hearing. This pissed me off even more. Because he was not hearing what I was saying to him so I switched to writing him, three to 4 page letters for weeks. Telling all the secrets I kept inside my core all my life it took all the strength I had to tell him what had happen to me with Stan, my brother, and my other family members. At one point, Sylvet said he did not want to hear it. I told him he was going to listen. I did a lot of yelling, crying and hanging up on him. I was literally fighting, for my freedom, life and my sanity from his grip on me. I told my father how I wanted to beat his ass the way he beat ours. Using the paddle and extension cord on my father's ass. I wanted him to feel our pain and for him to hear our cries. Every letter I sent to my father, I also sent a copy to each of my siblings so way everyone knew what I was saying to my father.

(BREAKING THE CYCLE OF ABUSE)

(NO MORE SECRETS)

My siblings did not respond the way I would have hoped. I knew they were angry with me for opening a Pandora's Box. It was either I let sleeping dogs lie, and keep caring this burden the rest of my life, and make my sister happy. Or make me happy by opening Pandora's box and start swimming to reach land. I was drowning. Telling my story was me saving my life. My sibling told me they read the letters and that was it. They just really want me to do what I have to do to make myself better. However, either way it did not deter me. I kept at my dad and I just kept coming at him with all my strength. Finally, on the night, before Christmas 2013 my father called, which was a surprise and it was good to hear his voice. Finally, my father gave me my apology I had been so desperately waiting for.

I waited for over 49 years. I could feel his apology was sincere, and he truly meant it. Also I could tell in his voice he felt bad with what he had done

My bonds and chains are broken. My father has finally set me free. My past is my past, and nothing else. My past has no effect on my present, no power, or control. My being able to tell my family everything kept me quiet, ashamed, and afraid. I truly wish I could have done it sooner. Now I am free and finally able to

The chains, that bonded my feet from walking forward, are broken. As I have said in the being of this book. My core has finally awakened. She is full of life, and there is no going backward. The need is to go forward into the future.

I wake up and every day, and I smile because I am still alive, and I am free.

I broke the CYCLE

I was going to be cliché and talk about myself. However, I would rather talk a little about a man raised all of us in dysfunctional family. Now he sees how his little girl has grown up as a strong independent woman who can actually say I am very proud of my father

Roman James Steward, here he is.

Aug of 2014 I am 53 years old, and I told him I wanted to ask him some questions about his life. You see he was never what you called an open book. He was not one to talk about his past.

1. "Were you born at home or at hospital?"

Roman - "At home."

2. "Did you have to pick cotton?"

Roman – "Yes, I think I was five when I started."

3. "What age did you stop picking cotton?"

Roman – "17 years-od."

4. "How far did you get in school?"

Roman – "I finished the 12th grade Graduated from Center High School, in Alamo Tennessee."

5. "How were you punished?"

Roman – "I was punished with a wooden paddle at school. At home, Othea used an Ellen switch, Sylvet used his fist and knocked the shit out of me, and he used paddle to beat my ass with."

(Wow, now I know where the paddle comes to play living under his roof as a child)

6. "Was school hard for you?"

Roman – "No. I liked school until I started smelling myself (wanted sex)."

7. "Did you play any sports while in school?"

Roman – "I enjoyed playing baseball, and I played second base."

8. "After graduating school what did you do?"

Roman – "His father sent him to Tuskegee Alabama for college. I had received a scholarship in baseball. I was excited about going to college. I was not scared at all. I was happy I did not have to milk cows anymore. I was there at Tuskegee for six months. My course of course of study was history, and English. I did make some friends while I was there. Those two courses interested me because I wanted to learn about history. With me coming from Tennessee we already had slang, I did not want to sound like the Mississippian's with "I am and I ain't and all shit." In addition, I did not want to speak with a dialect. To find a job while in college I had to go back to milking cows. I hated milking cows I left."

9. "When did you meet my mother? In addition, did she graduate?"

Roman – "Yes, she did, but I do not know when. I came back to Jackson; I was 20 years old. I had been back for two weeks and then I met your mother."

10." How did you approach my mother?"

Roman – "I met your mother at church, she lived in Atwood. There is only one-year difference between us. My mother had picked cotton growing up. We got married; it was a small courthouse in Durant

Mississippi, in 1954. Uncle Tom and Aunt Josie Pearson (were husband and wife) came with us to get married."

11. "How does the Midwest fall in to play?"

Roman – "I was talking to your grandmother Nover lee, and she had cousins were going to the Midwest, and suggested they follow them to Iowa, for a job."

12. "How long before Jeffery and I came along?"

Roman – "Two years."

13. "How did you find out about Jeffery heart condition?"

Roman – "He was taking baby medicine, and they found out. He did not swallow to good, but he could crawl. I took him to the UV of Minnesota just as I did my daddy (We found out Papa Curtis had Tuberculosis). "

14. "Are you my real father?"

Roman – "I don't know; I guess we will never know."

15. "Where were you at when Jeffery died?"

Roman – "When they called, and told me he was dead, they said there was nothing I could do so I stayed the rest of the day at work."

16. "Where did the idea, for you use wood to punish us?"

Roman – "From school."

17. "What was it about Dianna you liked so much?"

Roman – "I had a motorcycle, and Dianna kept asking, for a ride. I gave her a ride, and it started from there."

18. "How did you feel about my pregnancy?"

Roman – "I did not like at all. I felt you were way too young to have a child."

19. "Were you sad I left the house?"

Roman – "Didn't like it because I didn't think you would be able to handle yourself" Butt now I see I was wrong and I am sorry."

20. ""Why did Othea want a divorce?

Roman – "I do not know. Well is not true. We had been together, for over 25 years and I guess I just didn't want her to live on her own without me. Letting go was hard for me."

(I thought was the most truthful word ever came out of my dad' mouth I can remember beside the apology my dad gave me.)

21. "Do you miss all of us kids after we moved out?"

Roman – "Time goes and yes I do."

22. "If you can change anything from the past or present what would it be?"

Roman – "If I hadn't been so angry all the time. I wish I had smiled more! I also wished I could have loved you kids better."

23. "Where do you think came from?"

Roman – "Just knowing I was grumpy after the kids started coming, chores, raising a family, bills."

24. "Who were you closet to out of your siblings?"

Roman – "Malik."

25. "Where were you at when you found out Papa

Curtis was sick?"

Roman – "I was in Cedar Rapids, Ia. I went to Tennessee. I brought my father back to Iowa to see the doctors here. I took him two hospitals the University of Iowa, and to University of Minnesota. The doctors said "Papa Curtis had blood clots." I was 21 or 22 years old the time. There wasn't anything the doctors could do. He had, had that condition, for several years.

26. "While Papa Curtis was in Iowa was his health getting better?"

Roman – "No the doctor told us Papa Curtis was going to die. They gave him six months to a year."

27. "How long was Papa Curtis back in Tennessee? Before he passed?"

Roman – "I went to Tennessee, for Labor Day. I started to drive back home to Iowa and my daddy told me before I left. " I might not be here when you get back home to Iowa. He wasn't even a home a month before " Papa Curtis passed on Nov 22, 1963. Sylvet's mother had debilitating diabetes. My grandmother passed in April 25 1985."

For all its worth, I am glad I did not give up my fight to live. I can now see how the road was paved for my mother and my father both coming from the south back in the late 1930's. I can also see the lack of nurturing from both sides. Still there is not excuse, but now I can understand.

I wanted an apology, for over 49 years. In addition, I mean this with my very being. I am just glad I was able to get the apology before my father left this world. I am just very proud of the man who swallowed his pride, and gave me the apology I justly deserve. To be set free to live my life the way I want, and with my father in it. I wanted to celebrate at least one Christmas with my father in the new millennium. Finally, my prayers were answered. God is so good. I was able to spend Christmas with my father in 2015. When Steven and I arrived in Tennessee. We walked into the house I just smiled and I was happy to see him. My father met my husband Steven and was cool. Steven was happy because all he's has been hearing is I want to go home for Christmas.

The road my father and I traveled on has finally come to join as one. I love dad. With my soul and with my core.

To my parents Roman James Steward and Willie Edna Bryant. I love you both.

Here is Willie Edna Bryant

My mother grew up in the south, in Atwood Tennessee. That is where she met and married my dad. I do not know much about my mom. We were never close. As I moved on in life obviously so did she. I never called, or visited my mother when I found out my parents had divorce. I guess because she never called or visited me. I only started talking with her toward the end of her life. I visited her one time while I was living in Wisconsin. I was able to see her in 2006 and while I was at the hospital visiting, her she did say to me she raised me the best she knew how.

I guess that was her way of saying sorry. At time, I still have not forgiven her yet, but she knows it now. I drove in the middle of the night because my sister had called, and told me she was dying. I arrived at the hospital at six a. m. in the morning, and boy let me tell you she was very surprised to see me. Her eyes lit up, and I saw such a smile on her face.

I started to cry. As I walk over to hug my mother for the first in over 35 years she said, "Jaynie it is so nice to see you." A few months later on January 23 2007, my mother passed. Her passing was harder on my sibling then me. However, it did hurt me inside. My husband Steven and I came for the celebration of her moving on. I know she is smiling down on all of us. I said a few words at her celebration, and I would like to share them with you.

Dear Mom,

You were not there for me in my life growing up. I felt the distance. We are both sorry for that

You were not there for me, and I was not there for you when we went our separate ways. We are both sorry for.

Maye calls and tells me to open my heart; I tell her the door is locked. I threw away the key. I am sorry for.

With her tenacity, and persistence, I finally unlock door and it opens on its own. I am grateful for Maye's diligence not to give up.

Now you are on your last mile, and thank God, we are here for each other

Now the saddest day is here you have gone home. My memory is alive, and vivid with the time I shared with you. I know you are grateful for

I am throwing away the crying, the sadness from the past and replacing with pure joy we have given each other.

smile you showed me when I first walked in your hospital room early Thursday morning I will never forgot.

You said, "Jaynie so nice to see you! I am happy you came to see me.

It took you long enough. I didn't say anything back I just chuckled. She still has a sense of humor.

I have never seen your face light up so much as it did day. I know we will always be grateful for. We both know there are no needs, for sorries and forgive me's.

I just have the beauty the innocence of our relationship, for the first time in my life.

I will always cherish.

Your body no longer but your soul is alive, and here with me. With all of us. And it feels so good.

Words really can't express my joy and happiness. You are not gone Othea you are just out of sight.

I truly love you, and will always carry you in my heart. You are forever in my soul, my prayers.

I know we are both eternally grateful, for that.

Mom, we had a change of heart. I love you. W.E.B R.I.P.

As I finish the last pages of my book, I am 54 years of age. As you can see from 1963 until 2015, I have had a long road with many hills to climb, and a heavy burden to carry. I would like to share I have been married for 11 years. My husband's name is Steven. I am finding every marriage is work of two wills. I'm enrolled in college soon to be graduating with my Associates Degree. I am working on another book. Not sure, on how many more I will write. Finally, my closet is empty the world is my oyster.

All I know is I have no luggage on my back. Miraculously I have come full circle in this book. The ending to this book was good timing. I could not have planned this ending even if I tried. I was recently featured on an cable television show that aired on Aug 2015. The title of the show was Nobody knew I existed. The show is about uniting birth parents with their child they placed for adoption. I had a child Jennifer at the age of 17 years old. Her name was Jennifer. I was still in high school. I placed her up for adoption in 1979. I never thought our roads would cross. Well they did. She had been searching for over 20 years for me. A well-known cable television show liked our story, and the rest is history. He adoptive parents named her Leslie. It was nice meeting her, although we did not chat much. Now our roads crossed and now they have parted again. She would rather keep her life separate from me. It hurts me to think she doesn't want to include me in her life since she was the one who searched to find me. I just have to let go of the pain of knowing that we may never speak again. Since our reunion, I have been asked to be back on the cable television show to talk about what has been happening between Leslie and myself. And where are we now.

Thank you I am very touched. Also I am happy that the TV viewers liked our story that much. I also want to give thanks to the media for your support and kind words. I don't have any animosity toward Leslie at all, just love for her and her family.

Life is moving forward for me. I prayed to have this burden lifted off my shoulders and God took it away. Praise God. I hope one day that Leslie, becomes unguarded and grows to understand just how good of a life she had. Instead of being angry at the life, she would have had and hated including me.

The ground I walk upon is hard and I am steady.

Epilogue

My husband Steven and I rre leaving the Midwest soon. I have come to the end of my journey. I am ready. I just want to be out where I can see the ocean, breathe the air, and smile because I am and

I will always be a PROUD SURVIVOR.

I have a tattoo of a vine. It starts at my ankle and it wraps around my body up to my neck where it branches out.

Throughout the tattoo, there is writing, Chinese symbols. (Strength, Friendship, Courage, Truth, and Growth)

And the writing says

"Never Stop Living"

I am a walking talking testimonial. I fought to live.

I AM FREE

NO   MORE   SECRET

I HAVE BROKEN THE CYCLE OF ABUSE and I AM FREE

In the 55 years, I have been alive,

I have finally come full circle

If you would like to contact me, and remember, you are not alone.
Please contact me: janiece_corevine2015@yahoo.com

Albert Einstein and Mark Twain a once said "If you always do what you always done, then you will always get what you always got". I believe that till this day. However I believe in this statement even stronger. I live this statement every day and will for the rest of my life.

If you change what you want to change in your life.
Then you will never have to go backward to live for today.
The present is now and backward was yesterday.
By janiece Corevine

www.ingramcontent.com/pod-product-compliance
Lightning Source LLC
Chambersburg PA
CBHW031237090426
42742CB00007B/228